To: Coleen

SOWING IN TEARS, REAPING IN JOY

THE LIFE STORY OF FLORENCE MILLER MISSIONARY TO JAPAN

Florence J. Miller
II Corinthians 9:6
Ecclesiastes 11:6

SOWING IN TEARS, REAPING IN JOY

THE LIFE STORY OF FLORENCE MILLER MISSIONARY TO JAPAN

BY

FLORENCE J. MILLER

EDITED BY

LUCILLE D. LENGEFELD

www.bookstandpublishing.com

Published by
Bookstand Publishing
Morgan Hill, CA 95037
3897_3

ISBN 978-1-61863-526-6

Printed in the United States of America

Dedicated to the memory of

My parents
August and Clara Miller

who nurtured me in my Christian faith by example,
faithfully taking me to church,
encouraging me in my calling,
assisting me in getting my education and
praying for me all through my thirty-eight years of missionary service.

PREFACE

The material included in these memoirs was gathered largely from letters written to my family and to supporting churches. They were saved by my mother and some of my siblings. The letters were not originally intended for publishing in a book. Consequently, they relate a personal story of my life and missionary work in Japan.

I was encouraged many years ago by Gideon Zimmerman, Executive Director of the North American Baptist Conference, and more recently by Paul Ewing, Field Director of NAB in Japan, to record an account of the beginnings of the North American Baptist Mission work in Japan. Since I did not have access to official records, I decided to simply use my memoirs to tell my part in the work and leave to others more qualified to do a more historical record of the total NAB mission in Japan.

Florence J. Miller
January, 2013

ACKNOWLEDGEMENTS

I want to thank the following persons to whom I am indebted for the contents, editing and publishing of these memoirs:
My mother, Clara Miller, and siblings for preserving my letters;
A former North American Baptist missionary in Japan, Mrs. Lucille Lengefeld, for editing and reducing my six hundred pages to two hundred;
The Director of the North American Baptist Heritage Commission, Dr. Jackie Howell, for getting them printed and published;
Jim Landman, my kind deacon at my home church, Napier Parkview Baptist Church, for preparing the photos for publication.

INTRODUCTION

In October of 2011, Japan Field Director Paul Ewing, my husband Bill, and I visited Florence Miller in her home in Benton Harbor, MI, where she placed in our hands her "labor of love"—over 600 pages of information which we referred to as "Flo's Memoirs." Upon meeting with Dr. Jackie Howell, Director of the NAB Heritage Commission, we decided to edit the material down to a book of some 200 pages. I felt blessed and honored to be included in this project, the results of which you are holding in your hands.

I first met Florence in September 1971. She was a veteran missionary of twenty years' experience, and I was one of five new short-term missionaries. During the ensuing years, I came to admire and respect Florence as a woman of God, as the quintessential missionary, and as a precious friend. As I began the editing process, I soon discovered that the task required much more than inserting punctuation marks and deleting repetitious passages. I found myself relating to Florence in an even deeper way as she recounted her sorrows as well as her joys. It is my prayer that this account of her life will truly bring honor and glory to the Heavenly Father whom she deeply loved and diligently served.

Lucille Lengefeld
January, 2013

Table of Contents

"Those who sow in tears shall reap in joy. He who continually goes forth weeping, bearing seed for sowing, shall doubtless come again with rejoicing, bringing his sheaves with him."

Psalm 126:5-6 (KJV)

1

CALL TO JAPAN

Introduction

I was appointed by the North American Baptist Missionary Society as one of its very first missionaries to Japan. A young couple, Jay and Esther Hirth with a three month old baby, would be my co-workers. Jay had been in the Air Force stationed near Tokyo, and saw the need for missionaries to bring a message of hope to a people who were disillusioned after learning that all they had fought for was false.

The seeds of my call to Japan were sown in elementary school. My elementary country school teacher introduced me to Japan in a manner I could never forget, through poetry and art. She read us some Japanese *haiku* poems and asked us to write one. I also painted a picture in orange and black of a Japanese lady with an old fashioned hairdo, dressed in a kimono, sitting on a cushion on the straw matted floor, silhouetted in front of delicately papered sliding doors that opened onto a narrow verandah. Also, I saw a postcard of a Japanese iris garden that my aunt's stereoscope converted into a three-dimensional picture. I fell in love with Japanese gardens, especially iris gardens. These things were seeds of love for the Orient that God planted in my heart as a child, so that He could use them as magnets to draw me to Japan when the time was right.

That time came during my first year at the Moody Bible Institute where I heard missionary speakers from many countries tell of the spiritual needs of people around the world and how God was using missionaries to meet those needs. Every Friday night we heard missionary speakers, but one night there was no missionary. Instead, a student led the meeting and read to us from a book about India by Amy Carmichael, entitled *Things as They Are*. Amy was a single missionary from England who spent her entire life in India. In the book, Amy relates a dream she had. She said that she saw a long procession of people marching towards a precipice. She noticed that they were all blind and because there was no one to warn them of the danger ahead, they were falling over the precipice one by one and perishing. Then she saw another group of people sitting on the grass in a circle, singing and laughing and making daisy chains, blissfully

1

unaware and unconcerned about the perishing ones. When I heard this, it was as if the Holy Spirit had thrust a spear into my heart, as I saw myself among those making daisy chains, enjoying the teaching and fellowship of a wonderful Bible school but not really concerned about the spiritually blind who had never been warned of the danger of hell or told about a Savior who had come into the world to seek and to save the perishing. That night I made a promise to God that I would go somewhere where the name of Jesus was not well known. I had no idea then, where it might be. I changed my major to the Missions Course and from then on knew that God wanted me to be one of His messengers to the unreached. I regularly attended the Missionary Prayer Bands where we learned about the needs of different countries. I felt drawn to China at that time.

Childhood

As a very young child, my three older siblings and I were taken to the Clay Street Baptist Church in Benton Harbor, Michigan by my parents, August and Clara Miller. My father was born in Poland of German ancestry. My mother was born of parents who came from Germany so German was spoken in her home. German was spoken in our home also when we children were very young, so I understood a little German. Also, I learned to understand some German at church where our worship service was conducted in half German and half English, but I usually slept through the German sermon.

My parents were married in 1920 and purchased a 20 acre farm in Benton Harbor where they grew fruit. With the birth of four children just a little over a year apart they struggled to make the annual mortgage payments. The Great Depression years of the 30's intensified their financial burdens, but through it all, mother was determined to see that the family always attended church in town on the Lord's Day, even though it was always a temptation to work on Sundays to earn a little more money.

My mother came from a large family with ten children. Her parents and grandparents had immigrated to the United States from Russia. They were fruit growers in Benton Harbor also. On Sundays the family traveled by horse and wagon to the First Baptist Church in St. Joseph and later to the Clay Street Baptist Church when it was built in Benton Harbor. Mother became a charter member of Clay Street

Baptist Church. As a young girl she was baptized and wanted to serve the Lord as a Christian worker, but her education ended when she graduated from the eighth grade because the family could not afford more.

When the Miller children were born, unbeknownst to anyone except her, she dedicated each child to the Lord for whatever service He might call them to. My father had hopes that his children, and especially his only son, Edwin, would work with him on the farm. However, Edwin did not share that vision. When he was a senior in high school he told my parents that he felt God was calling him into the pastoral ministry. My mother was delighted to hear this but my father was disappointed. However, he did not stand in Edwin's way when he enrolled as a student at the North American Baptist Seminary in Rochester, New York.

The Miller children: Evelyn, Lillian, Edwin, Florence (about 5 years old)

Florence (about 10 years old) with Evelyn, Father, Mother, Edwin, and Lillian Miller outside our house

When Edwin returned home for his first summer vacation after one year at seminary, he brought with him a seminary friend from Canada who wanted to earn some money working on a farm. These two young men were very enthusiastic about their studies and their church work and awakened a thirst for Bible study and spiritual growth in the hearts of some of the church youth, including my sisters and me. My eldest sister, Evelyn, was already working as a stenographer. My sister, Lillian, was planning to train as a nurse in St. Paul. I wanted to study Home Economics and had been accepted at Michigan State University. However, strongly influenced by my brother, I felt the desire to attend Bible school instead of college. I cancelled my application to Michigan State and applied to the Moody Bible Institute in Chicago. My eldest sister, Evelyn, decided to give up her job and attend Moody also. My father seriously questioned the wisdom of our decisions, wondering what we would do for a livelihood after graduation. We did not know how to answer him but told him we were trusting God to lead us. It must have been very hard for my parents to see all four of their oldest children leave home and go off to school in two years, leaving them without the workers they badly needed on the farm. The only child left was a baby girl, Sherrill, not yet a year old, born to them when I was seventeen years old.

4

Preparation to Serve

I enrolled at Moody as a student in the General Bible Course. Evelyn and I were roommates the first year. It was a comfort and encouragement to me to have an older sister with me, since it was the first time for either of us to be away from home. For me, Moody felt like a little bit of heaven on earth, with over a thousand Christian students and wonderful instructors. I felt that I would like to stay there the rest of my life and enjoy that heavenly atmosphere. The one thing that was difficult for me was sharing my faith with others when we went out on practical Christian work assignments each week. I was quiet and shy and found it hard to engage in conversation with strangers, especially about spiritual things in which they had no interest.

While at Moody I attended missionary prayer bands where students prayed for missionary work being done in various countries. I was drawn to China and the China Inland Mission.

After graduating from Moody in December, 1945, I entered Wheaton College because I didn't feel adequately prepared for the tremendous task ahead of me. I was a Bible major, so I could transfer some credits in Bible from Moody, shortening my time at Wheaton, enabling me to graduate in June 1948 with a B.A. in Bible. At Wheaton there was a strong missions emphasis through the student-led Foreign Missions Fellowship which met every Friday night. Even before I graduated from Wheaton, I knew that I would be unable to go to China, because the Communists had taken over the country and all missionaries had to leave or be imprisoned or killed. So I began to consider another mission field. Before the war with Japan, I thought of Japan as just a small island country, but Japan had aggressively enlarged her empire by taking over Korea, the Philippines, Mongolia, Indo-China and parts of China, and had attacked Hawaii. When the United States declared war on Japan and our service men were being sent to the Pacific region, Japan loomed large on the map.

The war with Japan ended in August, 1945 with the defeat of Japan, but it required time for the people to adjust to the American occupation under General McArthur and to recover from the devastation of the war. After things became somewhat settled, General McArthur called for 2000 missionaries to come to Japan to help fill the spiritual vacuum left when the Emperor was forced to deny his deity.

The people felt an emptiness of heart, resulting from a lost cause for which many had laid down their lives. Many missionary organizations that had never sent missionaries to Japan before were beginning to send missionaries there after the war.

Since the door to China had closed due to the Communist take over in 1950 and the door to Japan had been opened, I began to pray about going to Japan. I had hoped to go out under our North American Baptist General Missionary Society and wrote a letter of inquiry to Dr. Dymmel, the Missions Secretary. However, he informed me that they only sent missionaries to Cameroon and Nigeria in Africa, but he would put my letter in his file.

After graduating from Wheaton, I enrolled at the Biblical Seminary in New York, graduating with a Master's Degree in Religious Education in 1950. After eight years of book learning, I still felt ill prepared for actual missionary work. I wanted more hands-on experience, especially in a Baptist Church setting. My brother, Edwin Miller, was pastoring the Erin Avenue Baptist Church in Cleveland, Ohio. He extended an invitation to me to come and serve for one year as the "Church Missionary." The church had had a woman serving in that capacity earlier so it was not a new idea. In actuality, it was very much the same as a Director of Christian Education position. I gladly accepted the offer and learned a lot about church work and evangelism through this job.

While I was working in Cleveland, I was actively engaged in applying to the Conservative Baptist Missionary Society. I met their candidate committee and was interviewed by them. As I prayed for guidance I received a letter from Rev. William Hoover, my pastor in Benton Harbor, in which he stated that our North American Baptist Conference had just decided to open mission work in Japan and that a young couple in Chicago were desirous of going there. He knew that I was considering going out under the Conservative Baptist Missionary Society, so he sent me an application for NAB. When I saw it I could hardly believe my eyes. It was as if the Lord had shown me a clear *green light* saying "This is the way. Walk ye in it." I had wanted to go out with NAB from the beginning, but since they had no work in Japan, I had no alternative but to seek another mission board. With this information, I felt that everything was falling into place and that my home church would support me since the pastor was backing me up. I applied to NAB and was accepted. Richard Schilke was then Missions

Secretary. My church pledged my full support. I was the first member to go out as a missionary.

Departure for Japan

Florence, Esther and Jay Hirth with Jeep station wagon

I met Hirths for the first time at our mission headquarters in Forest Park, Illinois. The mission provided us with a used Jeep station wagon, which we were to take to Japan, since cars were not being made there at that time. As we were driving through the mountains of California along narrow, curved roads, the Jeep stalled and the lights went out. Cars were coming from both directions, but they could not see us. One car almost rear-ended us, but the driver swerved to the mountain-side and managed to squeeze between us and the mountain. He shouted, "Grab your flashlights and let people know you are there." Then he took off his cap, showed us his scarred forehead and said, "See what happened to me! My car stalled once, too, but my car rolled over the precipice, down into the canyon. I have a rope in my trunk. I'll pull you to the nearest gas station." For five miles he pulled us along the dark, dangerous road, while I prayed, "Dear Lord, please protect us." When we reached the gas station, I unashamedly, audibly offered up a prayer of thanks to the Lord for his protection. We spent about a week at the Home of Peace in Oakland, California, making purchases of equipment and having it crated for shipping to Japan.

We boarded our ship, a freighter named "The Surprise," at 4:00 p.m. November 6, 1951, six years after the end of the war with Japan. "What an apt name for our ship," I thought as I walked up the gangplank, literally trembling, knowing it would take me far away from my homeland and loved ones, whom I would not see for five years. We did not leave port until the next morning. I got up early so I would not miss the experience of passing under the Golden Gate Bridge. As we pulled away I saw a huge red ball beneath the bridge. What an amazing view! I was on my way to the Land of the Rising Sun.

Florence at Pilot's Wheel

It was stormy thirteen days of the fifteen we were aboard. It was cold but we sat on the deck watching the waves that were as big as a house, bombarding our little ship with its nine passengers. I wondered if we would make it safely to Japan. At night we put pillows on either side of our bunks to keep from falling out. One night everything in the cabin was flying across the room. It looked like the morning after a drunken brawl. It was difficult to keep our dishes on the dining tables, even though there were railings around the edges. The crew told us scary stories of how ships could break in half due to the force of the waves and how ships sometimes collided in heavy fog.

We arrived at Yokohama on Thursday, November 21, American Thanksgiving Day. The cook had prepared a turkey dinner, but we weren't enjoying it because someone on deck called out, "I see Japan!" and we all rushed up to the deck to get a glimpse of our new homeland. What a thrill to see Mt. Fuji covered with snow, rising proudly above the other mountains. And what an appropriate day to make our arrival, Thanksgiving Day!

When we finally tied up at the dock in Yokohama, we were in our cabin looking out the porthole. I remembered what the officer had told us about guarding our belongings. I kept my valuables close to me and waited. I watched as the little longshoremen moved about on the wharf. They were wearing white headbands and looked to me like pirates. Soon the gangplank connecting the ship to the wharf was in place and these little men came swarming up into the ship's cabins and began to carry out our suitcases. I did not know where they were taking them or if I would ever see them again.

Because our mission was just beginning work in Japan, we were required by the Japanese government to have a sponsor, namely, a mission that was already in Japan, to be responsible for us. The Baptist General Conference had started work in Japan a few years earlier so they became our sponsors. One of their missionaries, Francis Sorley, was supposed to meet us at Yokohama, but no one was there when we arrived. When Jay told me that, he said that I didn't need to worry because he was sure that he could find his way from Yokohama to Tokyo with our Jeep station wagon. He said he knew a few Japanese words. I said, "I'm not getting off this ship until someone comes to meet us." We waited about a half hour and Mr. Sorley came to meet us. What a relief that was!

Jay and Esther Hirth and Linda

The Jeep station wagon had been anchored to the deck and was exposed to the waves that swept over the ship. The last night aboard, the waves were so big and heavy that the whole roof caved in, making it hard to open the doors, and the rear spring was bent. Moreover, the lights weren't working and we had to travel at night to get to Tokyo. It took quite a while to get all our baggage and the station wagon unloaded and cleared through customs. Finally we were ready to go. Since we had no lights, we had to follow closely behind Mr. Sorley's army Jeep, down the main highway, about a two hour drive to Tokyo.

We had to compete with all kinds of vehicles: bicycles, motorcycles, three-wheeled mini-trucks and even ox carts. It was a scary ride. I still wonder why we were not stopped by the police. When we finally arrived at the YMCA where Hirths would stay, I again said, "Let's thank the Lord for his protection all the way." And we did.

I had a tiny little room about 8 feet by 10 feet at the YWCA with room for only a single bed, a tiny dresser, a chair and tiny table and a small closet. My window looked out on a busy street in a district known as Ochanomizu where a lot of universities were located. My tiny room cost about a dollar a day, or 10,000 yen a month. A dollar was worth 358 yen. I discovered that other single women missionaries were staying at the YWCA which was very helpful since I did not know the language. Hirths and I had intended to find a house where we might live together, but until then, the YM and YW served as our temporary homes.

Our first Sunday morning in Japan we went to an English service at the Chapel Center, a U. S. government center for all kinds of religious services. Both civilians and servicemen came there to worship. It seemed strange to see so many Americans in Japan. Of course the reason was that the American occupation army was still there for at least another year.

A friend of Jay's from his time in the Air Force, Tetsua Kobayashi and his father, together pastored a small United Christian Church (Nihon Kirisuto Kyodan) only a few minutes from Sorley's house in Nerima Ku, Tokyo. We attended their church service one Sunday morning and later we were invited to the home of Pastor and Mrs. Kobayashi. As we entered the pastor's house, we took off our shoes in the entrance, put on slippers provided for us, stepped up about ten inches to the straw-matted (*tatami)* floor in the entranceway (*genkan*). We were ushered to the living room where we sat down on cushions around a low round table. We were served coffee, a special treat for Americans, which was rationed at that time. Tetsua spoke pretty good English and his wife Etsuko (whose English name was Emily) spoke English very well because she had studied for one year at a college in the U.S. Later we were served supper: shredded cabbage, a marmalade sandwich, a slice of something like coffee cake and coffee. Coffee, milk and sugar were a wedding present, so you see they gave us their very best. They said they would invite us for *sukiyaki* sometime. That is a very special party dish with delicious thin slices of beef and vegetables in a sweet soy sauce cooked over a charcoal burner in the middle of the table, as the guests help themselves from the pot with chopsticks.

We stayed for the evening church service. It was a new church with benches. The people all left their shoes in the entrance and put on slippers provided by the church. Jay gave a testimony in English through an interpreter. The services lasted from 7:00 to 9:30 p.m.

Japan has a Thanksgiving Day which they celebrate one day later than ours. Sorleys invited us and six other Baptist General Conference missionaries (Swedish background) to their home. Sorleys had a new American style home, built by their mission as mission headquarters. Everything was modern, western style, except for a kerosene heating stove instead of a furnace. We had a real American Thanksgiving dinner including pumpkin pie.

I ate two breakfasts at the YWCA cafeteria and found them quite expensive, so I decided to eat breakfast in my room and other meals in nearby restaurants as the other girls did. The weather was quite mild, about 60 degrees by day and much colder at night. There had been no snow yet that fall, but I was told it did snow occasionally in the winter. There would be no heat in my room until December, so I kept my coat on all the time I was in my room.

First Impressions of Japan

When I first arrived at Yokohama, a number of things struck me. Everything was very small in comparison to things in America. The people were small, their houses and buildings were small. Their vehicles were small. This was partly due to the fact that the country was very crowded with so many people. Also the country was impoverished by the war, so they had to make things cheaply. I also observed that everything looked dingy and colorless. The buildings were coated with brownish, blackish creosote to prevent deterioration. The roofs were made of gray tile. The floors of the houses were covered with woven straw mats about two inches thick. The interior walls were made of brown mud mixed with straw. The ceilings, doors and woodwork were all of unpainted wood. The primitive kitchens in some homes were blackened with smoke from charcoal burners or wood-burning firepots set in ceramic or brick "hearths". Bathtubs were oval wooden structures about two to three feet deep and just long enough to allow a person to sit with bent knees. Wood-burning firepots at one end, opening to the outside, were used to heat the water and a wooden cover was used to retain the heat in the tub.

I had never seen so many kinds of vehicles in my life as I saw on the streets in Japan. There were many bicycles, motor scooters of all descriptions, motor bikes, a few motorcycles, and many three-wheeled vehicles (some made like a pick-up truck in the back, others with a seat for passengers). The driver of these three wheelers straddled the motor like a motor-cycle. I was always amazed to see the loads that people pushed and carried. Some of the bicycles were loaded so high I wondered how the riders could ever keep their balance. Sometimes restaurants delivered food to individuals by bicycle and the riders held one hand on the handle bars while balancing a stack of five or six trays of food. There were all kinds of carts (ox-drawn carts, bicycle drawn carts, push carts), wagons loaded with wooden buckets, nicknamed "honey dew buckets" by the foreigners. They were filled with manure, both animal and human, and the contents were spread on the gardens and fields to grow vegetables. We were warned not to eat fresh vegetables unless they had been washed in detergent or dipped in some disinfectant. We couldn't very well refuse to eat food that was served to us, so we did eat raw cabbage, tomatoes, etc. Some missionaries advised, "Don't be too particular about what you eat. You'll get worms anyway, so just enjoy it and take worm medicine." There were many tiny cars like Austins or even smaller, Jeeps, army trucks of all kinds, and a few foreign cars, American and European. The missionaries brought the vehicles they needed with them when they came and paid high duty on them.

The weather in Japan was not as cold as I had thought. I had expected snow when we arrived, but I was told that snow usually does not fall until January and then, it only lasts a few days. However the dampness and lack of good heat in the buildings makes one feel cold much of the time. We got heat in our rooms at the YWCA on December 1st, so then my room was quite comfortable. Heat came on in the morning and in the evening when it was the coldest and off during the rest of the day when it wasn't so cold. I could understand why so many Japanese people had colds in the winter. They wear white masks to prevent the spread of germs to others. Also many of them still had tuberculosis which is very contagious at certain stages. Most Japanese homes were heated by *hibachi*, a large ceramic bowl

12

about the size of a canning kettle, filled with sand. On the sand is placed burning charcoal. It is surprising how much heat they give off when the *hibachi* is warmed up and you are sitting close to it, warming your hands on it, but they also give off dangerous fumes if you are exposed to it too long without fresh air coming into the room. Sometimes there was a wood or coal stove in the main living room with a tall pipe chimney going through the room or through a window. For cooking, many people used a charcoal burner, called a *shichirin*. Others had gas burners. I bought a Japanese electric hot plate to help heat my room before we got heat, thinking I could use it also for cooking, but it was very slow. There was a gas burner in the Y which we could use. That was much faster. The electricity often went off for several hours a day or perhaps two days a week. Because of the uncertainty about electricity, electrical appliances were not too dependable. This condition was particularly hard on refrigerators.

Our freight came on a different ship than we did, about a week later. After it arrived, it was not unloaded for about another week. The Hirths were feeling cramped in their small quarters with a baby and were eager to find a house. One night at a gas station, we met some American Baptist missionaries who said that they were moving out of their house and thought that we might be able to rent it. When Jay inquired and learned that we could, we were overjoyed. It was a large, semi-western house with five rooms for the Hirths and a maid on the first floor. There were four rooms on the second floor for me and two small rooms in the attic for storage. There was plenty of room to store our things. We could live in the same house, yet have separate quarters. It appeared that we would be able to move in very soon. We were anxious to get settled in our own place where we could do our own cooking and live more economically. We planned to have a house warming after things were in order and invite some of Jay's Japanese friends.

When we arrived in Japan, we thought that we would be able to immediately enter the Naganuma Japanese Language School, where most of the new missionaries were studying. However we were told that it was too crowded and that we would have to wait until January when a new class for beginners would start. For one month we were unable to communicate with Japanese people, unless they could speak English. Sometimes we used sign language in the shops.

13

At first we did most of our grocery shopping at the O.S.S. (Overseas Supply Stores) which handled only American goods and where clerks could speak English. We could get almost anything we needed there, but of course the items were expensive, having been shipped from the U.S. and having duty tacked on. Little by little we learned what things to buy from the Japanese markets at cheaper prices.

Jay and Esther moved into their part of the house the middle of December. My apartment (two rooms and kitchenette) on the second floor was still occupied so I had to wait until the first week in January.

Language school was to start January 7th, so I had a week to get settled before that. All of our freight arrived safely. We thought we had brought a lot with us but we were thankful for everything we brought, especially the food. Thus we rejoiced and gave thanks to the Lord for doing exceedingly abundantly above all that we could ask or think. Our housing problem was solved; we were able to enroll in language school even though it was very crowded; our freight arrived safely and we had a place to store it.

We visited one of the largest Shinto shrines in Tokyo, Meiji Shrine, where Japan's most loved emperor, Meiji, is enshrined as a deity. I found it hard to understand how an ordinary human being could be considered a god and worshiped as such. While we were there two Japanese young men asked to take our picture. Then they asked for our address so they could mail us a picture if it turned out well. We asked them to explain the shrine to us, but they said "We are sorry, but we cannot." Several days later we got a note saying one of them wanted to come to explain the shrine to us. We had a hunch, which proved to be correct, that he wanted an opportunity to hear and speak English with us. Jay spoke to him about reading the Bible. He said he had read some of it, but there were many things he could not understand. He said his eighteen year old sister was attending a Christian school and wanted to become a Christian, but his father said, "No." Jay invited him to come to our new home, if he wanted to speak with us again. He was very eager to do that, so he could learn English. We prayed that our conversations with him might be used of God to show him the way of life.

14

First Christmas in Japan – December 25, 1951

Christmas day passed with me feeling somewhat regretful over the way it was spent. I went with the Hirths to their home yesterday afternoon. On arriving there, we found the two Ishikawa sisters, Mine and Toshi, waiting for us. They had already waited an hour. They brought us a gift of a box of home-grown green tea of the finest quality. It was contained in a lovely painted tin box. We asked them to have supper with us, which turned out to be quite a feast. The sisters arranged the flowers they had brought for us, while we prepared supper. The flower arrangement (*ikebana*) consisted of two large, white pompom chrysanthemums, one large red poinsettia, and a tall willow-like stalk of green. These were made to stand in a large flat container. They were really lovely and looked very Christmasy. The girls were present when we opened our gifts, and fortunately we had purchased something for them. We had Bible reading, prayer and a few Christmas carols with the girls before they left. We were serenaded by two groups of carolers on Christmas Eve. One was the adult group from Dr. Kagawa's church which was only a few minutes' walk from Hirths and the other was a group of about ten orphan children from an orphanage a few minutes from our house. Esther gave the children cookies which she had baked and some of their American Christmas candy.

Mine told us that the young people from her church were going caroling for the Christian families in their area at 3:00 a.m. Christmas morning. I stayed overnight with Hirths. The next day I got out my slides and by means of the Hirth's projector got a glimpse of all of my family. I was very glad to have the slides, because they brought my family close to me. I did not feel homesick as I viewed them, but the night before, when I received letters from some of the family, my mind drifted homeward as I thought of how they would be celebrating Christmas. Those letters meant so much. I listened to *The Messiah* and some of the Christmas carols on my phonograph that had been given to me by friends in my home church before I left. I got out my little wooden Christmas tree with candles as a table decoration. Hirths had a Christmas tree with all the ornaments on it in the living room. Their rooms looked quite nice with the addition of some new furniture. It made me anxious to get into my little quarters. It won't be much to look at, but at least I could call it my own. I planned to move in a few days.

The day after Christmas about 20 Japanese young people came to Hirths for a kind of party and evening fellowship. I wanted it to be an evening of blessing to all as well. The Japanese in general, in the Tokyo area at least, know when Christmas is but it is doubtful that many of them know the real meaning of Christmas. They know only the merriment and commercialism of the Christmas season. To them it is a time of celebration like New Years. They know about Santa Claus and the giving of presents, because the businesses capitalize on this. We saw much hilarity and drunkenness on the streets on Christmas Eve by G.I.s as well as Japanese. It was heartbreaking to see the G.I.s go in for the immoral night life of Tokyo. Yes, the Japanese people do need Christ for there is open sin. There is also much theft. It is a standing rule that you never leave your house without someone (called a *rusuban*) to protect it from theft. Hirths have a dear old Christian lady who stays with the house and serves as a *rusuban*. She is also a baby sitter, cook, and housekeeper. She has served in this capacity for many missionary families. Many missionaries employ a maid so that they can give themselves to language study and to their ministry. I don't know yet if I will need a helper or not. It will depend on how busy I become after language school. I hated to think of eating meals all by myself, because I don't have an appetite by myself and I didn't relish cooking for just one person. But if it has to be, I will do it.

New Year's Celebration

New Year's celebration is probably the biggest holiday in Japan. Everything closes down for two or three days, depending on your work and how long you can afford to take off. Preparations for New Years begin about a month ahead and overshadow Christmas, which is regarded as a foreign thing.

Housewives enlist the help of the entire family to do a major house cleaning job before New Year's arrives, including removing the straw mats on the floor, taking them outside and beating the dust out of them and then putting them back in place. They also repair the paper doors and make everything look its best because many guests will be calling on them to thank them for favors done in the past year and requesting that they again favor them in the New Year. They will bring

16

with them gifts that reinforce their verbal expressions of appreciation. Of course a return gift must be on hand to give to the visitors. People who are in places of leadership such as government officials, school teachers, religious leaders, doctors and others who are considered benefactors must be called on and given a gift. Housewives must also prepare special New Year's food that may be kept for about a week, so that when guests come, they will have something to serve them. This allows storekeepers and housewives to have a little break from work when New Year's Day arrives.

Ending the old year and greeting the New Year in the right way is very important in Japan. Old debts must be paid and broken relationships mended before the New Year begins. If there have been failures or mistakes in the past year, one way of putting them behind you is to go to a drinking party, get drunk and forget all about them. There are many such "Forgetting the Past Year Parties" to attend, such as company parties, social group parties,and university student parties. They come at the same time as Christmas parties so it is sometimes hard to distinguish which one they are celebrating since non-Christian Christmas parties are usually drinking parties too, with the addition of a decorated Christmas cake, gifts, and possibly a Christmas tree.

On New Year's Eve almost everyone goes to visit temples or shrines or both to pray for good fortune in the coming year. These prayers are sometimes written on little pieces of wood, which are purchased and left there. Many buy "Good Luck Charms" at the temples and shrines to take home. Others buy a paper on which their fortune for the New Year is written. After reading it, they may fasten it to a shrub or tree nearby in hopes that it will, or will not, happen depending on the nature of it. At some temples sacred fire, lit by the priest, is taken home by worshipers to start the home fires. This is done by igniting a long piece of twisted straw at the temple fire and twirling it around to keep the flame burning until they arrive home. To us this all seemed like a lot of superstition, but for many Japanese, this is not only tradition but something they actually put their trust in. This is a good night to observe the Japanese as they practice some of their centuries-old religious traditions.

I spent my first New Year's Eve with three missionary girls at the Ochanomizu Student Center, where two of them lived. This Student Center was across the street from the YWCA in a district where there are many universities. This Center became a gathering place for small groups of missionaries on various occasions. My friends and I all brought our colored slides and had a slide-showing evening. I took my popcorn popper so we had popcorn and apples as we watched. Then we had a period of devotions and prayer as we passed into the New Year. I didn't hear any whistles blow as we did in the States, nor did we hear the bells of the Buddhist temples sound. We must have been too far away to hear them. These huge iron bells are struck on the side with a heavy wooden beam, pulled back by several men and then allowed to reverse course and hit the bell, thereby driving out the sins and evils of mankind, it is believed.

Emily and Tetsua Kobayashi, Jay's friend, took us to various places on New Year's Day and explained the meaning of many things. People visit the shrines and temples for about a week. It seems everyone goes, regardless of their beliefs. We were taken to a very famous Shinto shrine in Tokyo (*Yasukuni Shrine*), known as the Soldiers' Shrine. When soldiers were killed in battle, their spirits were said to return to this shrine where they somehow became gods which people honor and worship.

We went to the Imperial Palace, in the center of Tokyo. Here again throngs of people were gathered to worship or to pay their respects to the Emperor. There is a wide double moat around the palace, so you cannot get very near the palace, but the Emperor and Empress come out to greet the crowds.

1952 - Emperor Hirohito and Empress - greeting the crowds at the palace

18

We also went to a Buddhist temple which was quite similar in appearance to the Shinto shrines, except that there is always a statue of Buddha, whereas in Shinto shrines there are no images. It is really quite a shock to one who has lived in a so-called Christian country like America to see how few Christians there are here.

Tetsua told us that it is expected that Christian pastors visit all their members at New Years. This usually means that some kind of rice wine (sake) will be served to them. There is a special kind of sweet wine which women and children are served. These pastors usually come home from their visits with flushed faces, the result of many small cups of sake.

On January 2nd we were invited to the Ishikawa's house for a tea ceremony and for dinner. Three of the children, two girls (Mine and Toshi) and one boy (Nobuo) were by then good friends, so it was a delight to go there. We arrived about 12:00 noon. The two girls, Mine and Toshi, were dressed in bright kimonos. Mother and father were dressed in dark-colored kimonos. Nobuo, the university student, was dressed in a new blue suit. Children are often given new clothes at New Years. They also receive money called otoshidama.

On January 4th, we were invited to the home of Mr. Minagawa, the young man who had taken our picture when we met at the Meiji Shrine. He then contacted us at the Y, expressing a desire to learn English conversation. His sister attends a Roman Catholic school, but none of the family members are Christians. We were told by the son that his parents visit a shrine on the third of every month in addition to the worship in their home. From all this we gathered that it was a very religious family and we could understand why they did not want their daughter to become a Christian. As in Paul's day, like the Athenians, they worshiped they knew not what. The oldest son is interested in Christianity. He attended Bible classes while a prisoner in Korea. We had sukiyaki and eel. I didn't know it was eel until after I had eaten it. I never thought I would eat eel, but it wasn't bad. Esther has worms, so Jay and I probably do too since we've eaten the same food. The inevitable happened sooner than we thought.

In contrast to the Minagawa home is the home of the Christian minister whom we had come to know and love very much, Pastor Kobayashi, father of Tetsua. We visited his church in Nerima Ku last Sunday. His daughter-in-law, Emily sat beside us and interpreted in

English all that he said. It was a wonderful sermon, indicating far more mature Christian experience than many ministers in the U.S.

His wife was at the point of death, while he was preaching. Out of his experience of waiting upon the Lord in perfect trust during this trying time, he brought a message to the people to do the same, for the Lord was the only One who was the unchanging, eternal Helper in every circumstance. My heart was deeply stirred as I realized how this Japanese Christian minister was helping *me* through his message. There are few like him, however. In general the Christian church in Japan is very weak, having been strongly influenced by liberals and those whose emphasis has been mainly on a social gospel. When we see how few Christians there are in this land of 85,000,000 people, it is almost overwhelming.

My First Apartment

How exciting it was to move into my apartment above the Hirths. I moved in on a Saturday and as you can imagine my place was a mess for several days. It was such fun to open my boxes and pull out my things, especially the household equipment. I loved my little kitchen that had a nice tile sink, a two burner gas stove, cupboards and shelves all around. It was small, but just right for me. My living room had some old, old furniture: a large sofa and two huge chairs, plus a huge chest of drawers that looked like a pirate's treasure chest. I had a square table, about the size of a kitchen table at home, for my dining table in the living room. It was really too big but it was in the house so I decided to use it until I moved out of the house. I had a *tiny* desk, a very homely chest of unpainted drawers, a huge book case that held almost all my books, a four drawer steel cabinet that belonged to the house, a wash basin and spacious closet in my bedroom. I was so grateful for all the things that everyone gave me, because I could use them all. We enjoyed the phonograph player very much, especially the Christmas carols and *The Messiah* during the Christmas season. I took it with me when we went to Emily and Tetsua's house for *sukiyaki*. Tetsua's mother was very sick and not expected to live long. She used to be a very good singer, they said, and loved music, so we played the old hymns for her.

2

LANGUAGE SCHOOL AND EARLY MISSIONARY ACTIVITIES

January 8, 1952

We started Japanese language study at the Naganuma Language School. Our classes were 9:00 a.m. to 12:00 noon, Monday through Friday. The afternoons and evenings were to be given over to study at home. In our opening lecture by the president of the school, Mr. Naganuma, we were told that he had written to the heads of the mission boards, requesting them not to give their missionaries any regular work assignments if they expected them to learn the language effectively. With this advice and that of other missionaries, it appeared that language study would be a full time job. We started language study by learning the fifty sounds and symbols in the Japanese language. Each syllable has a consonant and a vowel such as *ra, ri, ru, re, ro*. There are five vowels, just as in English, and are always pronounced the same, regardless of the consonants preceding them. Some of the sounds are like English but others are quite different. We had to practice imitating them.

The Japanese language can be written in *hiragana*, the symbols that represent the fifty sounds in the language. This is the way that very young children begin to learn to read and write Japanese in school. There are another fifty symbols for the same sounds that are used for foreign words and names, called *katakana*. These two sets of symbols are quite easy to learn, but the Japanese borrowed over 2000 Chinese pictographs which must also be learned in order to read the newspaper. The Japanese language can be written using the English alphabet. This is called *Romaji* because it uses Roman letters. This is not the best way to learn Japanese because the Roman letters do not accurately represent the Japanese sounds, so one tends to pronounce words with an English accent instead of the true Japanese sounds.

Almost all of the students were missionaries. They came from many different countries and from many different missionary organizations. It gave us a wonderful chance to get acquainted with them before we were all scattered around the country to do our missionary work. We had both male and female teachers to acquaint us with the different ways that men and women spoke.

An Unexpected Happening: Fire!

February 6, 1952

We had been in our home and in language school for about a month when an unexpected thing happened. While Jay, Esther and I were at language school on February 6, we received a phone call saying that our house had burned. Assured that baby Linda and the Grandmother (*Obaa San*) who took care of her were safe, we hurried home, not knowing what we would find. Unable to get past the fire trucks, we parked our car and sloshed through the mud to view the charred shell of a house that remained. Mr. Ogawa, Dr. Kagawa's secretary, who is our neighbor, met us. He told us that the neighbors had seen smoke coming out of the windows about 9:15 and hurried over to tell Obari San, the Hirth's helper. She took Linda over to a neighbor and immediately other neighbors hurried over to save whatever they could. Most of Hirth's things on the first floor were saved, although many things were damaged. The majority of their clothes were destroyed. All of Linda's things were saved. My upstairs apartment looked completely burned out. The fire began in my bedroom, so there was no opportunity to rescue anything.

The chief of police, fire department and insurance companies began to investigate the cause of the fire. I was called in for a series of questionings regarding the heating pad and hot plate which were plugged into an outlet near my bed. That morning I had put both of them under my bed to make the room look tidier. The thing that grieved me most was not the loss of my things, but the fact that I was responsible for the fire, though unknowingly. The house was insured, but the loss was not completely covered. I felt so bad for the Toppings who owned the house and also for the Hirths. I acknowledged this responsibility and apologized sincerely to both Toppings and Hirths, but I could do little more than exhibit a repentant spirit. I prayed that the Toppings would not feel bitter about it and that their loss would somehow be made up. I knew the Hirths would be most gracious and forgiving.

Everyone was very kind to us. Several missionaries helped by storing some of our things and transporting them in their cars. The encouragement and help of all these people was a real comfort. The Lord helped me overcome the dreadful weight of guilt I felt, but it was hard to shake it off.

My clothes, shoes, bed, books, Christian education supplies, office supplies, and living room furniture were lost. My typewriter, phonograph, camera, some kitchen utensils, some linens and some food were left but all were damaged considerably. My valuable papers such as passport, birth certificate, etc. were also gone. I would have to begin anew, but somehow I did not dread it, because I had the confidence that it would be a precious experience of walking with the Lord, trusting Him to supply what I needed. I was especially sorry to lose my books and school notes, my snapshots and color slides, which could not be replaced. However, none of these things were so important that I could not live without them.

After a few days I decided to go back to the YWCA to stay. When I moved to the YW, I was met by the assistant manager who looked at my boxes and said "You still have many things, don't you?" I couldn't feel sorry for myself in a country like Japan, for when you think you have lost all, you still have more than many of the Japanese.

The Hirths stayed with a kind American Baptist missionary couple (Hinchmans) until they could find another place. Neither Hirths nor I had any insurance on our personal goods. The Toppings said that the rebuilding of their house would cost about $2800 above the insurance money. After Hirths and I discussed this with them, they said it would be satisfactory if our mission assumed half of that amount. I believe that the Mission gave them about that much from the contributions made by the churches, as a token of sympathy and to help them with their loss.

The students at the language school had prayer for us the day of the fire and then formed a committee to collect money and clothing for us. Their contributions were very generous and in some instances, sacrificial. As soon as NAB Missions Secretary Mr. Schilke heard of the fire, he sent letters to our supporting churches informing them of our needs and requesting that they contribute as much as they could. I had no idea where help would be coming from, but it was exciting to see God at work in ways I never expected.

I learned many important lessons through this sad experience. One was that when the worst thing happens, the best still remains, if one has God, because He is the source of every blessing. He is like the spring of water that never runs dry. I also learned that we must never set our hearts on material possessions. We can be supremely happy without owning much of this world's goods, for fullness of joy is found in the Lord's presence that can't be taken away. I prayed that I might never forget the lessons the Lord had taught me.

I was summoned to the police station some days after the fire to answer questions regarding the fire. I was there from 1:45 to 6:15. The police station, of course, was unheated, but they put a charcoal burner in the little room for my comfort. They did everything they could to make me feel comfortable and at ease, which is more than I could say for American policemen. The interpreter walked from the police station to the electric train station with me and on the way he said, "Speaking for myself, I would like to talk with you some time about religion." Upon further inquiry I discovered that he had some Catholic teaching while in Paris and that he had been baptized while in a hospital at the point of death. Since that time, he said his religion had been neglected. I made it clear to him that I believed differently from Catholic teaching and elaborated on some of the basic differences. He asked if he might write to me or visit me sometime.

I attended a mass Youth for Christ Rally at which the Moody film, "Dust or Destiny" was shown. I took Mr. Minagawa and his two sisters. When we got there, we were surprised to find that the older brother had come also, by himself. We had never had a chance to speak to him about Christ, so I hoped that this meeting would be a help to him. The building seated 2500 and it was crowded with people standing everywhere. The message was given through an interpreter. It was a fine message and they had a wonderful interpreter, so I believe the message really got across. I prayed that one of these days, Mr. Minagawa would take a stand for Christ. I didn't know how much he really understood or believed. I wanted him to take the initiative rather than for us to urge him to accept Christ.

March 23, 1952

Hirths now live in a nice Japanese style house. They have put in kitchen cabinets and remodeled the bathroom. It was rather expensive but the cabinets are removable.

Our Japanese language class is continuing to pray for one of our language teachers, a young man named Mr. Ando (Ando Sensei to us). One day last week he again introduced the subject of religion into the class by asking whether we were the same as nuns and priests. Fortunately, in our class we have only evangelical Protestants, so we could answer freely. Our prayer is that his curiosity about missionaries

24

might lead him to inquire further about Christianity and that little by little he will see the Light. Inter Varsity Christian Fellowship (*Kirisutosha Gakusei Kai*) is having a conference this week for university students. We are praying for this, too, because the university student group is so important in Japan. It is the group that leans most toward communistic philosophy.

One of the language school teachers asked if I had time to teach English to a girl who in turn could teach me Japanese. I had very little contact with Japanese people, so I consented. She will come to me twice a week and we will each teach the other person one hour.

April 27, 1952

We received word that a missionary couple by the name of Browne was moving out of their house. We were able to rent it and I moved into the house in April. The rent for the four room house was less than my small room at the YW.

I borrowed a table and a camp cot until I could send for a roll-away bed from the States. I wanted to live as simply as possible so that I would not become burdened down with possessions and so that I did not appear wealthy to the Japanese, for even when we thought we had just the bare necessities, they thought we had so much. They don't use a lot of furniture, sitting and sleeping on the floor as they do. Cushions take the place of chairs, and quilts on straw mats take the place of beds. These can be folded up and put away during the day. Even the legs on the little low tables sometimes were folded up to make more space. I really liked the little house, but I didn't especially like being alone at night. However, I knew that the Lord's presence was more real and constant than that of a friend. I knew that I had to learn to trust Him for protection and safety.

With the house, I inherited from the Brownes a Japanese Sunday School which they had begun in their home. They said about 100 children had been coming each Sunday morning. They had two sessions divided according to age. Mr. Browne taught the children in Japanese. I was not that advanced so I had to either find an interpreter or a Japanese teacher. I prayed that I could find someone quickly, so that the attendance would not drop off. My bedroom and living room became the Sunday School classroom. The children sat on the bare floor with no rug to soften it.

I also inherited an English Bible Class for girls which met at my house every Thursday night. I didn't exactly like *English* Bible classes. Although the students may understand some English, there is a lot that is going over their heads and not making sense to them. They might pretend to understand even when they really don't, because they don't want to appear slow in catching on or else they might think it would not please the teacher to hear that. I considered teaching the class with an interpreter, if I could find one.

I thought that living out among the people would be a real boost to my language study. I found out by experience, that unless one used the language, it didn't stay with you, regardless of how diligently one studied.

May 6, 1952

I feel that I have neglected my language study badly this term. I haven't done nearly as well this term as last. The change of teachers was one factor, my living in the Ineson home was another, and now my moving to this new place in Nakano Ku, and the added duties of fixing up a house, have hindered my study. I am glad to be out among the Japanese people here and to begin a little work of actually teaching. The first English Bible Class since being here will start this week. I hope to be able to begin the Sunday School next Sunday if I can get a Japanese teacher.

Just today, one of the missionaries from Sweden who is living at the YWCA offered to come to live with me for about two months. She thinks it's better for me to have some company, which I agree with. She has spent eight years in China. She speaks quite good English. We have had some good times of fellowship, so I am sure it will be a boost to my morale. She will move in with me in about a week. She has no furniture except a bed, which is perfect for my set up, because the rooms must be emptied every Sunday morning for Sunday School.

June 8, 1952

John and Lydia Rhoads were appointed by our NAB Mission to work with Youth for Christ in Japan. They are due to arrive June 12. They have two children and are expecting the third. Even though they will not be working with us directly, we do feel that they belong to us

26

and we are happy to have them come. If possible we want to join Youth for Christ representatives in meeting them at the ship.

I found an interpreter (*Praise the Lord!*) and our Sunday School has opened in my house. The first time there were 22 children. Today there were 25. I hope that as soon as the word spreads, more children will come. We have two classes, one for the little ones up to 5th grade and one for the older ones. I'm not too keen on English classes, because I know the girls don't understand very well, but since it had been started by the former missionary who lived in the house, I have continued it.

A young man is coming to my house every Friday night for personal Bible study in English. We are studying the gospel of John. The first time we studied chapter 1, verses 1-4 and discussed how Christ was like light. The young man opened up at the end of the study saying that his life was dark and gloomy and that he sometimes despaired of living. I tried to help him open his heart to Christ so that he might know joy and peace. We prayed together but I do not know what he prayed, since he prayed in Japanese. I asked family and supporting churches to send me left over children's Sunday School papers, large Bible story pictures and outdated teachers' manuals to help me with my work since these materials were not yet available in Japanese.

I went with some of the language school students and teachers on a trip to Kamakura to see the great Buddha statue. Kamakura is one of the strongholds of Buddhism. There are over thirty temples. Pilgrims travel from one to the other until they have visited them all. At one of the temples where the priests are supposed to meditate, we were invited in to look around, which is quite rare. The woman who talked with us explained that Buddha is the Japanese Jesus Christ. I almost lost my breath when she said that. How little the Japanese know of Jesus Christ or they would certainly never make that comparison. We also visited a little cemetery where we saw in front of the tomb stones rice bowls, chopsticks and tea cups. Food and drinks are sometimes placed there for the spirits of the dead. Actually, sometimes beggars come to eat the food that is placed there.

One day while we were up on the flat roof of the three story concrete language school building during recess, playing volley ball, we saw some buildings around us swaying. We thought it was very amusing. We did not know what was causing it. When we went downstairs, we discovered that the teachers had all gone out of the building because it was an earthquake. Earthquakes are frequent in Japan. This one was said to have been the worst in six years. There was no damage from it in our area.

June 15, 1952

Our mission family grew with the arrival of John and Lydia Rhoads and their three children. They will not be working with us directly, since they are on the Youth for Christ staff. They have an interest in our work and will be available for consultation and support. John is a graduate of Dallas Seminary and is a traveling evangelist. He plans to work with an interpreter rather than in Japanese. Jay Hirth, and possibly John Rhoads, are planning to take a trip south to view some of the needy provinces of Japan in order to determine just where we ought to set up our headquarters and establish our field of service. That was a very important decision about which we prayed much. I hoped that before long another single girl would be sent out to be a co-worker with me. Companionship means so much in a foreign country, especially when one tends to become discouraged.

July 10, 1952

I completed my second term of language study, from January through June, with examinations. In July I changed language schools to compare the merits of each. The school to which I transferred was held in a Missouri Synod Lutheran Church. I was told that they teach more religious vocabulary to the students and that the classes were smaller with two or three students in a class. This gives more time for all to participate. Otherwise I would have been in a class by myself and that would have been too expensive. Jay and Esther are glad that they changed. We are in the same class, but I am a little ahead of them since I went to school in July and they didn't. We had our first public reading class. Each student was to read something before others. We are assigned a teacher to help correct our pronunciation. Last week, every day for fifteen minutes I practiced alone with my teacher. In two weeks I must give my first speech. I will prepare a Bible Story to use with children. We could not have done this at the other school.

One night I was sitting at my desk studying at about eight o'clock in the evening. I looked up and saw something white flit across the window on the other side of the room. I quickly went to the window and saw a young man in a white shirt and dark trousers crouching beneath the window. When he saw me he took off. Without thinking, I ran out the door in pursuit of him. I chased him for several blocks but he outran me, so I went back to the house. I don't know what I would have done if I had caught up with him. I was terribly shaken up and decided I had better call the police, but I didn't have a phone. There was a police box several blocks away where a policeman was stationed. I decided to go there and tell him what happened.

Before going, I went to my neighbor and asked her to keep an eye on my house while I was gone. While I was talking to the neighbor, I saw the young man walking in front of my house from the opposite direction. When he saw me, he again ran off. I was afraid to go to the police box but I did go and reported what had happened. The policeman said there had been some break-ins in the neighborhood so I should put double locks on my doors and windows. That was all he did. I went back to my house and locked the doors and windows but I could not sleep that night or the next night. The second day after this happened, I was again at my desk studying when I heard footsteps drawing near my house and then they stopped. There was a little footpath in front of my house. I turned out the light and went to the window and saw the same young man tip-toeing in front of my house. When he saw me he again ran away. By then I was beginning to be a nervous wreck and wondered if it was wise for me to stay in the house alone.

I told my missionary friends in language school about it and one of them, Lorraine Fleischman, said "I need a place to stay. Maybe I could come and live with you for awhile." I didn't think twice about it and said, "Would you really come and live with me?" She said she would. What an answer to prayer it was!

November 4, 1952

We had a few days off in October from language school, so Jay and I both made trips to spy out the land in search of a suitable place for us to begin our missionary work. We consulted with other missionaries and read statistics about the locations of churches and missionaries before we went. We saw that many of the new missionaries were settling in the large cities, so we decided that it would be best if we went to some place where there were few churches and missionaries. Jay went alone to Yamaguchi Ken, the southernmost prefecture of Honshu, which is the main island of Japan. I went to Tokushima Ken, the northeastern prefecture of Shikoku, the smallest of the four main islands of Japan. I had been given the name and address of Pastor Eichi Itoh by our pastor friend, Kobayashi Sensei. Pastor Itoh lived in Kamojima Machi, a small town in Tokushima Prefecture. He was to be my main source of information regarding churches in that prefecture.

A young Japanese girl who had been helping me in Tokyo accompanied me to Shikoku. When we arrived at the Kamojima train station, we had no idea how to find Pastor Itoh's house. As we stood there with our suitcases, wondering what to do, a man came up to us and asked if he could help. I explained that I wanted to go to the house of Pastor Eichi Itoh. He said, "I am Eichi Itoh." I couldn't believe it! When I explained to Pastor Itoh the purpose of our visit, he cordially invited us to his house and spent time telling us about churches and missionaries in the area.

We intended to stay just long enough to gather information and return to Tokyo the same day, but he informed us that there would not be another ferryboat from Shikoku to Honshu until the next morning. He said, "You may stay overnight with us and leave in the morning." He also said that he would invite some of his church people to his house for a special prayer meeting to pray for God's guidance for us in choosing a workplace. He then got on his bicycle and rode around town asking people to gather for a special prayer meeting.

A short time before the people arrived he said to me, "It would be nice if you would say something to the people in Japanese." I told him I couldn't but he insisted, so I did my best which was terrible. It was the first time I had spoken in Japanese to a group of people. He had been accustomed to working with missionaries, so he interpreted my poor Japanese into good Japanese so that I could be understood. About 33 people came, with just about one hour's notice. I was amazed. The spirit of the meeting was wonderful. I sensed that there was real harmony among the people. There were a few young people present who understood a little English. They asked me to teach them an English song. I taught them a simple chorus containing the gospel very clearly. What a privilege to be in this pastor's home, poor indeed, but blessed by the presence of the Lord. In the six years that he had worked in Kamojima, a lovely church had been built and seven or eight preaching stations in nearby towns were established. He was truly an evangelistic pastor.

In the morning we took the train to the city of Tokushima and boarded a small ferry that carried only about 20 people. I was the only foreigner on the boat. The ferry was supposed to take us to Osaka but as it turned out, our course was changed due to very stormy weather. When we had gone about halfway to our destination, the wind became very strong and the waves very high. It was also very cold. The captain's mate brought out blankets for the passengers. Many were getting sick as our little craft was tossed about like a cork.

The Lord gave us the opportunity to speak to the mate about Jesus. At first he said he didn't believe in God and that the Bible was only fiction because the Japanese also had stories of creation and of gods. Gradually he told us about his past life. He said he wanted to believe in something. He accepted the gospel of John I had offered him and asked me where he might go to hear the Bible taught. He invited us to sit in the pilot's cabin. My companion and I sat on a straw matted ledge behind the captain as we continued the conversation. There the mate spoke plainly with us about God and the Bible, before two other crew members, so I felt that he would make an unashamed Christian if he ever decided to become one. He lived on a small island between Shikoku and Honshu called Awaji. He invited us to come there and teach him.

He pointed out a famous huge whirlpool near the island called *Naruto*. Many little boats have been caught in this whirlpool and gone down. In fact we saw the evidence of it. Some portions of a ship that had gone down were sticking up out of the water. This only added to our fears that our little boat might sink. I watched the face of the pilot as he struggled to control the boat, as it bucked the huge waves. In my mind I pictured the apostle Paul, as his ship was wrecked and he and his fellow passengers swam to an island. Was that going to happen to us? The pilot decided that it was too dangerous to go to the port of Osaka and headed in the direction of the nearest port, which happened to be in Wakayama Prefecture.

November 23, 1952

Today was Japanese Thanksgiving day. One year ago on our American Thanksgiving day we had arrived in Japan. We were eating our Thanksgiving dinner on the ship when we pulled into Yokohama

Harbor. The following day we had shared another Thanksgiving dinner with the Sorleys, the Baptist General Conference missionaries who met us at the ship. What an eventful year it was! We entered another year in Japan with the same anticipation, not knowing what this year would bring forth. However, we could confidently say "Hitherto hath the Lord helped us."

The big event in Japan recently was the proclamation of the Crown Prince as Heir Apparent to the throne. The thing that grieves the Christian's heart is to read that the imperial family are still devoted Shintoists. Every major event in the family must be reported to the gods at the shrine of the Sun Goddess in Ise in Mie Prefecture and to the spirits of the dead emperors at their mausoleums. One outstanding missionary said "As long as the Ise Shrine of the Sun Goddess stands, Japan will be Shinto at heart."

John and Lydia Rhoads, 3 children, Jay and Esther Hirth, Linda, Florence Miller

November 30, 1952

The Hirths, Rhoads, and I met for an important *sodan* (big council) to decide on our field of service, in view of the recent survey trips Jay and I had made. We compared facts and figures and decided that since we were just opening our work, it would be better not to get

32

too far away from Tokyo, the capital city. Jay had gone with John Rhoads and the Youth for Christ team to the city of Ujiyamada (later named Ise) in Mie Prefecture to hold street meetings during the summer. It took about 10 hours by train from Tokyo to Mie Prefecture. Ise had a population of around 60,000 people. They said they had had a good response to the gospel invitations. The city was located just thirty minutes by streetcar from the famous Ise Grand Shrine where the Sun Goddess was worshiped. This is the main shrine of Shintoism. The emperor is said to have been descended from the Sun Goddess so he and family members would come there on special occasions to worship. This was not an easy place to work because the whole city is centered around the Shrine. There was one Catholic Church and two Protestant churches in the city. To Jay this was a challenge. He wanted to live and work in the city of Ise. Consequently the decision was made to start our work in Mie Prefecture even though I very much wanted to go to Shikoku. I was uncertain about whether to live in the same city as Hirths or go to another nearby.

December 28, 1952

The Christian teacher at the high school was able to secure a large room for the Christmas program at the high school near my house. He paid for the janitors and the use of the stove, but the room did not cost us anything. I did not expect many parents, and only five came, but there were about 200 children in all, including some older brothers and sisters who did not come to Sunday school. The program went off quite well, but I wondered if it was worth the effort since so few parents came. After the program, about 50 of the older children and teachers went caroling along the streets, carrying lighted candles. It was very pretty and drew a number of people to the doors and windows of their homes to see what was going on. We gave out Christmas tracts as we walked. We prayed that there would be some fruit from it later.

Having decided on Mie Prefecture as our field of service I was praying about where the Lord would have me live. I really wanted to spend six months, or even a year, with the wonderful pastor whom I met in Shikoku, Pastor Itoh, in order to learn his approach to evangelism.

Some of the junior high school students asked some very significant questions in Sunday School. For the first time I began to understand how difficult it was for them to believe in Jesus. One girl asked about the Trinity. Another asked, "Who is a Christian?" After using the wordless book to explain the way of salvation, we read from Revelation 21 where it speaks of heaven and hell. One girl said she could not believe there is such a place as hell. I pointed out the people who would be there, among them the unbelieving and idolaters. This is very significant for Japan. She asked if all who worship in other ways, without believing in Jesus, would go to hell. "Those who believe in Jesus are so few," she said. It was hard to say "yes" when you know that their families are probably Buddhist and their parents, already fixed in their beliefs, may never be persuaded to change their beliefs.

The bed, refrigerator, and washing machine I had ordered from the States arrived. The customs was very high, $200 just for getting them into the country plus the shipping expense, which was very high too. I was almost sorry I had sent for them.

January 5, 1953

I am hoping to go to Shikoku to live in the town of Kamojima where Pastor Itoh lives. I wrote to Mr. Schilke about this. He said it must come as a recommendation from the field and be approved by headquarters. I talked to Jay and John about it and they are in favor of it. I will need a place to stay there. I would like to room with a Japanese family, so I won't have to move all my belongings down there. I want to leave my household things in Tokyo for the 2 to 3 months that I will be in Shikoku. I have been praying that someone without much furniture might want to move into my house and use my furniture for a few months; someone who could also keep up the Sunday School.

January 30, 1953

I got permission from headquarters to go to Shikoku to live for a few months. However, I was told that the mission planned to send out a partner for me this year and wanted me to hold the house in Tokyo for her. They did not know who it would be or just how soon she would come, so I didn't know whether to stay in Tokyo until her arrival or try to get someone to live in the house temporarily, while I am in Shikoku. My new co-worker would probably want someone to live with her, just as I did, so I said I would try to find a single girl who needed a place to live. Also I had to write to the Japanese pastor

34

to see if it was all right for me to live there. I felt confident that the Lord would work out all the details just right.

I was very thrilled to hear that a new missionary would be coming out this year. Jay went down to Mie Prefecture this week to buy the land for their house in Ise City. They expect to begin building in the spring. Esther is excited.

February 21, 1953

I sent an invitation to the police interpreter who questioned me after the fire to attend the Youth for Christ rally. I received a card from him after the rally, saying that he had attended and enjoyed the meeting very much, especially the speaker, Dr. Fred Jarvis. He said that during the message, two girls near him were weeping because of their sins and that if he had been younger, he would have wept with them. Being an old man, his heart had become like a rusty machine, the parts of which can no more be moved. He said he believed it to be divine providence that old men's hearts were not so sensitive or else they must always be weeping over their sins. He has been convicted of sin but still does not see the way of forgiveness for sin.

Yesterday my Japanese language teacher who is soon to graduate from Tokyo University, the top school in Japan, in explaining the word "bury" said, "When a cat or dog dies, you put it in the ground, place flowers and a marker with its name on the grave and pray." I was so shocked that I guess I sounded rude when I exclaimed, "You do that for a cat or dog?" I told him that I had read in the newspaper about Buddhist memorial services for cats that had been killed in order to make musical instruments from their skins. He said, "Yes, that is very common and so is praying for horses that were killed during the war, in the service of the country." Once again my face disclosed my astonishment and he asked me, somewhat surprisingly, "Is such a thing inconceivable to you?" I told him plainly that it was. He is soon to graduate from the best university in Japan but is still in spiritual darkness.

March 7, 1953

Last night I attended a prayer meeting where about 35 missionaries were gathered together. About a month ago, when one of the larger missions (The Evangelical Alliance Mission, known as TEAM) had their annual conference, the Lord met them in an unusual way and is continuing to work among them, as well as with other missionaries and also Japanese. It is a real revival. The Lord's power has been manifested in various ways, including the correction of a stammering tongue on the part of one missionary. The most glorious victories have been in the creating of a new love for the Lord and His Word, faith in prayer, and cleansed lives. We prayed that this would be just the beginning of the moving of God's Spirit and that it might spread throughout Japan, reaching into the most remote villages.

This past summer, Youth for Christ was concentrating all its efforts on Japan. Their plan was to organize about 50 teams to work with the Japanese Christians in an all-out effort to make the gospel known in every part of Japan. It seems that the Lord was beginning the work, which the Youth for Christ teams hope to accomplish. Japan had never had a real revival such as other countries have known. This could be Japan's opportunity.

On one of our school field trips, we visited the temple where 47 *samurai* (warriors) of many years ago, killed themselves to take revenge on those responsible for the death of their lord. This act was in keeping with the old Japanese *samurai* way of thinking, which placed loyalty to one's superiors as one of the most important principles of life. Thus these 47 men showed their loyalty to their master, even to the giving up of their lives. This act was lauded by all Japanese and many come to this grave to pay honor to these men. As we entered the gate, one of the teachers purchased some incense to place on the graves, which he said was according to Japanese custom. He also offered some to us, but of course we did not accept it. It was extremely disappointing to me to see the one teacher, who is supposedly a baptized Christian, take some of the incense and place it on the graves. They would probably argue that there was no religious significance in the act, but that it was purely according to custom, just as we placed flowers on a grave. I am certain that the use of incense is definitely related to heathen worship. These teachers are all university graduates and very scientific minded. They find it difficult to accept the Bible as the Word of God, but without any question follow a Japanese custom.

It was getting to be like spring in Tokyo with plum blossoms blooming and in a few more weeks the cherry blossoms would be in full bloom. Spring of 1953 was something of a goal for us. It meant the end of our formal language study at school and also making preparations to leave Tokyo. I had to wait patiently for the Lord's plan

36

to become clear to me. I was given permission by the mission to live with a Japanese family in Shikoku for a few months before moving to Mie Ken. I heard from one of the girls in Pastor Itoh's church whom I had met there. She said that the pastor had told them of my coming and they were glad to hear of it. She did not mention a place to live, so the problem was still unsolved.

In addition to this was the matter concerning what to do with my house. Mr. Schilke had written saying that the mission was planning to send three new missionaries: a couple, and a single girl to live with me, so I should keep the house for them. I did not know when they might be arriving, but probably not before summer at the earliest. I had to stay in Tokyo until they came to occupy the house or I would have to make arrangements with someone to stay for a few months, which could be rather difficult. It was hard to be patient when you wanted things to be definite right now. I trusted that the Lord would work out all the details.

Jay went down to Mie Ken to purchase land for the mission house where they will live. He planned to go again in April to begin construction of the house. The Hirths are expecting their second child.

An Ebenezer Experience

March 7, 1953

One night while I was still living alone, I had a most unusual experience. I had studied Japanese for about one year. At first I did quite well, but when we started getting many new *kanji* (Chinese characters) to memorize for each lesson, it seemed that I just could not remember them. I felt very discouraged and put my head down on my desk, saying to myself, "I can't learn this language. I just can't! " Then I heard a voice as clearly as if someone had been in the room speaking to me. The voice said, "But you *can* ask the Father in my name." I knew immediately who was speaking to me, because Jesus had said to His disciples words almost like that in John 16:23 "Whatever you shall ask the Father in my name, He will give it to you."

It was as if the light went on inside me as I realized that I had been studying very hard in my own strength and had not been praying about my studies. Faith laid hold of those words spoken to me and I *did* ask the Father, in Jesus' name, to help me learn the language, for without it I could not carry out my calling. After I prayed and believed the words of Jesus, I picked up my vocabulary cards and to my amazement, I was able to write them correctly! I knew this was not mere coincidence, but I wanted to confirm my conviction that there had been Divine intervention on my behalf. I said to the Lord, "If I can write my Japanese composition for tomorrow as well as I have written these vocabulary cards, then I will know for certain that it was really You answering my prayer." I wrote a two-page composition and took it to school the next day.

I handed my paper to my teacher, a middle-aged man. He read my paper silently in front of the class and as I watched him, tears rolled down his cheeks. I wondered what was going on in his mind. Then he told us this story. He said, "I was a *kamikaze* (suicide) pilot during the war. My little zero plane was supposed to have dived into an American ship and I would have died, but my plane crashed in the mountains. One of my companions died, another had both legs amputated and only I, though seriously injured, was perfectly well. Ever since I have been asking 'Why did all my buddies die and I remain alive?'" I don't remember what I wrote in my composition, but it may have concerned my faith or purpose in coming to Japan. At any rate, something I had written was used of God to touch his heart, because Japanese men do not weep in public.

What an encouragement that was to me to know that God could use me, even though my Japanese was imperfect! I wanted to know how many mistakes I had made and eagerly awaited the return of my paper. It had only a few red marks on it. I knew then that God had truly helped me. It was not mere coincidence. I called that my "Ebenezer Experience" because I could look back on it in the future when I again became discouraged over the language and say, "Hitherto hath the Lord helped me (*Ebenezer*) and He can help me again." I was burdened for my teacher and prayed for him, but I do not know if he ever became a Christian. He had been studying the Bible but was not yet ready to believe it. On the seventh anniversary of the plane crash, he planned to go to the site of the crash and meditate. I prayed that he would meet the Savior there, face to face.

The end of our school term is drawing near so I have spent extra hours studying in preparation for exams. As I reviewed my vocabulary cards, I was overwhelmed at the number I still did not know. This was our last term of language school before we move out of Tokyo.

38

Going to Shikoku

The Lord certainly was working out everything perfectly concerning my going to Shikoku. From the time the thought first entered my mind to go there, a number of problems were solved one by one. The two big matters of a place to live and someone to move into my house in Tokyo while I was gone, were taken care of. I received a letter from the pastor saying that it was all right for me to come to live with his family for a few months. I hadn't asked him if I might live with his family, but rather if he knew of anyone who would be willing to take in a foreigner. Maybe there wasn't anyone willing to do so, but anyway, I was happy about it, because they are such a grand family. I hope I won't be too much of a nuisance to them, because the pastor's house is a busy enough place, without having boarders.

The second problem was solved a little later. A couple in Japan with Youth for Christ, the Pools, attended the same language school I did. I told them about my situation and they said they would like to come to see my house. They liked it very much. They did not have much furniture, so my things would not be in their way. I told them that it would only be for a few months, because we had new missionaries coming. They were willing to move in for that time and would trust the Lord to provide another place when needed. They even consented to take care of my puppy, Susie, until I came back.

April 12, 1953

The Pools were to move into my house on April 15 so we three girls, Gudren Ingebretson, Lorraine Fleischman and I, had to be out by then. It was fun for us all to be packing and racing with time to clear out before the Pools moved in. I planned to leave some of my things for them to use, but it was still a real chore. I left my typewriter behind so I had to write letters singly and by hand after that.

When the pastor with whose family I plan to live came to Tokyo I asked him what things I ought to take with me. He said I would need a *futon*, a Japanese-style bed consisting of two heavy quilts, that I could have made in Shikoku.

I really looked forward to living in my new Japanese home. I didn't relish the twenty-four hour trip to Shikoku by train and boat by myself. At least I had traveled that way once before, so it wouldn't all be new and strange to me. I knew I would be missing all my Tokyo missionary friends to keep me company, so I would have to rely on letters from them.

Esther had a really hard time before her baby was born. She was in the hospital once and went back home but nothing was happening. She finally delivered a baby girl on April 2. They named her Sharon Lynne. I went to see them. Mother and baby were doing fine. Mom wanted to send something for the baby so Esther suggested something for a year old child like a pair of corduroy overalls.

May 2, 1953

I am living with pastor Itoh's family in Shikoku now. The house is perhaps average or a little below average. The family consists of grandma (Pastor's mother), father, mother, one son aged 10 and an adopted nephew, aged 14, who was orphaned. The first Wednesday night I was here, the pastor was to be absent so he asked me to lead prayer meeting. I tried to refuse but couldn't, so I prepared a little talk and read it, but even the reading of it was poor. There is nothing so effective for producing humility as going to a foreign country where you have to learn everything like a child. I pitied those who had to listen to such mangled Japanese.

Pastor and Mrs. Itoh had been missionaries in North China to Japanese who migrated there after Japan took over parts of that country. They experienced many hard things which taught them to lean hard upon the Lord. When I heard of what they were willing to suffer for the Lord's sake, I couldn't help but feel that I was unworthy to work with such a man as Mr. Itoh. He was always praising people for their good deeds. He had confidence in everyone and was willing to commit responsibility to people others would probably not trust. Consequently he was loved by almost everyone.

Pastor Ito was limitless in his energy, from early morning until late at night. I felt guilty taking a nap now and then in the afternoon, because they never did. Missionaries have a reputation for taking afternoon naps. We were encouraged to do so by older missionaries for health's sake, since more sleep seems to be required in a foreign country, especially from the beginning when the body was not yet adjusted to the climate. Just being a foreigner takes energy and so does trying to think and speak in Japanese. Mrs. Itoh sometimes told me about the other missionaries who lived in this town and are now on furlough. You can't keep anything private. Either the maid or the neighbors or someone will spread the news of your private life around, so you have to exercise utmost care about what you do and say.

May 10, 1953

The pastor's wife occasionally asked me to go visiting with her. I didn't contribute much to the conversation, but I learned a lot. Upon entering a Japanese house, after taking off your shoes, you step inside the entrance way and make your presence known by saying, "Excuse me." When the lady of the house comes to the entrance, she greets you with a deep bow and asks you to come up into the hall which is covered with straw mats. This begins a series of bows and greetings. It is rude to stand in a Japanese house, so you immediately assume a position of kneeling and sitting on your heels. Then you say something like, "Good afternoon, thank you for all the nice things you did for me when you visited me recently." "I was very rude to you for which I am sorry," etc. As you can imagine, my bows were always very short and shallow. Not knowing all the flattering humbling phrases, I either said nothing or muttered something no one could understand.

Of course you are always served tea and usually some little cakes as well. Most of these little cakes are filled with a kind of jam made from sweetened beans. I'm learning to like it, but at first I could hardly stand to eat it.

During the course of the conversation, many of the needs and problems of the people were expressed. It was clear that they trusted the pastor's wife or they would not have shared them with her. We visited a mother who was concerned about a wayward daughter who got into trouble and, to protect the girl and the reputation of the family, she was sent away to live with her grandmother. Another Christian woman was burdened down because her husband, a doctor, had a serious drinking problem. A young Christian girl, at the death of her father a few days before, was left to support her mother and younger sister on a salary of $15 a month.

May 30, 1953

I was praying for a Japanese helper to work with me when I went to Ise. I learned about a Christian girl about my age, who would like to work as a maid and at the same time study for the Lord's work. She had only gone through junior high school. I asked the Lord to guide me clearly in making the choice of a helper.

3

BEGINNING THE WORK IN ISE

June 28, 1953

I received a letter from Jay saying that Esther was in the hospital with a nervous breakdown. At first they thought that rest was all she needed, but she got worse instead of better, so the doctor said she had to go home. It was impossible for her to take care of the children, so Jay had to go along. Jay and Esther and the two little children flew home to Chicago immediately. The plane trip was 36 hours long. It was uncertain when, and if, they would return to Japan. I left Shikoku and went to Tokyo immediately after receiving Jay's letter and helped them get ready to leave. They could take only 120 pounds so they left practically everything behind. Jay planned to talk to the new missionaries who were coming out, to see what they could use of their things. The rest would be shipped to them or sold. I lived in Hirth's house and tried to take care of their things as best I could.

Mr. John Rhoads took over the business end, such as the bookkeeping and the supervising of the new house which was under construction. There were lots of decisions to make and all kinds of little things to do. I was so glad that the Rhoadses were able to help. Until then, they had been somewhat unrelated to us because their work was with Youth for Christ. Esther's illness came as a shock to everyone. Not even Jay ever suspected that anything was wrong, except that he knew she tired easily. The three-week delay in waiting for the baby, plus the difficult labor seemed to bring to a head all that had been building up for a long time unknown to anyone. She spoke freely to the doctor about all the things which had been troubling her. I thought that with Jay, the children, and the many young couples who were friends of theirs, she surely was not lacking in friendship and social life. If I had had any idea that I was failing to be the friend I should have been, I would have done something about it. I prayed that I would learn from this for the future.

Our new missionary family was scheduled to arrive about the first of September. Walter and Barbara Sukut have a little girl a few months old. Walter studied at our NAB seminary and pastored one of our NAB churches for a few years. A single girl, Lois Lechner, from Chicago, was to be sent a little later. I prayed that we would all be able to work together harmoniously and be zealous to see souls saved. I planned to stay in Tokyo until Sukuts arrived and help them get settled before going to Ise.

I had a good two months in Shikoku. I felt it was really profitable in many ways. I came to love the Itoh family and the people of their church, even in that short time. Four of the ladies, including Mrs. Itoh, came on the train with me from Kamojima Machi to Tokushima City where I boarded a ferry. They brought tickertape and told me to hold on to the end of it while they held onto the roll. As the boat pulled away from the dock, the tape gradually unrolled until it slipped from our hands and the tie was broken. I felt as if I were going back to America instead of to Tokyo.

Before boarding the ferry, we discovered that Mrs. Itoh's sister, Mrs. Iwai, who was almost blind, was going to Kobe on the same boat. She wanted to visit her son who was studying at the Methodist seminary and pray with him concerning a problem. It was dangerous for her to travel alone, but there seemed no other way. I was able to go with her all the way to where her son was and they in turn saw me off for the train going to Tokyo. Her son was a handsome chap and had a real love for the Lord.

July 18, 1953

When I got back to Tokyo and Hirths had returned to the States, I felt very much alone. I received a cablegram from Mr. Schilke saying, "Prepare to go to Ise."[1] I was very much afraid to go to Ise alone. I was expected to supervise the building of the mission house but I knew nothing about construction. John Rhoads came to my aid and made a trip to Ise to check on things. I shared with John my need for a Japanese helper. He was doing evangelistic work with Youth for Christ and had just returned from some meetings in the city of Yokkaichi in Mie Prefecture.

Jay had a long talk with Mr. Schilke and they drew up a list of recommendations in view of the emergency created by Esther's illness. One of the decisions was that Lois, the new girl, is to come down to Mie Ken to live with me instead of staying in Tokyo for language

---

[1] The original name of the city was Ujiyamada, but when a second train station was built it was called Ise. Eventually the city came to be known as Ise, but the original station was called Ujiyamada.

44

school. It will be rather hard for her to adjust to a completely Japanese situation so suddenly but, of course, I'll be able to help her a lot.

The new mission house was supposed to be finished about the end of August. Mr. Rhoads came down and looked it over this week and found that there were quite a few things needing correction so he is sending down another contractor. This will delay the building for a time which really put me on the spot, because I had requested a room with Mr. Onishi, who is building our house, until the house was finished. Then Mr. Rhoads and he had a little disagreement about the way the house was being built. I didn't know if my coming would make things better or worse, so I came down on the train, not knowing where I was going to live.

Jay had employed a young man, Mr. Fujii, to come with him as his interpreter and helper. They lived in a small three room house owned by the main carpenter. When Jay left, this young man stayed on, having Sunday school. I went to see this young fellow today and was surprised at what I saw. The house was open and about a dozen children were romping around. Although the Mission told us to keep him as an interpreter and language teacher upon Jay's recommendation, Mr. Rhoads and I decided it wouldn't be right for me to work with a man, for it would be putting me in many awkward positions and it wouldn't be good for him either.

It seems, in many ways, I have come into some knotty situations. I would much rather have come into a place and began on my own from scratch, than to a place prepared by someone else, but that's the way things are and the Lord will have to straighten things out.

I just returned from Sunday School. I did not teach this morning because I did not have time to prepare anything in Japanese. Moreover, I wanted to listen to Mr. Fujii teach. There were about 25 children present this morning. This afternoon there will be another class of older children. Then there is an adult meeting this evening. I am going to speak in English to the adults tonight, since Mr. Fujii can interpret for me. After this I shall have to do it all in Japanese as best I can. The responsibility for the work will be upon my shoulders from now on.

John Rhoads had held evangelistic meetings in a church in Tomida Hama, a town near Yokkaichi in Mie Ken. A missionary by the name of Miss Elizabeth Whewell was in charge of this church called Mino Mission. She had been in Japan before the war and was regarded as a real pioneer missionary. She had a reputation for being very strict about living the Christian life. There was a spinning mill in Tomida Hama where many young Japanese women worked. They lived in the company dormitory. Miss Whewell held gospel meetings in this dormitory and a number of the girls were saved. They attended her church and were trained to become Sunday School teachers.

She taught the Christians that they should not work on Sunday because the Bible said, "Remember the Sabbath Day to keep it holy." When five of the Christian girls who worked at the factory told their employer that they could not work on Sunday, they were fired and were without jobs or income. One of them, Yoshiko Yamamoto, felt that perhaps the Lord was leading her to give her life for Christian service. She was only twenty years old and had very little education. She and two brothers lived in the mountain area of Gifu Prefecture. She was just 15 years old when she had to go to work in the spinning mill, away from her family. She said that the first time she heard the gospel, she believed in Christ. After she had attended church for a time, she was taught how to teach the Bible to children. She became a very good story teller and had a lot of enthusiasm when she taught. Mr. Rhoads had met her and thought she might be willing to be my helper. I went to Tomida Hama, and met Miss Whewell, Miss Yamamoto and some of the other girls. I talked with them about my need for a helper and asked if Miss Yamamoto would be willing to come and live and work with me in starting a new church in Ise. Miss Whewell encouraged her and after we had prayed together Miss Yamamoto consented to be my helper. It was a real step of faith on the part of both of us because we knew so little about each other. It seemed that the Lord had brought us together and so we agreed to follow His leading.

August 4, 1953

I moved to Ise and am living in the little Japanese house owned by the carpenter who was building the mission house. My Japanese helper, Miss Yamamoto, is living with me. I am truly grateful to the Lord for providing me with such a fine girl. She has a very sweet disposition, which was a rebuke to me when I run out of patience. She was always full of joy and never moody as I was at times. She was so eager to witness and is much bolder in talking to people than I am. My important task, I felt, was to be able to guide her and then to turn her loose, for she could accomplish so much more than I, being at home in the language and being Japanese.

We didn't have any glowing reports to make concerning our work during the beginning stages. In fact, our attendance at both Sunday school and adult evening meeting is lower than when Jay's interpreter was here. However, we felt confident that little by little, the Lord would increase the work. Today we had the privilege of informally telling a group of five boys, and later five girls, the story of Jesus' birth and the prodigal son, by means of my story-viewer. These children were from the neighborhood and were always peeping in at the windows, so we invited them in to hear the stories and see the pictures. We had a large sign in front of our house announcing the meetings and occasionally people came up close to the house to read the sign. One lady with a baby on her back came while Miss Yamamoto (Yoshiko) was outdoors fanning the charcoal burner to heat water for dishes. Yoshiko San[2] immediately gave her a tract and witnessed to her. She talked with her for over 15 minutes. In the meantime the fire had died out but nobody cared, because it might be the beginning of a spark of life in the listening one's heart. Our house was quite isolated from the others and not very conveniently located for church meetings. We asked permission to rent a kindergarten building. It would be grand if we could get it because everyone knows the school building.

In addition to the church work, I was supposed to be supervising the building of the mission house. Mr. John Rhoads made all the big decisions and I made the little ones, such as choosing the color of the bathroom tile. In Japan, bathrooms always have tile on the floor and walls. The bathtub is also made of tile.

Lois Lechner, the single girl who is supposed to join me soon, wrote saying that she still had not received final word of her acceptance by the Mission Board due to her medical examination which classed her as a Class B candidate. I also received a letter from the Sukuts today which contained their prayer card, the first picture I had seen of them. They will be sailing to Japan August 16 and arriving about September 1. They have a little girl, Nora Jane, about a year old.

---

[2] "San" is a polite term that is added to the name of a person and is the equivalent of Mr., Mrs., or Miss.

They will go to Tokyo to study for a year. It will be good to have all of our missionaries out of language school and into the work. I must be patient, for it took a good year and a half before I arrived in Mie Prefecture.

August 18, 1953

The mission house is gradually nearing completion, although we have had some problems. The man we have supervising the house said, "If you build another house, let us draw up the plans for you and you'll have a much better house." I can't get enthusiastic about moving into it for several reasons. In the first place, I feel it will tend to isolate me from the people, for I am quite sure they will not feel as free to come there as to an entirely Japanese house. Secondly, it will be only a temporary residence for me and I don't feel like fixing up a place just for a year or so.

The Sukuts will be arriving in Japan in about two weeks so I will again be going to Tokyo. I expect to bring all of my furniture down at that time, plus my little pooch. She had three puppies. We'll have to cure her of that. The owner of the house in which I lived in Tokyo wants it back, so the missionaries (Pools) now living there will have to move.

Lois is supposed to arrive about September 20. She is about 30 years old, a few years my senior. The Sukuts appear to be younger than I, from their picture. I'm having a problem finding a maid for Sukuts. The girl who worked for Hirths says she cannot work for people who do not know any Japanese because she knows no English.

October 6, 1953

I went to Tokyo to meet Lois. She is a lot different from me in many respects. She is very talkative, for one thing, which might make up for my usual quietness. She is the kind of person that would stand up for her rights, while I would probably let people trample all over me. Maybe we can learn something from each other. My prayer was that we would be spiritual leaders in the true sense and not in name only.

Since Sukuts brought a car with them, no one was using the Jeep station wagon which Jay and Esther had used. Since Lois and I both drove a little, we decided it might be nice to have a car in Ise but how would we get it there? It takes about 10 hours by train from

Tokyo to Ise so we figured it would take about twice as long by car, since the roads were very poor. We debated back and forth whether or not we could make it. Finally, we decided to try it. The mountain roads were rather treacherous because of curves, though we had no mishaps. Every time we saw a truck which had slipped off the road, we breathed a prayer of thanks for the protection of our Heavenly Father. There was only one main highway, so after that we couldn't get lost. They call it Route 1, but actually that is unnecessary because there isn't any other route. My nearest description of the roads was a Chinese checkerboard, because it was so full of potholes. When we arrived home, we laughed when we saw the license plate hanging by one screw!

Miss Yasuko Kitahara, one of the girls from Mino Mission in Tomida Hama who lost her job because she would not work on Sunday, has come to help me with household tasks, so that Yoshiko Yamamoto can be my full-time church worker. I must pay Yasuko Kitahara but Yoshiko San is paid by the mission. With the arrival of Lois Lechner, there are now four of us living in the little three room house and we are beginning to find it a little crowded. The new mission house is still several weeks from completion so we may not get into it until the end of October.

Lois in front of little three room house

Our church attendance is very poor with only one or two or three at each meeting. Some said that they were believers in Christ but

49

no longer attend regularly, only when it is convenient, which is not very often. We pray especially for the man living right next door to us. He attended our meetings quite often and seems eager to know more. I wanted to reciprocate for his kindness to us so I invited him and his wife for a meal. He came by himself. I learned later that it was not customary for a husband and wife to go out together since she is expected to stay at home and look after the children in the house. It is all right for the father to take a daughter with him but not his wife. We live and learn by our mistakes.

October 20, 1953

I received a letter from Jay today saying that Esther had gone home three weeks ago. The children were being cared for by someone else. We still do not know anything about their return to Japan, if or when.

Pastor Itoh, with whose family I lived in Shikoku, asked us to hold meetings once a month in a factory. He lived too far away to do it himself, but he had a contact there and said he would introduce us to the factory head on November 5. From then on we would have the opportunity to hold meetings there. The workers live in dormitories so it is very convenient for meetings with them. There are about 400 employees in the factory. We are also doing a little hospital visitation, one afternoon a week. I am still not able to undertake too much, because of my language study.

Our language teacher is very helpful in every way and is a good teacher. We are very grateful, especially for Lois's sake, since it is quite a sacrifice for her to come here to Ise to live with me and study the language with a tutor, instead of being in language school in Tokyo as I was and Sukuts are. Lois studies two hours and I one hour with her teacher each morning at his house. Today I asked my teacher to correct my Bible message which I gave at church last Sunday. Not only is this an opportunity to have my message in good Japanese, but also an indirect means of getting the gospel to him. He is familiar with the Bible and Christianity in an academic way, but I do not yet know clearly what he believes about Christ.

November 30, 1953

We had a gospel meeting in a silk factory in a town about two hours away by train. About 200 girls turned out for the meeting when we were there. I don't know where the men were. I felt so inadequate to speak, or rather to read to them, but I know the Lord helped me and gave me unusual freedom to conduct the meeting. One of the young girls, only 17, met me after the meeting and said that she believes in Jesus and waits eagerly to hear more from the Bible. The field is so white unto harvest but the laborers are so few. How I realized it there! I prayed that the Lord of the harvest would send forth laborers into His harvest field.

The Lord has been blessing the Sunday School and it looks as if we are going to need a larger meeting place. We had nearly 80 children last Sunday. Now we have some middle school and high school students coming. One of the middle school girls expressed her desire to be saved at a special meeting we had when Mr. Rhoads came down to attend to the house business. I know I dealt with her very poorly and yet I prayed that she might continue in her faith, if it was sincere.

A week ago, a young high school boy lingered after the meeting to tell us about problems he had with his math teacher. There had been something said in class which angered his teacher and since that time, he had been making it very difficult for the student. We suggested that he speak to his teacher and if there were anything needing confession on his part, to tell his teacher he was sorry. Then we prayed and asked the Lord to give him the necessary courage. The next time he came he said, "The heavenly Father gave me courage to speak to my teacher." Even though the teacher was not yet on friendly terms with him, he was grateful to God. Then he asked if God was able to save such a sinner as he. For a young person to say such a thing was indeed rare, for it seems that for the Japanese people, the fact that all men are sinners is one of the hardest doctrines to accept. We assured him that Jesus would cast out none who came to Him and then we prayed together. He prayed his own stumbling prayer, without any coaching on our part, also very rare. His faith is simple and childlike, and I do believe that he has been saved. Some who have been coming from the very beginning and who have said that they believe in Jesus have been very irregular in attendance and are still unable to pray. I pray that they may learn to do so.

One of the high school students who has been attending our church regularly for the past month is the son of a Buddhist priest. He spent a year studying for the priesthood, since it was expected that he would follow in his father's footsteps and eventually be a priest of the temple, but it had no appeal for him. A week ago he purchased his own Bible. His mother knows about it but his father does not. Last Sunday he brought his cousin, a young woman about 19, so it seems the Lord has definitely been convincing him of the truth. I prayed that he might be able to make a clear cut decision for Christ, even though it may mean real persecution in his home.

An old man came to church one day and told us that he had had seven operations and that he now had tuberculosis. He said that he believed in no god other than the Japanese Sun Goddess. Every morning he worshiped the sun and prayed, but having received no help, he came to our church to see if our God could help him. We sought to make him realize his greater need for forgiveness from sin. We tried to make him understand that unless he prayed to the true God and believed in Him, his prayers would never be answered. He is the second one who has come asking for physical healing. Japanese religions lead people to seek physical and material things, rather than spiritual. I pray that we might know the mind of the Lord, so that if it should please Him to do a miracle of healing, we would not be lacking in faith, that His name might be glorified among the heathen.

One Sunday we had a first time visitor at our little house church. She was a plump little lady who came puffing up the hill from her home, quite a walk for her. She looked curiously around and then took her seat on a cushion on the straw-matted floor, along with the others who had come to the service. We sang several gospel songs, including "Tell it to Jesus." I gave a Bible message as best I could, reading my notes written in *romaji*. The service ended and everyone went home. I wondered if anything I said had been understood and if she would come back again.

The next Sunday I was surprised to see Mrs. M., the little plump lady, at the meeting again. In fact she came every Sunday after that, rain or shine. When I got to know her better, I learned that the first time she came at the invitation of the blind masseur who had been coming to the church. He told her about the foreign church on the hill where he heard about Jesus. When she entered the church she expected to see a foreign god but she was disappointed to see only a foreign woman sitting on the floor. What was it that spoke to her heart and brought her back each Sunday to hear more? I believe it was the message of the gospel song we sang, "Tell it to Jesus."

52

"Are you weary? Are you heavy hearted?
Tell it to Jesus. Tell it to Jesus.
Are you grieving over joys departed?
Tell it to Jesus alone.
Tell it to Jesus. Tell it to Jesus.
He is a friend that's well known.
You've no other such a friend or brother.
Tell it to Jesus alone."[3]

Unbeknownst to us, she carried a burden of grief because her husband had committed suicide some years before and she had found comfort in talking to Jesus about it. Sometime later she made the decision to receive Christ as her Savior and was baptized.

Another whom the Lord directed to our little church was a young girl eighteen years old. She attended four times and stopped coming. I called on her at her home and discovered that she lived with her father in a tiny two-room house with few windows. I found her lying on her mat in a dark room with an umbrella over her bed, because the roof was leaking. I learned from her father that she had tuberculosis. I asked him why she was not in the hospital. He said that there was no room in the hospital. I went home thinking, "She will never recover like that. Something has to be done to help her." I did not know what to do. I had been in Ise only a short time and did not know many people. The only doctor I knew was one who signed my application for a driver's license saying that I was in good health. I decided to go to talk with him. I discovered to my amazement that he was the head of the City Hospital. When I told him about the sick young girl, he said, "Bring her here at once." I went home and told her father what he said. She was admitted to the hospital that very day. Later, I was told that I had to go to the City Office because I had not gone through the proper channels, but to myself I was saying, "The Lord knows how to take short cuts."

We visited her in the hospital and had private Bible Studies with her. She told us that she had believed in Jesus after just four times in church. Soon she was inviting other patients to her room for the Bible Study and some of them became believers. Unfortunately, after two years in the hospital, she died. It was the first Christian funeral our

---

[3] Lorenz, Edmund. S. 1876 (trans. Jeremiah Rankin) Tell it to Jesus. (public domain)

little church had. We were uncertain how to conduct the funeral since the body was cremated. I went to the crematory with the father and elder sister. We sat in the waiting room singing hymns to drown out the roaring sound of the nearby oven. Eventually the attendant brought out a little pile of bones and ashes and gave the father a pair of chopsticks to pick out certain bones and put them in a little jar. I had dreaded seeing this, but to my surprise my reaction was totally different as I realized that this was just the remains of the house in which she had lived and that her spirit was present with the Lord. Walter Sukut made a large cross covered with flowers, and displayed it along with other flowers. He then gave the message of hope that we as Christians have of the resurrection of the body some day, because Jesus had died for our sins and had gained victory over death through His resurrection. We sang one of Reiko's favorite gospel songs, "O happy day that fixed my choice on Thee, my Savior and my God." Non-Christians who attended the funeral were surprised at the difference between a Christian funeral and a Buddhist funeral which speaks of eternal separation. One of the neighboring families began to attend the church as a result of the message of hope.

Reiko's funeral

Lois and I differ on many things. I need prayer that I would not assume an attitude of knowing more, but be all that a more experienced missionary should be to a new missionary. My Japanese helper, Miss Yamamoto, also needs prayer. The Lord was very good to me in giving me a wonderful Japanese helper. Although she had not gone much beyond the fourth grade, she seems very mature in her comprehension of spiritual things. I have learned much in the matter of prayer and momentary waiting on the Lord through her. However, not having had much education or Bible school training, she is very conscious of her need of instruction and is very dependent on me to help her with her adult messages and with Sunday school lessons. Considering that she really does trust the Lord and attempts things the average person would refuse to do is indeed admirable. She never says she can't but she sometimes gets very discouraged, particularly when I have been overly rushed and have not helped her sufficiently. I get discouraged too, when I am pushed for time and it seems that deadlines can't be met. Last Saturday night we worked until 4 a.m. preparing messages, which left us both rather beat for Sunday.

Life in Ise has its interesting occurrences at times. The Sukuts and Mr. Rhoads came down from Tokyo for a few days, just before Thanksgiving, so we celebrated Thanksgiving together. The Sukuts may live in Ise if the Hirths are unable to return to Japan. Our second Thanksgiving was at the home of Glenn and Claire Johnson, the Presbyterian missionaries living at the opposite side of the city who work with the Kyodan church. Claire said they were inviting all the Americans in the city for an old-fashioned American Thanksgiving dinner. The only other Americans beside us were two single men, Catholic priests. It was an awfully long evening, not knowing how to converse with them, but the turkey, dressing, and pumpkin pie with whipped cream were wonderful.

December 28, 1953

Our Sunday School held its Christmas program a week ago Sunday in a rented hall. The Lord answered prayer marvelously in providing a meeting place. It had straw mats on the floor, Japanese-style, with no seats, so we could crowd quite a few people into it. We estimated about 250 children came but we were very disappointed that only two or three parents were there, even though we had sent two invitation letters home with the children. After the program, the older ones sang Christmas carols in the streets as they returned to our house for refreshments. I showed them some of my colored slides of America, and of course of my family, which interested them very much. After they left, 10 young people and adults remained for a very light lunch and fellowship around the table. They opened up and spoke more freely about their faith than I had heard them do at church, which was very gratifying. The Buddhist priest's son said that he was not yet willing to commit himself to Christ because he realized it must be a life decision. If he later went back on his decision, he would be worse off than before. He knows he is a sinner and reads the Bible. God is working in his heart. I pray he will put his trust in Jesus soon.

I had the opportunity to go to Tokyo for a few days at Christmas. While in Tokyo I was privileged to hear both Percy Crawford and Dr. Bob Munger. When I was at Wheaton College, Dr. Munger spoke in chapel every day for the spiritual emphasis week on the Holy Spirit. I was tremendously helped then, so I really look forward to hearing him again.

I am still bewildered about what God wants to do through me in Ise. I am asking the Lord to show me His plans and lead me into them. I am not one to blaze the trail and yet, here I am blazing trails. May God enable me and my coworkers and fellow missionaries.

January 24, 1954

I received some books for Christmas: two volumes of Lange's Commentary, *Thiessens's Theology, Thiessen's Introduction to the New Testament*, and Free's *Archaeology*. I mentioned the archaeology book to my language teacher and he seemed quite interested in it because books are his best friends. He considers himself a scholar and in many respects, I guess he is. He is a perfectionist, not content until he has investigated everything he does not understand. Last week he helped me with my message on the subject, "Do Men Become Gods (the Japanese idea) or Did God become Man (the Christian view)." He was so eager to help me with it. We spent two days from 9:00 to 2:00 the first day and from 9:00 to 12:00 the second day. At times I sensed a real interest in understanding the Christian idea but maybe it was simply interest in studying English, because I did not have time to write it in Japanese. We worked from the English copy.

Takashi San was saved on the first Wednesday of the New Year. The Lord has been speaking to him for some time and working on his behalf. He is a high school student and the son of a local Buddhist priest. As the eldest son in the family, it was expected that he would follow in his father's footsteps and become a priest, but he said he did not want to be a priest. He had seen too many things he disliked. At our watchnight service he received the Scripture verse, "Except a man be born again, he cannot see the kingdom of heaven." He did not understand it and asked me to explain it. The next Sunday I spoke on the New Birth and the New Nature. The following Wednesday he asked how he could be born again. In speaking with him, he said that he had believed earlier but, because he dared not tell his father, he had held back from making it known. He was almost in tears and it seemed as if he just could not take the step for fear of his father. I told him to put his faith in Christ first and even if he did not tell his father immediately, he could be saved. However, that was a mistake, because he relied upon my words that he need not tell his father more than I realized. When the next Buddhist festival came, he was supposed to help his father in the ceremonies. A few days before, he came to church and left a note saying he did not want to, but he could do nothing else. I realized then that nothing would do but that he plainly had to tell his father of his decision or he would never be able to break off from his old ways. I apologized to him for misdirecting him and urged him to tell his parents. His father is living in Osaka most of the time, returning home only twice a month, so he could not tell him immediately. Today he prayed for the first time at church thanking the Lord for giving him courage to tell his mother. He still has not told his father.

January 30, 1954

I wrote in a letter to the Erin Avenue Baptist Church in Cleveland as follows: I wish that each of you might have the privilege of speaking to someone about Christ who has never heard of Him. We meet them here almost every day, and while it is a privilege to tell them, it is also a grim reality that while you are speaking to one who has not heard the gospel before, there are thousands of others living in the same city who have never heard. May I share with you two incidents which will be representative of two attitudes of those who hear the gospel for the first time. One of the ladies who attends our church receives massage treatments from a blind man. This woman is still not a Christian, to our knowledge, but she comes regularly. She is a very troubled and despondent person and the impression she has received of Christianity is that it is a joyous religion. She told this to the blind masseuse and also told us about him. Yoshiko Yamamoto went to see him first and found him very open to the Gospel. The second time I went with her and found him eager to hear the Bible read and explained. We offered to pick him up every Wednesday night, so he has come twice now. Last Wednesday after Bible study he asked this question, prefacing it with, "This is the first time I am hearing of Jesus, so would you please explain to me about Mary. Tonight you said she was the mother of Jesus. Is Mary God?" The time I spoke with him, I mentioned that Christmas was Jesus' birthday. Apparently he was surprised because he asked "Who is Santa Claus?" He had always heard of Santa Claus in connection with Christmas. He wanted to learn the hymns we sing so that he could sing with us. He seems to have childlike faith, accepting whatever is told him as truth. We believe God will save him. His name is Mr. Yamamoto, which is a very common name. He plays the *koto*, a Japanese musical instrument, something like a harp. It has three strings which are plucked with one hand while the other hand presses down on the strings.

An incident occurred a few days ago while Miss Yamamoto was doing home visitation by herself. She came to a very small, poor house that seemingly had few or no windows. She found a middle aged woman in the house by herself. She attempted to give the usual invitation to church, but she hardly mentioned the word Christianity before this woman began a verbal attack upon her saying that she was much older than Miss Yamamoto and did not need to listen to what she had to say. Moreover, she had all the gods inside of her, including the Christian God. She proceeded to open her kimono to take from her waist a bundle of papers on which the names of many gods were written. She kept these wrapped about her body, sure that she had the help of all the gods there were. She said she was poor and had to work all day long and did not have time to listen to teaching. In her own way, she was worshiping the gods. She closed the door and told Miss Yamamoto to go to the rich people who had time to listen to her.

You see that not all who hear of Jesus, even though it is the first time, are willing to listen. Satan has held sway in this land for so many years and souls are not easily snatched from his grasp. We wrestle not against flesh and blood but against spiritual powers and only by spiritual weapons can we hope to conquer. Don't forget that there are some like these two people in your neighborhood, in your factory, in your school, to whom you, too, must witness.

February 21, 1954

Our Sunday schedule is a rather busy one: Sunday school from 8:30 to 11 a.m.; outdoor children's meetings in parks etc. from 1:00 to 2:00; adult meeting in the church from 3:00 to 4:00 p.m. This Sunday was a rather restful one for me although it was the usual Sunday schedule. The reason was that today Miss Yamamoto brought the message instead of me. She usually teaches the book of Matthew on Wednesday nights but we didn't have a meeting last Wednesday, so I asked her to take today's meeting.

Last Friday night we had a special evangelistic meeting here with Pastor Itoh from Shikoku, the pastor with whose family I lived for two months. He had to go to Tokyo and offered to have a meeting with us on the way. We had about 50 to 60 children present for the first part of the evening which was geared to them. Then we had a meeting for adults. About 35 were present. Pastor Itoh had a good message and quite a few raised their hands as an indication of their desire for prayer.

He stayed overnight with us, so I had a chance to ask him many questions I had concerning the work, such as going to the shrine for reasons other than worship, going to the graves on special days, marriage between believers and unbelievers, etc. His answers were very different from what I thought about these matters. I really respect Pastor Itoh and I know the Lord has given him a wonderful ministry. However, I don't quite know what to think about some of these problems. The more I ask people their opinions on them, the more confused I become.

The girls who work with me are of the extreme fundamental type. Sometimes I wish they weren't quite so rigid about some things. Today, for example, an old lady wanted to buy a songbook. We gave it to her and Miss Yamamoto told her to bring the money on Wednesday, but she insisted on paying for it then. Miss Kitahara wanted to explain to her that we did not sell anything on Sunday but I told her to let it go, for it seemed to me it would become an issue in front of all the others and I did not see any harm in it. We do not put books on display or ask people to buy them on Sunday, but if someone asks for one, I feel that it is not a matter of selling so much as providing them with something helpful. However, I know that the girls feel strongly about it because that is what they were taught at Mino mission.

A letter from Jay and Esther stated that Esther had gone to Texas with the oldest daughter, Linda, to stay with Jay's cousin until the end of March. Someone was apparently taking care of the baby. Jay hinted that they were willing to accept the Lord's leading to work in the States, if they could not return to Japan. Until now he has not mentioned the thought of not returning.

April 5, 1954

I took the night train to Tokyo to attend the wedding of a missionary friend who is with the Conservative Baptist Mission. Once in a blue moon on the mission field, wedding bells ring so it is cause for celebration. Unmarried men on the mission field are very scarce, so Carrie is a lucky girl. She let me in on some of her plans and I believe it will be a most unusual wedding with Japanese flower arrangements and hostesses in kimonos at the reception.

A week ago I spoke on the meaning of baptism and told our people that we planned to hold a baptismal service for those desiring it in June. Thus far, three have indicated their desire to be baptized but I hope that before that time, others will be willing to receive baptism, because I know there are others who are saved. Baptism holds much more significance here in Japan than it does in the U.S. It means a break with the old religions of Shintoism and Buddhism. My prayer was that I would be able to guide them adequately with my limited Japanese, so that they might live a separated Christian life.

Yesterday, after the adult meeting, I asked if any of them would like to come with us to hand out tracts. It is cherry blossom time in Japan and the Japanese all love cherry blossom viewing. There is a beautiful river near us and along its banks for a long way are many, many cherry trees, a regular fairyland of beauty, especially at night when the lanterns are lit. The whole city seems to turn out to go blossom viewing. As you can imagine, some of the parties turn into drinking parties and flower viewing becomes an excuse for indulging. We decided to take advantage of the crowds so near us, by giving out tracts. I was surprised when six of the church people volunteered to help. There is also a large exhibition going on in the city, which will continue for two months. One section of the exhibition consists of objects related to the Grand Ise Shrine located in Ise and in particular, those "treasures" especially created for use in the ceremony of rebuilding the shrine last summer. This is the first time these articles are being shown to the public. I was tempted to go to see them, but am not sure if the shrine receives any of the profits or not. Also I do not want to encourage the church people to participate in any of the functions pertaining to the Shinto worship.

April 18, 1954

This is Easter Day and, for some of our church folks, it was their first celebration of this holy day. It was a joy to hear several of the new Christians pray this morning, giving thanks for this first Easter day of their lives. We planned to have a sunrise service outdoors beside the river but it rained, so we had it indoors at 5:30 a.m. In spite of the rain and the early hour, 18 turned out which is good for our little group. I had a hard time getting through the message this morning. Maybe it was the early hour. Also the message was rather long and my tongue got weary, making all these foreign sounds.

Lois is in language school in Tokyo. She did not like being in a country area, isolated from other foreigners and social opportunities. Mr. Schilke's last letter suggested that the Sukuts not come to Ise but that they choose a field of their own and that I continue on here for another year, until it is known definitely whether Hirths will be back or not. I hate to think of being here alone for that time, but somehow I know His grace will be sufficient.

May 17, 1954

The Lord has been good to me in many other ways too. Since Lois has gone to Tokyo there have been a few times when I longed for letters from home more than usual, or when familiar faces of dear ones start creeping into my dreams. To meet this need of fellowship, the Lord has sent, from time to time, fellow missionaries, unexpectedly, from far places to encourage my heart. About a month ago, the Swedish girl who lived with me for a short time in Tokyo, stopped in to see me while on a sightseeing trip. A few weeks ago, a young Japanese woman, who spoke perfect English, came to see me. She said she was born in America and at the age of eight, came to Japan where she was reared. She returned to America for a year of college and there was saved. She is now doing evangelism in her own village, entirely on faith that God will supply her needs. She came to Ise to visit a friend and, learning that there was a Baptist missionary in the city, felt led to come to see me. Last week, I received a letter from one of my dear missionary friends, Peggy Winter, my college roommate and seminary classmate, saying that she was planning to spend a few days with me. She is coming all the way from Tokyo, ten hours away by train. The Lord knows even these little desires and needs of our hearts and does exceedingly abundantly above all we ask or even think.

On June 6 we will have our first baptismal service. As it seems now, there will be five. Several others desire baptism but will wait until later. We have held two special instruction classes for them thus far. Last week I asked to hear a testimony from each of them. They are very typical of converts at home, I believe. Some seem eager and joyous, some are quiet and reserved. I find it difficult to decide which ones are really ready for baptism. People's personalities make a difference in the expression of their faith. Some must be drawn out; others volunteer readily.

Last Wednesday, one of the girls told us, in tears, that her parents would not consent to her receiving baptism because they had always been Buddhist and all the relatives also. She came the next night to ask advice as to whether to go ahead, in spite of her parents' opposition. We decided that, first, we would speak with her parents and if they still objected, we would go ahead without their consent. However, the following day, we received a telephone call from her saying that they had told her she might be baptized. It will not be easy for her, because they are devout Buddhists. Three times a day, candles are lit, incense burned, food offerings made and prayers said for the spirits of the ancestors at the Buddhist altar in their home. Refraining from this daily worship immediately cuts her off from her family and makes her a foreigner in her own home.

Yesterday, Miss Kitahara, one of my helpers, went to see Mrs. Matoba, one of our new Christians. She is the one who always seemed so depressed and sorrowful. Recently she has appeared much brighter and says confidently that she is saved. Miss Kitahara found her reading a book on comparative religions. She said she knows she must tell others of Jesus and she is trying to prepare herself for it by learning how to approach those of other faiths. She is from a strong Buddhist home herself. We are praying for her husband that he and the entire family may one day belong to Christ. The churches in Japan have few entire families that are Christians. There is strength when the family is united in their beliefs.

June 14, 1954

Our first baptism took place on June 6 in the Miyagawa (Shrine) River which runs quite near our church and also through the beautiful park surrounding the Sun Goddess Shrine. Although six people came to the special baptism instruction classes, at the very end two decided to wait until they understood more of the teaching of the Bible. I felt it was wise in view of the fact that there were some doubts in their minds and was glad that they were discerning enough to make the decision themselves, rather than receiving baptism prematurely. When two people decided to put off baptism, I was fearful lest I had planned for a baptismal service too soon and that the others too might be desirous of backing out. I was much troubled that night, and the next morning I received a telegram from the North American Baptist Central Conference with congratulations and prayer for our first baptism. The Erin Avenue Baptist Church in Cleveland, where I had served for one year before going to Japan, also sent a letter with words of encouragement, which was a great stimulus to my faith. I certainly felt, for the first time, the great responsibility of guiding new believers and laying foundations for the work here. The instruction I gave was not adequate, I know, due to both my lack of ability in the language and also to my lack of experience and knowledge of the Word. In view of all the handicaps, His work is the more evident and His glory the greater.

First baptism

The four who were baptized were: Kammori San, a young woman about 20 years old, who comes from a Buddhist home; Mrs. Atake, a mother of six children whose husband is a Shintoist; Mrs. Matoba, mother of three children, who has dabbled in many religions before trying to find joy and peace; and Takashi San, the Buddhist priest's son. These four had been among the faithful attendees from the very beginning. Some had believed almost as soon as they heard the gospel, others after a long inner struggle. The process of nurturing these and keeping the vital faith alive is our task now, plus of course, bringing the other unsaved to faith in the Lord Jesus. I talked at length about God to a young man today who came to fix the car. His attitude is so typical of the people here, and I suppose almost everywhere: "You cannot know anything for sure about God, since there are so many religions, so we must content ourselves with what we know, namely the things of this life and how to live peacefully with one another." He believes the most important thing in the world is developing the right spirit of love and peace in the hearts of men, but all of this without God.

One of those newly baptized has volunteered to teach in the Sunday School, for which I am very grateful. She used to be a primary school teacher, so she knows and loves children, but to teach the Bible is still quite different from teaching reading, writing, and arithmetic. It will require some training. It rained all day on the day of the baptism but they were truly showers of blessing. A Japanese pastor from Mino Mission performed the baptism and John Rhoads officiated at the communion service which followed. Quite a few of the church people gathered at the river to witness the baptism, in spite of the rain.

July 4, 1954

I wish I could bring my co-worker, Miss Yamamoto, back to the U.S with me on furlough. I believe people in America would really like her. I am sure she would be a challenge to all of our young people at home, for I have not seen among our youth anyone so devoted to the Lord and zealous to witness for Him. She is extremely gifted in handling children in the Sunday School. When she tells a story, it is so interesting that even I am fascinated by it, although it is all familiar to me.

My household helper, Miss Kitahara, is off duty on Sunday so I have to do my own cooking and dishes, etc. Miss Kitahara teaches

Sunday school in the morning and helps pass out tracts in the afternoon. Today, for the first time, two of our new converts taught in the Sunday school, thus increasing our staff to four teachers. We cannot lay claim to a model Sunday school by any means, but I was happy that we still have a large number of children attending regularly, around 100 usually. The big problem is training teachers and I'm afraid I'm not doing much of that. I speak at the adult service at 3:00 PM on Sunday afternoons with the limited Japanese I know, and though it must be very painful to listen to, 15 to 20 people usually turn out. This is not always the same group, however. How I wished that we could have 15 to 20 truly born-again Christians on fire for the Lord. There again comes the matter of setting the pace, which really smites my conscience.

A new couple, Clemence and Sylvia Auch, were appointed as missionaries to Japan and are supposed to arrive about the middle of August. They are close friends of the Sukuts, having gone to NAB Seminary together. Mr. Schilke is still searching for a single girl to send in place of Lois Lechner who resigned from the Mission. So far no single girls have applied.

I thought I would be going to Kyoto for further language study in the fall but the latest developments are that, unless Sukuts can find an interpreter very quickly, they won't be able to come to Ise in the fall. That means that I stay in Ise, carrying on as best I can under existing circumstances. I was disappointed, of course, but it seems there is no solution, because interpreters are scarce. So perhaps the Lord wants Sukuts to get another year of language study before coming out. I am sure they will be grateful for it when they do come, because it is hard to study down here without a good teacher, along with the responsibility for the church.

The hot water heater finally got hooked up, so I had my first real bath in about nine months. I wish everyone in the U.S. could experience a Japanese bath. They would never go back to bathing American style of sitting in your dirty bath water, filled with soap and grime. Here, we rinse it all off first, outside the tub. The water goes down a drain in the tile floor. Then you get into the hot water that comes up to your neck and sit and soak and relax.

July 17, 1954

The Sukuts have a new baby, a little boy named Mark. It seemed that he would be born prematurely, but all is well with mother and child.

I have heard from Lois only once since she resigned and that in response to an inquiry I made about our finances and also to let me know what to do with some of her things.

The Lord has blessed us again in our services, although it seems like such a small witness amongst so many people. We rejoice for those who come to hear the word of God. The Lord has helped me with the language, although many is the time I have said in unbelief, "I cannot do it this week." How I praise the Lord for the victory He wrought when he called out the Buddhist priest's son to be his child. Now he is willing to teach VBS. He is very diligent in his preparation and I believe he will be a real channel of blessing. Already the number of boys in Sunday school has increased. Before we had only women as teachers and the older boys were few in number. He now has a class of about 11 boys. I would like to be present to supervise the VBS but perhaps I would just get in the way. The teachers will have a great opportunity for growth without me, I am sure. In all we expect slightly over 100 children.

More and more it seems the Japanese people are becoming anti-American. Not that I feel any personal abuse but the policies of the US are strongly objected to, both in the newspaper and in the conversations of the people. Not long ago I spoke with a high school teacher who is a member of the Kyodan church in Ise. He teaches current events and so, of course, he is very political and social minded. The biggest negative influence, of course, is the H-bomb and the effect that the experiments are having on both the people of Japan and the surrounding Marshall Islands. There is a great loss to the fishing industry of tons of tuna that are dumped, if found to be radioactive. The desperate economic situation calls for social reform and the Communists are only too happy to propose this to idealistic youth.

Auch's arrival is scheduled for August 17, 1954 so we will go to meet them in Tokyo.

July 29, 1954

Right now, I am in Karuizawa. The Japanese Sunday School teachers are busy in Ise conducting two weeks of Vacation Bible School. The Primary Department has one week and the Junior Department has one week. In all, we expect about 100 children. None of the teachers have ever had this kind of experience before, but they were willing to go ahead without me. For this I was very thankful to the Lord. Among the teachers is the Buddhist priest's son. What a triumph for our God!

Karuizawa is one of the finest summer resort towns in Japan. It is located in the mountains north of Tokyo, a trip of several hours by train from Tokyo. It is where missionaries from all over Japan come for a week of spiritual refreshment and to escape the heat of summer. Sukuts came to Karuizawa at the beginning of July for the summer term of language school. I enjoyed sitting beneath a beach umbrella beside the pool when I came for the conference. I welcomed the cool mountain air after the heat in Ise. For about 10 days we enjoyed listening to some of the world's best spiritual guides: Norman Grubb of England, Joseph Carroll from Australia, and a man from the West Indies Mission.

I had resigned myself to stay on in Ise for another year and Sukuts were prepared to stay in Tokyo for another year of language study. Those plans have changed because Sukuts were able to find an interpreter, so it looks as if we'll be exchanging places as before planned. They will go to Ise and I will go back to language school. The interpreter is well spoken of by many and is also capable of teaching Japanese, so it seems that he will be a valuable worker. He is married and has a 12-year-old boy. This means that he will probably be more stable and dependable than a single worker who might stay only for a short time. Their housing is a problem yet to be solved which we are praying about. Houses are really scarce and so are apartments. If the Lord can supply a worker, surely he can supply a house for him also.

4

KYOTO EXPERIENCE 1954-1956

September 16, 1954

Miss Yamamoto and I began to pack for moving to Kyoto where I would return to Japanese language school and Miss Yamamoto would enroll at a small Bible school started by Evangelical Free missionaries. Miss Kitahara would remain in Ise to help the Sukuts. We made a few last-minute visits to people we wanted to see before leaving. We arrived in Kyoto about September 9. The church people in Ise had a little farewell for us. We had supper together with about 30 people and then had a little meeting afterwards. I was deeply touched by their prayers for us. The Japanese are said to hide their emotions, but I believe they are far more emotional than we Americans. There was more than one with teary eyes. The Buddhist priest's son was the worst of all. He cried like a baby. It made me feel so unworthy, for I have not done anything to cause them to regret my going. At the same time it deepened my love for them.

The Lord answered prayer in regards to where to study Japanese and where to live. There is a Naganuma Japanese language school branch in Kyoto. I learned about an Evangelical Free missionary living in Kyoto named Mr. Hanson who was in charge of the little Evangelical Free Bible School in Kyoto. I called him and asked if he might know of any place where Miss Yamamoto and I might live if we move to Kyoto. I also asked about the possibility of Miss Yamamoto studying at the Bible school. Mr. Hanson found a two room apartment for us, just a short distance from the Bible school. It was in the home of a Kyoto University professor, Dr. Uchida. His wife was a Christian but the husband was not yet, although he seemed sympathetic towards Christianity. Other missionaries had lived in their home for several years, so they were accustomed to foreigners. The apartment had one Western-style room for me, and one Japanese-style room for Miss Yamamoto, plus a little kitchen. We would share the bathroom with the family. It seemed like an ideal setup for us and for them. The family felt the same way, since in Japan it is always good to have someone in the house when you are gone, to watch the house.

The Lord answered prayer in every respect so that all our needs were met. The Uchida family is very kind. They have three young children, Yoshine (10), Minako (8), and Toshiki (6), so it is quite a lively household. Miss Yamamoto will help me with the household tasks and in return, I will provide her with food and a little money for living expenses, so she can go to Bible school while I'm in language school. She will not be able to do a lot of work, because she has a full schedule at school. At least, she will feel that she is earning her education, rather than being given it outright. It felt good to be back in language school where there are good teachers and time for study. I wanted to take full advantage of that year of study, so I did not plan to do much else. There were only three students in my class, so there was plenty of opportunity for recitation and asking questions. I was ahead of the other two, so the first part was review for me but I didn't mind, because I had forgotten almost all the Chinese characters I had learned. Having had to use Japanese all the time, my speech had become quite fluent, at least more so than those who had only been in language school, but my reading and writing were neglected.

I went back to Ise to be with Sukuts and introduce them to the people on their first Sunday. We plan to go back occasionally on weekends to do a little visitation with the people for a time. Sukuts have a good interpreter, but he has been a Christian only about two years, so he doesn't know the Bible very well. Walter said he was scared after the first Sunday.

When I was in Karuizawa, I had a physical examination and found that I was still anemic, which probably accounts for my being tired most of the time even when I am not doing much. I had been trying to eat a lot of liver to correct that. It was cheap, because most Japanese do not eat liver. It was regarded as a kind of medicine for sick people. The doctor gave me iron pills and told me to get liver shots for two months. I waited until I got to Kyoto to get them, because I knew there was a Southern Baptist Hospital there.

October 17, 1954

Last Friday after language school, five of us students biked from school to one of the temples to watch a Buddhist festival. By the time I got home, it was almost 7:30 p.m. Mr. Uchida was singing hymns when I arrived home and he seemed to be in a receptive mood, so when Mrs. Uchida asked me to play her organ for them to learn some new songs, I gladly consented. Later we listened to part of *The*

70

Messiah on my phonograph. It was then about 9:30 p.m. and I was beginning to feel aches and chills and fever, all at the same time.

I took a hot bath, hoping that would relieve me, but there was no help. That night and half of the next day, I had a temperature and continuous headache, stomachache and all my muscles and bones ached. Yamamoto San and Mrs. Uchida prayed for me. I asked Yamamoto San to put some ice water in the hot water bottle for me. I went back to bed and immediately broke out in perspiration. My fever was gone by the time she brought me the ice water bag. When prayers are answered so suddenly, one almost tends to attribute the results to other reasons but I do know it was of the Lord's mercy that I was healed.

November 23, 1954

It seems as if we are going to lose the Rhoads family from our NAB Mission, because he feels called to do mass evangelism and at the same time train evangelists. The mission policy, thus far at least, has not had much room for that; its aim is to establish churches following a pattern something like that which we have followed in Ise. John does not feel the Lord wants him to locate on one station and work there as a pastor might. Walter and I both wrote letters to Headquarters asking them to keep the Rhoadses in the mission in a special capacity by loaning them to Navigators, with whom they have been and want to continue working. It seems that this will be the most satisfactory with everyone.

When I went to Ise, Walter told me that Takashi San, the priest's son, had decided to stop coming to church because he did not have time. He wanted to go to college and had to study hard to pass the tests. I had talked to him about this once before I went to Kyoto and he seemed to have made a strong decision then, to continue going to church, but the devil keeps bringing up this problem. In addition to this, he says his faith seems to have no effect upon his life. It does not seem to help him, so he thinks it is a waste of time to go to church now. Also he has been having many doubts about the Bible being the Word of God and Jesus being the Son of God. I did not know then that he was having so many personal problems with his faith. I spoke with him for several hours. Some points seemed to be cleared up but when he left it was with the same general attitude. I believe that the power of God can move mountains.

It seems that the devil has been working overtime in relation to me. Since Miss Yamamoto and I have been living together in Kyoto, we have been getting on each other's nerves, or maybe it would be fairer to speak only for myself. I tried to analyze the causes of the situation, for from the beginning we got along very well. I had to admit that the main reasons were pride and lack of love on my part, but having to live so intimately, sharing meals, going to church together, having no one else to share things with regarding work or personal affairs also contributed to the problem. I wondered what the right relationship between us should be. She was my helper whom I employed for service, yet we were co-workers in that we shared the ministry of the Saturday School, which we revived in the Uchida's home. Also, we were supposed to be friends because we lived together, ate together and went places together. Some missionaries say that it is wise to keep a distance between yourself and your worker, lest you find over-intimacy spoiling the relationship. I did not want to lose Miss Yamamoto, because I considered her a fine Christian and a good church worker, but I desired a co-worker who was capable of advising me in case of problems I might be creating. We foreigners make many mistakes, doing what we think best, and are not even aware that we are doing so.

I battled with myself over how to change my attitude yet seemed unable to do it, even though I prayed earnestly about it. One day I was reading John, chapter 11, about the resurrection of Lazarus. When Jesus said to Martha, "I am the resurrection and the life. Do you believe this?" it was not a *doctrine* to believe, but a living Christ with power to raise the dead who was speaking to me. If He could raise Lazarus from the dead, then surely He could revive my cold heart and make it warm and tender again. As I began to put my trust in Christ to do this miracle in me, little by little my heart attitude began to change and our fellowship was restored. This was an unspeakable blessing and a definite answer to prayer. Had this not happened, it would have been impossible for me to carry on any kind of work at all. We had a long talk one day and I hope that it will help.

Uchida family with Florence

Mrs. Uchida and I have begun a close friendship. She is a doctor's daughter and is quite refined. Also, because she is a new Christian, she tends to look to me for guidance in her Christian life. She is the one who wanted me to revive the Saturday School in her home. When the previous renters moved out, the Saturday School ended. Dr. Uchida seemed happy about that but Mrs. Uchida wanted it to continue. However, she did not feel that she could go against her husband's wishes. She said to me, "If I ask him, he will say 'no' but if you ask him, he might consent." So I asked him for permission and he agreed. He even agreed to my having an English Bible Class.

December 27, 1954

Christmas has come and gone but our missionary family will not be getting together for our fellowship time until the 29th. My first Christmas celebration began on December 11, with our Sunday school program. Last week I had the Guenthers (Rubena, a Mennonite Brethren missionary, and her parents) here for supper. I had my apartment decorated for Christmas with a little tree, candles, Christmas cards, etc. so we made it a Christmas affair too. After supper we gathered around my little organ and sang some of the old fashioned secular songs. It made me think of our hymn sings around the piano when we were little and Mom played the piano. It was so nice to have the two generations of Guenthers here to give a little perspective in age to our missionary fellowship. We don't often have grandmothers or grandfathers around us. I am sure their presence here made a real impression on the Japanese, because they seldom have the chance to meet a man who has walked with God 70 years as Mr. Guenther has. Then to see the parent-child relationship between an adult missionary and her parents was a good experience too, I am sure, for many Japanese think that old people in America are to be pitied because they do not live with their children as they do here in Japan. They think that American children neglect their parents. I am sure they were able to see genuine love and respect in the relationship between Rubena and her parents.

December 31, 1954

While almost all the Japanese were making last-minute preparations for the big New Year's celebration, we celebrated Christmas at the Uchida house. It was not anything really exciting, but it was a blessed time. Our first event was the children's Christmas program. We had a simple program with carols, the Christmas story presented by means of a series of large pictures illustrating all the events in the story, a quiz on the Christmas story with questions for each grade and caramels for rewards, a dramatization, and a little story by me. We gave the children each a little treat of candy and cookies, plus a little children's hymnbook. We hope that by means of the hymnbook, the children would be helped in learning the songs and at the same time, the parents would receive at least an indirect witness. I know that the children in the Uchida family were making good use of it, singing all the songs they knew and of course, the parents must listen.

The next day was a little Christmas party for the English conversation class students. Mr. and Mrs. Uchida were students too, so Mrs. Uchida was hoping that through that fellowship her husband's attitude might be restored to normal and it was, so that the next evening we were able to celebrate Christmas with the family. At the party for the students, we sang Christmas carols, of course, and afterwards I read the story from the Bible. The week before I had shown them a number of selected Christmas cards and spent the evening explaining the meaning of the symbols used for Christmas such as the star, bells, holly, and candles. I took for granted that they knew the Biblical story of Christmas, but when I showed them cards with the wise men and shepherds, they had no idea who they might be.

74

They are not yet interested in the Bible it seems, but I gave them a New Testament in colloquial Japanese for Christmas and prayed that it might awaken some interest. They gave me a lovely Japanese doll and a beautiful silk wrapping cloth which is used in place of wrapping paper. The Uchidas gave me a pretty pillow for a sofa made of hand dyed fabric called Rokketsu, or wax dyeing. It is very expensive.

Mrs. Uchida told me that, after she was led to faith in Christ by a Pentecostal missionary who rented a room from them, she was baptized secretly, because she knew her husband would never consent to it. He was the eldest son in a family that was in charge of a Buddhist temple and, as such, felt obliged to support it. When she returned from her baptism, her face was beaming and he guessed what had happened. He asked her if she had been baptized and she confessed that she had. He said, "You go right back there and cancel it!" Of course, she couldn't do that. When she stopped worshiping at the Buddhist altar in their home, he became very angry with her. He broke up the altar and blamed it on her. At times he seemed more tolerant of her faith, allowing her to attend church and even to take the children with her. Later on, he must have felt very lonely Sunday morning, because he forbade her to take the children to church. She never wavered in her faith, although it was sorely tested. Instead she grew to be a real witness for Christ to others.

The Wednesday before Christmas, I went to Ise to get in on the Christmas party at the Sukut's. There were about 35 present. I could not help but recall the previous Christmas, when there were only about 14 and only two or three Christians. My heart rejoiced at the increase, but there was one heartache. Takashi San, the priest's son, was not there. He has been experiencing a lot of doubt about the Bible and has been struggling over the problem of whether he can take time from his studies to attend church twice a week or not. He says he must study as much as the other students or he will not be able to compete with them when they take the college entrance exams. Only ten percent of those taking the tests will be admitted. Walter said that Takashi San had told him that if he failed to pass the test, he would curse God. It seems that something has come in, the devil of course, and is pulling him in the opposite direction. It's a difficult situation and I still feel that he is a born again child of God and that God will not let go of him. It was just a year ago at New Year's that he was saved. He needs a lot of prayer support just now.

Walter Sukut, Clem Auch and I went to several little villages around Ise to see what would be the best plan for expanding the work and where I might live after I finish language school in Kyoto. After looking around, none of them seemed to me to be the place that I would like to really settle down in. Walter and Clem thought we should have a recommendation concerning the matter to give at the field council in Tokyo after Christmas, so I was much troubled about the matter. I did not like to make an important decision in a hurry. They said, "You had a whole year when you lived in Ise to think about it." Finally Clem came up with the suggestion that if the mission decided to change our terms from 6 to 5 years, which is the average for missionaries in Japan, that, after language school I would have only one more year before going home on furlough. It might not be such a good idea to begin a new work that might not be continued. He suggested that Sukuts go back to language school in Kyoto for a year and I go back to Ise, where I know the people and they know me, for my final year. That way I could probably do more in a year's time than I could by going to a new place. We agreed on that and sent that as a recommendation to headquarters, not knowing if the mission would approve the shorter term of five years.

The Sukuts found a new location for the church which made it more convenient and also more conspicuous to people. This building was located on a busy street, not very far from where the mission house was. It was about the same size as the former place, but since no one lived in it, all the space could be used. We decorated it the day before the Christmas service. Many passersby stopped in to see what was happening. I think that accounted for the large crowd at the meeting in the evening. About 60 people crowded into the little building. I trusted that the good attendance would be only a token of the Lord's blessing on the new building, which we dedicated to the Lord.

A lady who lived in a nearby village came to see Sukuts to talk about the things of the Lord and then offered her home for meetings each Saturday night. There were almost as many people attending there as at the usual church service in Ise. Yamamoto San and I went out there on Saturday evening and spoke to the group. On Sunday the children's Christmas program was held in Ise in the morning and Sunday evening we missionaries went to Tokyo for our field council from Tuesday to Wednesday.

January 20, 1955

After the mission meeting, I left for Sendai to spend a few days with Lorraine Fleischman and then with Peggy Winter in Akita Ken. It felt really good to be with American friends with whom I could talk freely about anything. The Conservative Baptist Mission, to which both Lorraine and Peggy belong, lost quite a few of their staff due to illness. Three of their single girls went home and one of the wives had a nervous breakdown. I don't know what it is about Japan, but all the mission boards say that there are more missionary casualties in Japan than in any other field.

The day after I returned to Kyoto from Akita almost proved to be a fatal one for me. I was sitting on the floor, beside my heating stove that had an open gas flame, having my devotions. I fell asleep. About 30 minutes later, I awoke with an awful sickening feeling in my stomach and my head was so dizzy I couldn't figure out what was happening. I felt an urge to go to the bathroom, but when I tried to stand up, my legs wouldn't hold me. I finally staggered out the door of my room into the hall way, but had taken only a few steps when everything blacked out. Yamamoto San, whose room was nearby, heard the thud on the floor when I fell and called Uchidas. By then, the cold air in the hall was reviving me and I was semi-conscious. They immediately suspected the gas stove, but later when we had a man check the stove, he said the stove was all right. The oxygen in the room must have gotten used up because the room was closed tightly. God miraculously preserved me again!

February 3, 1955

Each day finds me pressing on a little further with my study of Japanese. It seems that no matter how far you progress, there is still so much more you need to learn that you never get over the feeling of just resigning yourself to being a foreigner who will never be able to speak as a native Japanese anyhow, so why try. I will be studying through July and then in the fall I will return to the work in Mie Ken.

It has not yet been decided definitely if I will return to Ise or not, but as it appears now, I probably will. The work there is steadily growing, but not, of course, without setbacks and heartaches. The Sukuts are working through an interpreter, which is not an ideal situation, but in spite of this the Lord has been pleased to bless the work. A youth group has recently been started and seems to be of real help and interest to the young people. The young man who was acting as leader of the group is hoping to enter Bible school in the spring and give his life to the gospel ministry. We are praying that he will be accepted by the school and that he will be able to find a part time job to help pay his expenses.

Dr. Uchida applied for a Fulbright scholarship to go to the US to do research but was rejected because of his lack of fluency in English. He was told to study English more and apply again. I felt led to help him an hour a day, so we began by using the English newspaper as our text book, but some of the language was difficult to understand and the grammar was not always correct. I suggested switching to the English Bible. This is the first time that he is reading the Bible, although there has been a Bible in his home for about three years. It is a little difficult to explain some of the deep things of the Bible in simple English, such as the Trinity, demon possession, etc. I kept our study rather objective so that he wouldn't feel I was trying to cram the Bible down his throat. I prayed that the Lord would awaken a thirst for spiritual things in his heart and convince him of the truth of God's word.

June 30, 1955

Walter Sukut and Clemence Auch came to Kyoto to look for housing last Monday. After just two days, we found two quite nice apartments, but the rent is pretty expensive. It looks as if Sukuts will be permanently located in Kyoto, so the Mission may approve building a house for them. Another missionary couple, Edwin and Meraleen Kern, will be coming out the end of this year.

John and Lydia Rhoads are leaving our mission, so the coming of the Kerns doesn't really increase the number of our mission family. There has been a long correspondence between the Rhoadses and our mission trying to work out some plan whereby John could remain with the mission and still do the work he wants to do in cooperation with the Navigators. It seemed best that, if he wishes to join their work, he sever relations with our NAB mission. I felt for quite some time that if his heart was with the Navigators, then he ought to be a part of their staff, since his only connection with us was the financial support from NAB churches through our mission.

September 12, 1955

Sukuts moved to Kyoto the end of August where they will probably be permanently stationed. Mrs. Uchida urged us to begin a church in her neighborhood. The mission bought land for a mission house near the Uchida home and construction began. We hoped that some of the contacts I was able to make while in Kyoto would form a little nucleus for the new church which was to begin in the Sukuts' home.

The mission approved our recommendation to shorten our term of service to five years, instead of six, so after I serve another year in Ise, I will be going home for my first furlough. The Auchs will probably be coming to Ise after they finish their second year of language school to take my place when I go on furlough.

I was really afraid to go back to Ise, wondering how I could possibly prepare three messages a week in Japanese, besides doing visitation, Sunday School, youth group, etc.

The Lord provided a wonderful helper for me in preparing messages. The neighbor boy, a university student, was home recuperating from tuberculosis. One day he came over, asking me to help him with English conversation. I suggested that if he would find it useful, I would appreciate someone helping me translate my message from English into Japanese. That would be a kind of English study for him also. He agreed, so four days a week he came to help me. I was very grateful because I still needed someone, both as a language teacher, and as a helper with preparing messages.

There have been a string of problems following on the heels of the other and all of them rather serious. Were it not for the promise of God concerning casting our burdens upon Him, I am sure I could not have slept or worked for thinking about them.

One of the Sunday School teachers, our oldest and most faithful Christian, or so we thought, committed adultery. The man involved, a non-Christian, would not admit it, but when I talked with him and told him that she had confessed it to me with tears, his attitude revealed to me that it was true. I did not know how to handle the situation. I suggested to her that she apologize to his wife and she said she would, if the man would apologize to her husband, but he wouldn't. I asked her whether she would confess her sin to the church, because, as a result of it, many were staying away from church. She said she could not and for a while she stopped coming. Now she is coming again but we have not taken any steps to bring it before the church. We asked her to give up her Sunday School class and stop playing the organ. Most of the church people do not know anything about the problem. I am sure it would shock them if they did. Of course the family would suffer from making it public. I didn't know what to do about it.

Another serious problem has arisen because Mrs. S., in whose home we have our Saturday meeting, no longer makes offerings to the spirits of the dead ancestors at the Buddhist altar in her home. Her husband is dead and his younger, non-Christian sister, who lives in the home, wants to put Mrs. S. out of the house that belonged to her husband's parents. The neighbors have all come to think badly of Mrs. S. for causing a quarrel with the family.

Another of our new Christians seldom comes to church and reports have come of his getting drunk. However, others are showing a desire to serve the Lord and to help in the church work so we are grateful for these.

November 1955

John Rhoads and his interpreter, Jingu San, came to hold an evangelistic campaign in Ise for a week. When I was in language school in Kyoto, I had met two sons of Pastor Iwai who lived in Shikoku. Kiyoshi and his brother, Ken, sang together very nicely. When I went to Ise for the second time, I kept in touch with them and asked them to come to Ise to help us during the evangelistic meetings.

They consented and were a real help to us singing at the meetings and at the street meetings we held during the day. Every night there were responses to the invitation to come forward for salvation. Mr. Rhoads preached very good salvation messages every night and the power of the Holy Spirit was felt. There were about fifty in all who signed decision cards. After we called on these people and found out which ones seemed likely to continue as new believers, they were not so many. There were about ten, but not all of them continued to attend. Some were not sure of salvation and did not attend regularly, so it is hard to say what fruit will remain.

Street meeting

A few days after we held a street meeting in connection with the evangelistic campaign, a lady came to my door and asked if we were the people who had held a street meeting. I said, "Yes." She said, "I have been looking for you, because I was listening to you and thought you might be able to help me with my problems. I went to the nearest church, which was the Catholic Church, but they said they did not hold street meetings. However, the priest was willing to listen to me as I told him about my problems, but he did not give me the help I wanted." I asked her what problems she faced and she told me this story: "I live in a small town about two hours from here. My husband is a pearl merchant and a prominent man in our town. He attends geisha houses and sometimes brings geisha to our house who are pregnant. He expects me to take care of them. When a baby is born, she and the baby disappear. I am about to have a nervous breakdown. I came to the hospital in Ise to get help for my emotional condition, but I need more than medicine. When the priest heard my story, he offered to help me get a divorce but I don't want a divorce. I want to learn to live with my husband and my problems. Can you help me?"

I was shocked to hear her story. I knew that I was incapable of helping her solve such major marital problems, but Miss Yamamoto and I did what we could to present the gospel to her and offered to go to her house to talk with her further. She bought a Bible and a hymnal before she left. We did go to her house one day when her husband was

81

not at home and tried to explain the gospel to her, but we realized it was too far for us to continue visiting her. We did not hear from her again. What a sad story!

January 17, 1956

After the Christmas programs at the Ise Church were over, I went to Kyoto for a day of fellowship with our missionaries. There I met Edwin and Meraleen Kern, our newest missionaries, for the first time. Meraleen is expecting in February sometime. She plays the vibra harp which is a delightful and enriching gift which the Lord can use in our work. Both Ed and Meraleen play the piano. Sylvia Auch also plays the piano. Gradually, we are acquiring new talents for the Lord's service. After a goose dinner at the Sukut's new home in Kyoto, we had a time of singing Christmas carols, accompanied by Meraleen on the vibra harp. It was really an enjoyable time. The next day my two helpers, Miss Yamamoto and Miss Kitahara, came to Kyoto and we had a little fellowship with all the Japanese helpers and co-workers. This was the first time the entire mission family and helpers were together. The girls enjoyed seeing where the missionaries lived and getting a little look at the big city. The next day we returned to Ise together.

Walter Sukut and Edwin Kern came to Ise for New Year's and preached the watch night service and also at the New Year's Day service. The next day I went back to Kyoto with them for our annual mission business meeting. Of chief interest to me was the date of my furlough and what I would be doing upon my return to Japan. It was comparatively easy to decide on the date of my furlough, since it would come due in November and that date seemed to be the most satisfactory for all involved. We did not find the second question quite as easy to answer. Sometimes I thought I would like to work on the same field as a couple, so that the man could do the pastoral work and I could fill in on other things, like a church missionary. After looking at the problem from all angles, it seemed that the best thing would be for Auchs to move to Ise in September and I stay in Ise until my furlough in order to bridge the gap until the church and Auchs could adjust to each other. If a single girl did not come to join me, then the work might be turned over to the Kerns, who would be ready to go out into the work, following two years of language school in Kyoto. This might mean another possible change for me after a year of work in a new area. I really don't think I am the pioneer type, but the Lord has pushed me out into two new areas so far, which have become our present two locations, Ise and Kyoto. Now we must pray that the Lord will definitely lead in the choice of the new area.

February 6, 1956

On February 23rd and 24th Billy Graham will be in Osaka. My two Japanese helpers and I are planning to attend the rally. We are really thirsting for showers of blessing. It seems we all are spiritually empty and lacking in power. This morning the girls and I had a long time of prayer and Bible reading together, seeking to find out why the showers of blessing do not come. We had a good time together but still we have not received what we are looking for. If we ourselves are not filled to overflowing with joy and peace and love, it is not very likely that the church people will be either.

I was challenged by what David Brainerd, a missionary to the American Indians, wrote concerning himself and his work. At one time, he felt that all his work had been in vain, seeing no fruit except that of his interpreter and his wife. He felt he was a burden to the missionary society that was supporting him and felt that he ought to resign. Even in the midst of that discouragement, he faithfully carried on his witnessing and that was when the Lord first began to move in the hearts of the Indians. Even in discouragement, we are to carry out our duties, never knowing when the seed sown will spring up to eternal life.

February 27, 1956

It is Monday, and my mind is very carefree as it usually is on Monday after the heavy schedule of Sunday is over. We are advised to take one day a week off to rest up, so I usually write to my family on Mondays. The Lord has been good in giving us all health and when we think we are all tired out and can't go anymore, he sends some friends from out-of-town that make us stop what we are doing and relax. Peggy Winter, my college roommate, and Lorraine Fleischman, both Conservative Baptist missionaries, are coming to see me and will spend four or five days here.

Billy Graham came to Japan this past week, with two meetings in Tokyo and two in Osaka, one night for missionaries and one night for Japanese in each place. My two helpers and I attended the Osaka meeting February 23rd-24th. Before going we had a long time of prayer and Bible reading. There were about 1000 missionaries and foreigners present from all over southern Japan. The next day there were two meetings for Japanese, one at 5 PM outdoors and one at 7 PM. There were about 15,000 present. The message was just a simple presentation of the way of salvation and yet many responded.

We held the baptismal class for seven people who have requested baptism. All of them were coming to church before the evangelistic meetings, except one. This one was a young man full of enthusiasm and eager to serve the Lord. We truly rejoiced over him. Many of the benefits of the meetings will not be evident immediately, for some who were touched then will attend occasionally upon special invitation. We look forward for fruit in the future. None of the seed sown will be wasted, I was sure. After Easter we planned to have three nights of meetings, especially for the young Christians, to help ground them and lead them into a closer walk with the Lord. I invited a missionary from South Africa, Percy Luke, whose wife is part Japanese, to be our speaker. He is a very spiritual man and very fluent in Japanese. These three nights begin April 18.

April 9, 1956

Mr. and Mrs. Edwin Kern took my place in Ise for four days, so that I could go with Miss Yamamoto to her home in the mountains of Gifu Prefecture. She warned me in advance what to expect, so I wouldn't be too surprised. Still it was somewhat more primitive than I had anticipated. The mountain roads which the bus traveled were really dangerous. It was night, so I couldn't see all the dangerous curves and precipices, which was probably a good thing. The countryside was beautiful with mountain streams rushing along the river beds full of huge, beautifully shaped rocks. We finally arrived at her home at 7:30 PM.

Miss Yamamoto and her two brothers and a sister had lived in Manchuria. After the war they had to return as refugees, having absolutely nothing. While I was having breakfast, the little 12-year-old son of the married brother came rushing into the house wearing a big smile and holding in his hand a little fish which he had just caught. His mother said that he had prayed before going to the river that he would catch something, especially for me. When I heard that I thought, who is worthy to eat such a precious fish? Surely not I. I wondered how

Peter and the other disciples felt when Jesus told them to cast their nets on the other side of the boat and they landed 150 huge fish.

There was no furniture in the living room except for a little round table and three cushions. I sat on the newest and fattest of the cushions and used the little table with legs about 9 inches high as a desk, although it really was the dining table. The walls were wood and both walls and ceiling were blackened by the smoke. The kitchen was somewhat like the living room, in that it had a fire pit cut out in the middle of the floor. Instead of a stove, there was simply a fire built in the earth pit. Over the fire an iron kettle was suspended from a hook at the end of a long iron rod, hung from the ceiling. I tried to imagine myself preparing a meal on such a stove, especially if I had guests.

Last night, all three of Miss Yamamoto's brothers and sisters were there. Her oldest brother's wife was the only Christian. She became a Christian a year before and was doing her best to lead a Christian life in spite of much difficulty and opposition from relatives. The oldest brother seemed to be quite open to the Gospel. In fact from his attitude we were quite sure that he is a believer.

Tonight the people of the neighborhood gathered for a meeting, about 12 in all. All but one were relatives. Many seem to be really seeking and were consenting to the truth of what we said, but the story is always the same: "For us to give up worship of the god which the rest of the family worships is impossible. If everyone believed, it would be different, but for just one, it is impossible."

Both our Ise and Kyoto churches had Easter sunrise services. About 25 attended in Kyoto and about 50 in Ise. In Ise we had breakfast together after the morning service, followed by Sunday School. The baptismal service was at two o'clock in spite of the cold and the rain. Eleven people were baptized. During testimony time after the baptism, they all said that they were worried about the weather, but when they got out of the water, it did not seem cold at all. Their faith was tested and strengthened by it. At 4:30 PM those previously baptized and those baptized this time had a time of fellowship together with everyone giving testimonies and then having supper together.

I rejoiced that Takashi San, the priest's son, was present for the Easter services and for the baptism. During the past year and a half, he has hardly attended at all, because he said he had to spend all his time studying in order to prepare for his entrance exams for University. Consequently his spiritual life withered. I always felt sure that the time would come when he would realize his mistake. After he had taken his exam, he began coming to church again. Two weeks later he heard that he had failed his exams. He told me that he was beginning to realize that his way of thinking had not been right. He did not participate in the Lord's Supper Sunday night. Afterward he told me that he did not feel right about partaking, because he had not attended church for a long time. He said he wanted to talk and pray with me about it sometime. I feel that the Lord is really speaking to him. I prayed that he might again give himself whole heartedly to the Lord as in the beginning.

April 1956

As the number of baptized believers increased, we felt that it was necessary for them to have an organized church to which they could belong as members. Last Sunday we had over 100 children in Sunday school, but the children of believing parents were only a handful. I knew how important the religious instruction of parents was and longed for the day when there would be a strong Christian church, where parents bring their children to church and teach them in their homes.

Last week Friday, we had our first church business meeting at which we elected three deacons, ushers, a librarian, and the leader of the women's group. We did all the nominating and voting by secret ballot. The man elected as head Deacon was not the one we hoped would be chosen. We pray that the Holy Spirit will teach him and that the church may grow in discernment through experience.

Before the election, I asked my two helpers whether they would be willing to join our church, because, if they did not, they would not be able to vote. I expected both of them to say "yes" since they had both been working with the church for a long time. Kitahara San, the girl who helps me in the house, plus teaching Sunday school and other things, said that she would not join. Also, she feels she cannot work with us any longer, but I think she will stay until I go on furlough. I was sorry to hear it, but we cannot force anyone to stay. We still do not know where Miss Yamamoto will go in the future or whether she will stay here in Ise. She would like to go to school while I am gone, but we are trusting the Lord to make His will plain when the time comes.

May 23, 1956

I am in the home of two Australian girls in Shiga Prefecture. I met one of them when I lived in Kyoto. Last summer, she invited me to spend two weeks of summer vacation with them in their mission house in Karuizawa. Thanks to that kind invitation, I was able to attend the missionary conference in Karuizawa. Now I am spending three days at the home of these girls as a little retreat from the work in Ise. Today I determined to do nothing but loaf and write letters and sleep. I would have felt rather conscience stricken about it, were it not for the fact that I felt it was absolutely necessary. My head has been bothering me again. The least little worry causes an inproportionate headache, and I find myself losing sleep and not having energy to do much the next day.

Last week I went to Kyoto to try to be of some help to a family there. The son broke into eight homes in the neighborhood and stole considerable money. Nothing was done, except to reprimand him strongly and to withhold his allowance from him for a time. This time the police were the ones who discovered him and he was taken to the juvenile home for investigations. However, they, upon hearing his story, felt his crime was due primarily to the unhappy home situation and were intent on remedying that, rather than punishing the child. His stepmother was a young woman about 22 years old. The boy was 14, so there wasn't so much age difference between them.

The mother is a moody person and her attitude toward the son is not good. They definitely do not like each other and the son says he cannot stand being at home with her. When I talked with him, he asked me how he could overcome the devil. He also asked me to pray for him. He seemed sincere in wanting to overcome temptation, but there did not seem to be adequate sorrow for his sin. Love is not easily reborn in a family when the embers have almost grown cold.

I was hoping to return to the States in September, but Auchs would like for me to be here and stay at least a month after they arrive in Ise to take over the work to bridge the gap between them and the people. Mr. Schilke has written saying that he plans to come to Japan this fall for a survey trip and he would like me to stay here until then. Sukuts are expecting their third child the first of October, so they are suggesting that Mr. Schilke come in the middle of September. It may turn out that I will stay until he comes and go home with him. I would like to take the next boat home because I am of no use right now.

May 23, 1956

As I reflected on my experiences, I remembered F.W. Boreham's thoughts on fishing for men in his book *Mushrooms on the Moor*. It was an encouragement to me. He wrote:

"It is a great art, this human angling, and needs infinite tact, and infinite subtlety, and infinite patience. And, above all, it needs a resolute determination never, on any account whatever, to be soured by disappointment. When I am tempted to wind up my line, and give the whole thing up in despair, I revive my flagging enthusiasm by recalling the rapture of my earlier catches. What angler ever forgets the wild transport of landing his first salmon? What minister ever forgets the spot on which he knelt with his first convert? In the long and tedious hours when the waiting is weary, and the nibbling vexatious, and the bites disappoint, let him live on these wealthy memories as the bees hive in the winter on the honey that they gathered in the summertime. Yes, let him think about those unforgettable triumphs and let him talk about them. They make great talking. And as he recalls and recites the thrilling story, the leaden moments will simply fly, the old glow will steal back into his fainting soul, and long before he has finished his tale, he will find his fingers busy with another glorious prize."[4]

June 14, 1956

I went to Tokyo about three weeks ago for a meeting concerning evangelism in prisons and detention homes. It was all in Japanese, of course, and very polite, difficult Japanese, so I understood almost none of it. It was very discouraging after spending all that money for the trip and taking time out of a busy week. I felt I had really been foolish in going to the meeting in the first place. To ease my conscience, I went to see Elaine Nordstrom and spent the night with her. After a few days in Tokyo, Elaine came to see me and only then, did I realize that I, too, needed a rest. My mind just would not function and I was having bad headaches almost every day. I called Clem Auch in Kyoto and asked whether he could come down for several Sunday nights. Then Elaine and I took off for two weeks. We had some lovely hills near here, so we alternated between going to the

---

[4] Boreham, F. W. *Mushrooms on the Moor*. New York: Abingdon Press, 1919.
(Public domain)

hills for a quiet time alone and taking a walk between the paddy fields where the farmers were working, or into the mountains beyond. We also went to Kyoto over Sunday, because I felt it would not be wise for me to be around and not attend church. We went to watch the fishers using cormorants to catch fish. They tie cords around the necks of these waterbirds tight enough that they can catch fish but not swallow them. The fisherman then pulls in the birds and removes the fish.

In a letter to Ed (brother) and Mary I wrote, "Don't let yourself get too busy." That is one thing I think the Lord has been teaching me during this time that I have been on the shelf, so to speak. Sometimes we do people more good by not being so busy. God, no doubt, is happy for a chance to talk with us, too. I hope I can remember this lesson myself, once I get back on my feet again.

I heard a lovely song last night. I played a record from "Gospel Recordings" intended to encourage weary missionaries.

> "He giveth more grace when the burdens grow greater.
> He sendeth more strength when the labors increase.
> To added affliction He addeth His mercies,
> To multiplied trials, His multiplied peace.
> His love has no limit, His grace has no measure.
> His power has no boundary known unto men,
> For out of His infinite riches in Jesus,
> He giveth and giveth and giveth again." [5]

June 25, 1956

After loafing or taking a sick leave or whatever you want to call it, to clear up my headaches and get a new perspective on the work and all, I'm getting back into the routine again. The Christians took over some of the responsibilities during that time and now I hesitate to take them back, because this is a step toward an indigenous church. This process of starting a church from scratch, when no one really knows what a church should be, is more difficult than I anticipated. We have elected three deacons and some minor officers, but already we have some jealousy and evil speaking about these. No one is free from criticism, but to be able to live above it, takes all the grace that God can give.

---

[5] Flint, Annie J. He Giveth More Grace (Public Domain)

Missionaries at a Japanese inn

Our missionaries are planning a little spiritual retreat here about July fourth. It seems that when we get together, it is always for business and somehow or other, we don't have enough of that spiritual unity that we need. We are hoping that several days of fellowship together and of studying the Word together may bind us together more than before. We are planning to study the Sermon on the Mount during our devotional times. I am taking the Beatitudes.

August 1, 1956

I was blessed to be able to flee from the heat for two weeks by going to the mountain resort town of Karuizawa to attend the Deeper Life Conference for the fifth time. Afternoons here are still hot but mornings and evenings are wonderfully cool. Mornings and evenings are taken up with meetings, the afternoons are free. This time I stayed in a Bible school dormitory along with 45 other missionaries. We have meals together and take turns doing dishes, serving food, cleaning, etc. It reminds me of school days.

Our conference speakers were Mr. Friend from South Africa and Mr. Love from Florida. Both men were a blessing and a challenge to us. The opening address was on the topic "Is revival possible?" based on Isaiah, chapter 40. How wonderful to remember that God, almighty, yet gentle, loves both the pastors and the flocks that belong to Him!

Clem and Sylvia Auch finished two years of language study in Kyoto and moved to Ise. They came to live with me on July 12. I occupied one room and a bit of the study. My furniture and some of my books were stored up in the attic. Sylvia Auch prepared meals for me and did my laundry. She said she was unable to help with the church work so she might as well free me to do it. Miss Yamamoto and Miss Kitahara moved over to the little Japanese house where we first lived. We had two DVBS sessions this summer. One was in Kurose, a nearby village, for the first time. We expected about 50 children there and about 100 in Ise. It is impossible to find teachers. Maybe, if we didn't have any co-workers, the church people would pitch in better, because they would have to bear the responsibility. Auchs still do not have a co-worker. Clem still needs an interpreter and language teacher to help him get his messages into Japanese.

August 27, 1956

A letter from Edwin (brother) was waiting for me when I came back from Karuizawa. It was just the right time because, after having been with many English-speaking friends, there was a little bit of a lonely feeling when I walked in the door of my home. Ed's letter fixed that in a hurry. I didn't know how to account for the funny feeling that crept over me. I hated to admit it but I knew it was a longing to talk to someone, so I sat down and wrote some letters to my missionary friends, all of which were necessary anyhow, so I wasn't wasting any time. I heard the mailman come at ten o'clock. No sooner had he dropped the mail in the box, than it was in my hands. It's funny how the Lord knows what we need and when we need it. No, I guess it really isn't strange at all, just very wonderful.

So many things have been happening, not big spectacular things but quieter, internal things of the heart. They surely make a big difference. While I was in Karuizawa, I had a big struggle over my singleness. It's a battle in the realm of my affections. I wanted a word from the Lord that would help me accept my singleness, if that was to be God's will for me. I went outdoors to a quiet place by myself and sat down under a tree with my Bible in hand. As I read and prayed, it seemed that the Lord asked me what I wanted most of all; whether I really believed that the Lord Himself was the most desirable person in all the world and whether I really believed that if I possessed the highest good, I would be satisfied without some lesser things. I had been desiring a marriage partner, a lesser thing, and no matter how I prayed about it, I had no assurance that the Lord heard and would answer my prayer.

Then He fixed my eyes upon the beauty and strength of the Son of God and I found myself praying that the beauty of Jesus might be seen in me. When I opened my eyes I saw that my Bible was open to Psalm 21:2 "Thou has given him his heart's desire, and hath not withholden the request of his lips." Then I knew how I ought to pray and what I ought to desire. Back home, I found it necessary to be reminded again and this time the Lord spoke to me from Psalm 45:2 "Thou art fairer than the children of men." And then in verse 10, "Hearken, O daughter, forget also thine own people and thy father's house; so shall the king greatly desire thy beauty: for He is thy Lord; and worship thou Him." Could anything be more pertinent? Well, needless to say, when I follow this advice, the whole world looks different than it did before.

Yesterday as I was preparing my final thought for Sunday morning, the meaning of the familiar words, "Whosoever shall call upon the name of the Lord shall be saved" became applicable to almost every situation imaginable, not just the moment of believing for salvation. Whoever would really believe that Jesus is the Savior and would call upon him in the way that a dying man would for help, would surely be saved from that sin or weakness with which he was struggling, be it physical or spiritual. It seems like a *master key* that fits every door. This key was the means of enabling me to bring the message that morning with a sense of the Holy Spirit upon me. God brought to that meeting four or five who were not yet born again, but for whom we had been praying. I had no way of knowing if there was any response in any heart, but after the meeting, Mrs. Sekoguchi, the Christian woman in whose home we have a meeting in Kurose, asked if she and her son could come to talk with me. I thought it was the mother's idea and while I was very glad to have them come, I did not know how much to say to the son about spiritual things. Although there had been signs of a spiritual awakening in his heart before, when we called on him in the hospital, he seemed embarrassed when we talked about God. It turned out that he wanted to talk about faith.

I asked him what he believed about Christ and he gave all the answers a Christian would be expected to give. I asked, then, if he had confessed his sin to God and asked for His forgiveness. He said "No".

When I suggested that he do it then, he agreed to it. That was what he had come for, it seemed, and I didn't know it. I had to leave in about 15 minutes, so we had a hasty look at some Bible verses and a brief prayer and the contract was made. Tonight I am invited to their home for a "thank you" celebration to the Lord. I remembered how the shepherd called in the neighbors when he found his sheep. That mother was so surprised and happy she could hardly believe it was true.

September 18, 1956

Miss Yamamoto has decided to stay on with us, for which we really praise the Lord. After working here in Ise for one year, she began to wish for an opportunity to go to school. I had the same hopes for her, so she was able to attend a small Bible school in Kyoto for a year. Then, when it looked as if she and I would not be able to continue working together anymore due to our differences, the Lord wonderfully undertook and again gave us love for each other. Now our desire was for her to stay to help the Auchs. We promised her a week of rest after the busy summer was over. Her brother would like to move to Ise because it is difficult to make a living in the mountains. If they could find work in Ise, it would be wonderful. They could be free from the village prejudice, attend church and grow spiritually. They would be an asset to our church too, but the Lord must lead in this.

We wanted Miss Kitahara to stay too, but she had previously told us that she could not agree with us on some issues and so we expected to lose her. When Miss Kitahara announced her decision to go back to the church where she was saved in Tomida Hama, Miss Yamamoto felt that was the Lord's leading and she could stay here. Miss Kitahara left us last Monday with a good attitude, almost wishing she could stay on, yet feeling the Lord had led her otherwise.

A young man named Hisashi Murakami has come from Kyoto to help Clem Auch with his language study. He was a student at Ritsumeikan University in Kyoto and lived in a one-room house in front of our mission house in Kyoto. He began attending our English Bible classes and then went to our church in Kyoto, where he became a Christian. He has a humble spirit and seems eager to learn, so we are grateful to the Lord for him. He hopes to continue his education in Kyoto, but one never knows how the Lord may lead him in the meantime.

We have had to give up our meeting on Friday night in Mrs. S's house, due to opposition from her single, non-Christian sister-in-law who lives with her. Mrs. S's husband died so the sister-in-law acts like the owner of the house. I called on Mrs. S one night and her sister-in-law asked me to please stop the meetings. I told her that it was not my decision to make. We had been invited to come and if Mrs. S asked us not to come, of course, we would respect her decision. We left it up to Mrs. S, hoping she would continue the meetings but she asked us to give them up for the time being, because it was unbearable at home. We felt badly about it, but we also sympathized with Mrs. S. We trusted that there would be other homes open to us so that we might reach out to the people who may be seeking.

Sukuts have a new baby boy, Donald Dwight, born this morning. He is their third child.

We are planning to have evangelistic meetings in October from the 9th to the 14th. A Japanese pastor from Wakimachi, Iwai Sensei, in Shikoku will be our speaker. Two of his sons are studying at Kyoto University and have consented to come and help us. They came last year when John Rhoads was the evangelist. They both sing very well and can play the organ as well as preach. We are very grateful for their willingness to come and pray that the Lord may use these meetings for the salvation of many.

Mr. Schilke will not be coming to Japan this year as we thought so I am free to return to the States as soon as I am able to get a booking. Fall is usually a crowded season, so it may be a little difficult. I am waiting for word from the travel agency. I packed several trunks, just in case the notice comes suddenly and I don't have much time to get ready.

October 13, 1956

We have been receiving showers of blessing from the evangelistic meetings which will close tomorrow evening. We have never had less than 50 at any meeting and last night there were over 70. Our speaker is Pastor Iwai, brother-in-law of Pastor Itoh. We young missionaries have been lapping up his messages as a wonderful course in how to do evangelism. The Kerns came for four days. Mrs. Kern plays the vibra-harp which has added a lot to our meetings. Even now, I find myself tending to coldness of heart and unbelief, in the midst of all the blessing. How unprofitable can one become? But as I recall the Lord's promise that He would pour water on him who is thirsty and that He bids us bring our vessels, as many as we wish, and He will fill them all, I find new hope. Iwai Sensei is always giving thanks. It's hard to be around him and stay downhearted.

Yesterday Yamamoto San and I visited the juvenile home where we have gone for two years now. I couldn't even say a decent farewell to them, just a few jumbled sentences between the tears and dewy prayer. I don't look forward to farewell services. I'd almost rather just part, as if you expected to see everyone tomorrow.

My ship leaves Japan November 1. It will probably take about twelve to fourteen days to get to San Francisco. It is a Japanese freighter that is supposed to go directly to San Francisco. I am planning to spend a day or two in California before starting east. I still don't know where I will be going to school, but I hope to spend some months in study, if permitted to do so. I wrote to my siblings asking them to come to Benton Harbor to celebrate Thanksgiving with me this year, a big selfish wish. I expected to be home about the 21st.

5

MY FIRST FURLOUGH 1956-1958

After five long years in Japan, with so many adjustments, so many things to learn (the biggest challenge being the Japanese language), so many responsibilities thrust upon me as the trail-blazer of the mission and so many lonely days with no one to converse with in English, I was totally exhausted and ready for a rest and a return home to my family and my homeland, where things were familiar and I had a sense of belonging.

I was booked for a voyage on a Japanese freighter named the *Kosoh Maru*. Miss Yoshiko Yamamoto, my Japanese co-worker, and my good friend from Wheaton College days, Elaine Nordstrom, went to Yokohama with me to see me off. Miss Yamamoto was feeling somewhat deserted, not knowing just how her life would change working with other missionaries. I was excited and full of anticipation about going home. We said our goodbyes and I promised to return after a year in the States, visiting family and supporting churches.

It was a very peaceful voyage of twelve days. The captain told me it was because a missionary was aboard. Finally we entered the San Francisco harbor, but had to wait for a tugboat to guide us in and pull us up close to the dock. When the tugboat came alongside our ship, the passengers all gathered on that side of the ship to watch. We were told that we would have to remain on the ship over night, because the longshoremen had gone off duty. What a disappointment!

That evening as I stood on the deck and watched the pilot climb up the rope onto the ship and interact with the young Japanese passengers who were observing him carefully and began to converse with him, I had a strange experience of identifying myself with the Japanese, rather than the American.

It so affected me that when I went back to my cabin, I took out pen and paper and wrote down my feelings which I wanted to capture before they vanished and then pondered over what had happened to me while I was in Japan.

This is what I wrote:

"A Missionary Comes Home"

"The engines of the ship have been turned off. The tossing of the ocean waves has ceased. We are lying at anchor in San Francisco Bay. It is 11:00 p.m. and there is no possibility of disembarking until morning, although we are so eager to set foot on American soil. After completing my first term of missionary service, I was longing to get back to my own country and see my family. It had been a hard, lonely five years for me as a single missionary. I was one of the first missionaries to be sent to Japan by our mission. There were no senior missionaries to welcome us or to help us get oriented to the country. I knew no one and not a word of Japanese. The task of establishing our first little church had left me physically and emotionally exhausted. I needed the rest and comfort of being back home among my own people. I could not wait for a booking on an American ship. I took the first available ship, a Japanese freighter that carried about twenty-five people. When I boarded the ship, I discovered that I was the only American passenger. The majority was young Japanese going to America to study or visit relatives.

"From the first glimpse of light in the east, we stood on the deck thrilled with every new discovery as more and more lights came into view. We looked through the ship's giant binoculars and reported to the other passengers what we saw. We shivered with the cold but no one thought of going back to his cabin. It was too fascinating as we distinguished the lights of the Golden Gate Bridge and the Oakland Bay Bridge, brilliant against the dark sky. Was it real? Was it a dream? Yes, for many of the passengers it was a dream come true, especially for the young Japanese who had come to study, to travel and to live. For me, it was like waking up from a dream and finding it reality I had known from my childhood. Japan seemed far, far way, although we had left it only a few days ago. I wondered where I really belonged.

"My thoughts were interrupted when the pilot who would guide our ship safely to the pier climbed aboard from his little motorboat. He was a big, husky American in a heavy overcoat wearing a large felt hat. The Japanese young people were eager to greet him and began to ask him questions. He was in no mood to talk. He had a job to do. I heard some English words spoken in a loud, gruff voice in answer to a question by one of the passengers. I cringed a little as I felt myself drawing back from him, trying to blend into the group of

Japanese. One of the girls moved closer to me and called my name, like a little frightened girl. I could almost read her mind: "What are Americans like? Are they all big, unfriendly, and rough like this one?"

"I recalled the day I had arrived in Yokohama and had my first look at the Japanese longshoremen from the deck of an American freighter. I clutched my purse tightly and watched anxiously as my baggage was removed from my cabin. Where were they taking it? Would I ever see it again? Yes, I could understand Yano San's fears, for even now, I felt a bit of it too, in the presence of my own people. Why should I hesitate to speak English, lest the pilot recognize me as an American and speak to me? Was I ashamed to admit that he was one of the people to whom I belonged? Or was I afraid that I was no longer recognizable or acceptable as an American? There wasn't time to analyze my feelings. They were just there.

"Back in my cabin at midnight, gazing at my Japanese roommate who had already gone to bed, I tried to sort out my feelings. In the morning I would say "Goodbye" to my fellow-passengers, and we would go our separate ways. I would probably not have another intimate contact with Japanese for a year. I would miss them.

"I remembered the kind Japanese pastor and wife who allowed me to live in their home for two months to give me a chance to understand and participate in Japanese family and church life before I attempted to minister to the Japanese people. I recalled the family in Kyoto that permitted me to rent a room of their house and share in many of their family experiences. I especially thought of the two Japanese girls who came to live with me and help me with my church work. Unconsciously my life had intertwined with theirs. I knew that something had happened to me during my five years in Japan. Some of Japan had entered into me and some of me had been left behind in Japan. Without realizing it, my identification with the Japanese had begun."

In the morning of November 13th, we were allowed to disembark and go through customs and immigration. Rev. Clarence and Mrs. Dorene Walth, who pastored the Willow Rancho Church in Sacramento, came to meet me. I recall riding in their car along the streets of San Francisco looking at the buildings and houses that were painted all colors of the rainbow and thinking, "How garish!" Once again, I realized that I was looking at America through Japanese eyes. I did not know until then how much I had been affected by Japanese culture and values. For the first time, I understood what it meant to identify with others and with Christ.

Philippians 2:5 "Let this mind be in you which was also in Christ Jesus." Identification with Christ means to think, feel and act as He does, because we are one with Him. I was glad that I had absorbed some of the Japanese qualities without even being aware of it and thus, I could better understand and fit in with them.

When I arrived back home in Benton Harbor, my parents were still living on the eighty acre farm. While I was home Mom and Dad sold the farm and moved into their city home, after the tenants moved out.

My youngest sister, Sherrill, was nine years old when I first went to Japan and had grown to be a typical fourteen year old teenager. She was quite a different person from the one I had known five years before. It took a little adjustment on the part of both of us to see how each of us fit into the family that now consisted of four members, instead of the three that she was accustomed to. Her world and the world I had been living in were altogether different.

I was totally exhausted physically, mentally, emotionally and spiritually from my five strenuous years in Japan. I had struggled with learning a difficult language, loneliness, assuming full responsibility for the first NAB church plant, discipling new believers, and working closely with Japanese and missionary co-workers.

As much as I wanted to remain at home with my parents, I felt that I needed to be away from home in order to be renewed in soul and body and mind. I thought of spending some time at Wheaton, a place I had come to love in my college years, and to take a course of study, free from all other responsibility. Mrs. Clara Anderson, Esther Hirth's mother, had a rest home in Wheaton where she ministered to weary missionaries by using Swedish steam baths and massages. She invited me to spend a few days with her and get some healing treatments. It sounded good to me, so I spent a short time in Wheaton as a client of Mrs. Anderson. I also took a short course at the college before I began to visit churches.

When my parents moved into their city home in the fall of 1957, I had the privilege of going shopping with them for some new furniture and carpeting for the house. I wanted to give them a gift for the new house, since they were allowing me to live there while I was on home assignment. When I was at the Biblical Seminary in New

York, I had a course in religious art. Among the paintings that our instructor introduced us to was one called, "The Presence." I discovered that I could get a print of it at the Palmer House in Chicago, so I bought it and had it framed in a gold frame. It shows the interior of a beautiful cathedral that looks dark and almost empty, except for the area surrounding the altar, which was bright with gold finished objects that immediately caught the eye of the viewer. At the extreme rear of the cathedral, one can see the figure of Christ, standing in the shadows and lighting up the area around him, revealing the form of a woman kneeling behind the last row of seats. Christ is not looking at the brightly lit altar where the human action appears to be occurring but is looking down at the humble, praying woman with an arm outstretched, as if to help her in her time of need. The artist focuses on this encounter between a seeking soul and a loving, merciful Savior who is eager to help her. That is where the Presence of Christ can be found and where He does His work. This painting was hung over the fireplace in my parents' home.[6]

While I was home, in November, 1957 my home church completed the laying of the foundation and the cornerstone of the new church building which was to be called Napier Parkview Baptist Church. It had previously been called Clay Street Baptist Church but the old building was sold to German immigrants and a new church constructed in Fairplain in Benton Harbor, Michigan. Rev. William Hoover was the pastor at that time and the church had grown to about 600 people. The new building would accommodate 700 and had a very modern architectural style.

I had planned to return to Japan a year after my arrival home, which was November 13, 1957, but I did not feel that I was emotionally and psychologically restored enough to leave at that time, so I requested permission to stay home a little longer. Permission was granted, so I was able to spend a second Christmas with my family. My new departure date from Benton Harbor was December 27th and from San Francisco on January 7th, 1958. I will once again take a freighter to Japan, this time called the China Bear.

---

[6] In 2013 it had a prominent place in my room at the assisted living home, The Willows.

November 13th was designated "Florence Miller Sunday" at our church. On that day the church sought to raise the full support of $2,000 for me. I spoke at the evening service. It was wonderful having my siblings and their families home for several days. Some young couples had a surprise "Bon Voyage" party for me. I was given a projector and record player. I had received a tape recorder before, so I felt really outfitted with all the things I thought would be nice to have but couldn't afford.

Trip Back to Japan

January 20, 1958

This is the 12th day at sea and there is another week ahead of us. I was told at Oakland that we would arrive at Japan in 14 days but it appears now that it will more likely be 18 to Yokohama and then two more or so to Kobe, where I disembark.

The weather has been rough from the time we set out. The ship had a reputation for being a rocker to start with. On top of that, stormy seas made the trip anything but restful. Even though I took pills to prevent seasickness, I was sick for about three days. Almost all the passengers were. The first couple of nights were really hectic. All during the night our suitcases, chairs, shoes, flower pots, etc. flew back and forth, banging with every roll of the ship. Little by little, we learned how to pack everything away tightly, so that nothing could jiggle loose. We also began to discover how to use pillows and life jackets to prop up one side of the mattress to retard the rolling.

We have all taken our turns at going spinning, like tops, across the room and then bouncing back to hit the other wall. It has been some fun at the table too. The tablecloth and pad are always kept wet to try to keep the dishes from sliding, but even then, it is nothing to see a bowl of soup or a cup of tea go sailing off in the direction of a passenger. The cook sprained his arm. One of the waiters ran head on into the wall with both hands full of dishes. The captain told us that the ship is built to allow a 45 degree list of the ship, but one night we were tipping 47 degrees. Logically speaking, there was no reason why the ship couldn't have tipped over, but the weight of the cargo in the hold acted as a balancer and brought it back up into position. The stormy weather has accounted for the delay in our arrival. We went off our course to escape some of the stormy weather and then we had to slow down our speed also.

January 14th proved to be a double birthday celebration. A young passenger turned eleven on the same day that I turned 33. Her parents planned a little party for her and invited all the passengers. They provided us with cokes, mints and nuts for refreshments. I supplied the cookies my friend sent along with me. I saved all my birthday mail for the ship. I snitched a little and read the card from Mom on the 13th. I thought it wouldn't hurt to spread the joy out a little over several days.

All of my fragile things, such as accordion, amplifier, recorder, and record changer are in my cabin, so I think they will come through all right. The first class cargo in the hold has been getting very severe treatment, according to the first mate, so I am a little apprehensive about that. He seemed to indicate that the passengers' baggage was alright. He said he had not seen such damage done to the cargo on any ship yet, like this.

February 11, 1958

My ship arrived at Yokohama on January 26th, 1958. I got off and spent a day in Tokyo before returning to the ship because my destination was Kobe, the seaport nearest to Kyoto where I would be attending Japanese Language School for six months. The night of the 26th, there was a storm and a ferry boat carrying about 150 people went down between two of the islands of Japan. I arrived by ship at Kobe on January 29th. Auchs, Mr. Kern, Mr. Moore, Mrs. Uchida, Miss Yamamoto and Miss Yamada came to meet my ship about 8:00 a.m. but we didn't dock until 9:00 p.m. They spent the whole day walking around Kobe and were cold and tired. I felt sorry for them. It was wonderful to see them though. Ed Kern and the Moores went back with me to Kobe the following day to get my baggage through customs. The officials opened every box but charged me nothing, for which I was very grateful.

6

AFTER FURLOUGH ASSIGNMENTS

February 11, 1958

I had all my things stored in Ise, so I went there to get them. Soon after I arrived in Ise, two of our Christian young people were married. The bride wore a Japanese bridal kimono, black with red designs, and a white veil. She carried a little bouquet of flowers too, making it semi Japanese and semi Western. Clem Auch performed the wedding. Not knowing any other way to do it, it turned out to be very much like our weddings in America. It was held in the mission house in the afternoon, so those attending were only the immediate relatives and a few of the church people. The bride's father was dead, but her mother wanted the groom to take the bride's family name, Yamaoka, since the bride was an only child and the family name would not be continued otherwise, nor would there be anyone to worship the Yamaoka ancestors. This is a common practice in Japan. The mother of the bride is also a Christian, so we thought it strange that she would be so concerned about these things, but I suppose that some of the relatives were putting pressure on. At any rate, the couple was married in the groom's name. The next day, the mother called asking if it were against the teaching of Christianity for the name to be changed to Yamaoka.

After getting back to Kyoto, we missionaries gathered together for our annual field council but since two of the wives were sick with the flu, we disbanded. The two men came over to help me unpack. It sure was a boost. Fred is quite an electrician. He fixed up my transformer for electrical appliances and put a shelf in the kitchen.

The Kyoto church had a little reception for me in the evening. About 40 were present, some who hadn't been attending for a long time but may have felt obligated to come out of courtesy to the missionary. There are about twenty attending services regularly. There should be more. Some have grown cold spiritually. A young man who previously led our youth group but had drifted away from church was there. He has been attending quite faithfully but the joy seemed to be all gone from his face. In fact he would not even look at me. When the service was over, he was the first one out. I hoped I could get a chance to get close to him again to discover what his problem is.

105

Miss Yamamoto is still living in Ise. She came up to help me unpack some of my things and then returned. We have not yet decided where she should serve. She had planned to go to school but now she feels it would be too difficult, since she has not even finished Junior High school. She said she would rather just stay on with me, helping with the housework and doing as much in the church as she is able. The Japanese have often told her that she does not seem to be like them but more like the foreigners in her manner of speech, etc. She is not quiet and reserved like most Japanese girls but rather free and aggressive. If she stays on with me now, her opportunities for further education are probably over because she is already twenty five years old.

At our missionary field council a number of important things had to be decided. Of chief interest to me was my placement and the nature of the work I would be doing. We had to decide about sending one of our young men to Bible School in the spring, where to send him and how much financial help to give him. We also decided to encourage Miss Yamamoto to attend Bible School. If she does, she and I will not be together for about three years, or maybe never again.

March 24, 1958

After more than a year in the States using only English, I felt the need to get a short refresher course in the Japanese language before getting involved in my second term of work. The mission agreed to allow all missionaries returning to Japan after their first furlough to have six additional months of language study. Permission was granted for me to attend the Naganuma Language School in Kyoto. An apartment for me was found by our missionaries in Kyoto, Sukuts and Moores. It was a two-storied house with two apartments, one upstairs and one downstairs. It was located almost next door to a prison. It was little wonder that it was available. I had the downstairs apartment and the upstairs was vacant. It was a lonely, dreary place to be. In addition, I had a problem with my neighbors whose house faced mine. It seemed to me that I was not welcome in the neighborhood. Also I was a bit fearful about being so close to the prison. When I mentioned this to my fellow missionaries, the Fred Moore family offered to let me have two rooms in their large upstairs apartment. The landlady lived in the rooms on the first floor.

106

March 24, 1958

Last night I went to talk with Dr. Uchida. Mrs. Uchida and the children stayed downstairs, so I could talk with him privately. I felt it was a good talk and he still seems open, although he has not come to church since last Christmas. He recognizes God in a hazy sort of way as the power behind the universe but he cannot reconcile Christ as being that power. I continue to pray that he may not harden his heart having come this far.

April 13, 1958

A problem has arisen regarding the building we are now using. It belongs to a weaving factory. We signed a contract to rent it for a year. About a week ago, they informed us that they would like to break the contract, so we must get out the end of the month. We had purchased curtains to divide the classes but now they cannot be used. Last Wednesday night, we talked with several of the Christians about what we should do now. The man who more or less was in charge of getting the building said he would talk with the others about it. This morning after church, he made an announcement that we would have to get out at the end of the month. We would then be meeting in the missionaries' home, as before. This came as a surprise to us, because the missionaries had not been consulted nor had the rest of the Christians. From this, we sensed a division and a lack of cooperation between our people and the missionaries. It seems that we are not respected now as leaders of the church. We do pray that the Holy Spirit may melt and bind our hearts together in Christian love and that the gap between us may be closed.

Fred and Pat Moore and their three children and I are renting the upstairs rooms of a large Japanese house. The landlady lives downstairs. I am finding life here with the Moores very satisfactory thus far. They are our newest missionaries and are in language school. I have two rooms, a sitting room and a bedroom but no kitchen, so I have meals with Moores.

Since Pat is also in language school, they have a maid who comes at 8:00 a.m. and leaves at 5:30 p.m. She prepares lunch for us. I help Pat prepare breakfast and supper and help with the dishes. The maid does my laundry when she does Moores' and also does my ironing. This frees me for study.

Joy Moore had a birthday today. She is now four years old. She has an older brother, Stephen, and a baby brother, Jimmy. I enjoy watching the children and listening to their conversations. I like to hear their comments when we have devotions. It helps me in my Sunday School work.

One day Joy came to my rooms for a little visit. After she returned home, her mother found her crying. She asked her what was the matter but Joy did not reply. Finally, after much coaxing, she said that she had taken a cookie from my cookie jar when she was at my house. Apparently her conscience was bothering her, even at that young age. Her mother talked with her about it and soon they were both at my door, with Joy making a sorrowful apology for her deed. I assured her that she was forgiven and that if she wanted a cookie again, she could ask me for it and I would be glad to give it to her. This incident provided me with a good illustration to use in Sunday School.

I am going to begin a teacher training class in our church starting next Sunday for about three months. Trying to demonstrate effectively in inadequate Japanese is no easy task. Our Sunday School now numbers about 40 children on average. We decided to have our English Bible Class during the Sunday School hour before the worship service in hopes that some of the students might remain for that. This morning three stayed, so we are praying that they may find it helpful. There were about 13 adults in the morning worship service, not counting missionaries.

Miss Yamamoto has gone to Yokohama, where she is now engaged in study at the Kyoritsu Women's Bible School. I have not yet heard from her although she left a week ago. She did not know for certain whether she would be admitted until after a personal interview with the teachers there. However, we felt quite certain that she would be admitted as a special student, even though she had not completed high school. She seemed a little blue when she left here, but I am certain that once she gets adjusted to the school, she will like it.

Our new mission worker for Ise, Mr. Yoshio Akasaka, should be arriving in Ise tomorrow. He was married a week ago and will be bringing his new bride to their new home in Ise. Mr. Clem Auch's helper, Mr. Hisashi Murakami, will probably be moving to Kyoto to help Ed Kern, because Ed's former helper, Mr. Sekoguchi, has gone to the Japan Christian College in Tokyo. The church in Ise became attached to Mr. Murakami and did not want him to leave. They said that there had been so many changes in leaders already. We have decided to let him stay for a little longer, at least until the people get used to Mr. Akasaka. We hope there will not be any rivalry between them and that they can work together harmoniously.

May 25, 1958

We completed a fairly successful Sunday morning, considering the problems we have had in the church. Four men and one woman have stopped coming to church. That is about half of our regulars, so it was really a blow. Two of the men who no longer come were Sunday School teachers so we had just one teacher left. She and I carried on for two Sundays. Then Mr. Murakami came to live in Kyoto. He is now going to help Mr. Kern for at least one year, before going to Seminary. He is a fine young man and, with his help, we hope to make up for lost time. He is now taking over the Sunday School superintendency and is also teaching a class. In addition, he will be preaching every other Sunday and helping with the young people's work. My responsibility is still that of working with the Sunday School teachers. We have resumed our teacher training class. Mrs. Uchida has offered to teach Sunday School, so we again have three teachers. She had given it up before, because she lived a long distance from church and also because she was not feeling well. She says that as long as she can remain physically well, she is willing to teach. Sunday School attendance was down to thirty-five today. However, I feel that we now have a group of teachers who are willing to spend time in preparation and who are eager to learn. The attitude of all is good and that means a great deal in working together.

We have been burdened for another lady who made a decision for Christ several months ago. Her husband has led a very bad life. He has been dishonest in business and has been unfaithful to his wife. He has made debts which have burdened the whole family. The son, 24, is now following in his father's footsteps. He is drinking heavily and recently has been mistreating his mother terribly. He says he is being persecuted by his employer (uncle) because his mother is a Christian. He has told her not to go to church. One night he beat and kicked her so badly that she was bruised all over. Then, on top of that, he almost strangled her with his belt. Her hands were cut. He even gagged his little eight-year old sister, so she would not cry out. Both mother and daughter ran away in the middle of the night to the home of a nearby Christian. The violence is now over, but still the son comes home late at night after drinking heavily and keeps his mother awake insisting that she massage his body. The father has begun to realize his own sin and is open to the gospel. He was in church this morning. The little eight-year old girl has been a real source of joy and strength to her mother in that she, too, believes in Jesus. When her mother was suffering at the hands of her son, she said to her mother, "I know it hurts when he strikes you, but please don't resist him or scold him. They put nails through Jesus' hands and He bore it quietly." This little girl has been laughed at, at school, because she prayed out loud before eating her lunch. Now she bows her head and prays quietly. The teacher thought she was sick at first, but when she inquired, the girl said that she was just praying. The teacher told her mother this and encouraged her to continue going to church, because she had noticed a real change in the girl's conduct recently. May this be the testimony of all who are called by Christ's name.

The first Rakuyo church building

We are hoping to buy land, both in Ise and Kyoto, for our future churches. Land for Ise has been approved by the Mission and we are waiting for the money. Over half has been pledged, but we need the rest of the money immediately. We found a lot which we think is suitable and want to buy it before it is purchased by someone else. Lots for houses are too small for a church. To find a lot in a good location is extremely difficult, because land in Japan is not as plentiful as in the States. On top of that, land prices are rising rapidly. In just a few years, they have doubled. To wait means we may lose the lot we have in mind and may have to pay a very high price for a lot less favorably located.

June 17, 1958

We are having special meetings at the church this week with a Japanese evangelist. We had a fairly good attendance on Sunday but the evening meetings are poorly attended. The students are busy studying during the week, so we don't expect to see them very often. Last night there were three new people present. We distributed announcements of the meetings in the neighborhood. So far only one family has responded. The husband came the first night. He said he and his family used to attend a Baptist church in Okinawa but, since returning to the mainland of Honshu, they have not been attending anywhere regularly. We still are not sure if he is a true Christian. His wife came last night. We discovered that the husband is a teacher at Kyoto University. He knows Dr. Uchida who also is a professor there. Dr. Uchida has not been to church since Christmas. I stopped in Sunday night to give him an invitation but he did not come as yet.

One of my language teachers invited me to speak to a group of women who were graduates of the college from which she graduated. I spoke on the first and greatest commandment, "Thou shalt love the Lord thy God with all thy heart and soul and mind," as the need of all men, in every generation. In post-war Japan, a course in morals is starting to be taught, as it was in pre-war days. I proposed that we follow the first great command in the Bible, namely, letting the true God, as revealed in Jesus Christ, be the standard of what we are to love and obey. All of these women were graduates of a Methodist College, but probably only one or two were truly Christians. My language teacher seemed happy for it and another language teacher asked if I would give the same message to their women's group in her church.

Today when I went to my lesson, my teacher told me that one of the young women who had been at the meeting had taken poison the previous night and died. She left a note saying that it was the result of a problem which had persisted from the time she was married. No one really knows what is involved in that. The Japanese people have the highest suicide rate in the world. A church member shocked me the first day I arrived back in Japan by telling me that she had almost turned on the gas the previous night, because she and her husband had a disagreement over one of the children. For a Christian to have such thoughts as this was really a shock to me. Our lives are not our own to do with as we please. God has said that he who destroys the temple of God shall be destroyed. Lack of faith leads to our seeking a foolish way out that can only make greater difficulties and leave great sorrow and heartache behind. There is also selfishness in it that wishes to make another suffer. It's a kind of vengeance, though in a negative way. However, I need to remember that this lady is still a young Christian and may not think as a mature Christian would.

June 28, 1958

We are in the middle of the rainy season. It started late and only recently has really become hot. When it rains, it is fairly comfortable but when the rain stops, it gets muggy and stuffy. You need a bath every day and sometimes you feel like getting in the tub more often. I have only two more weeks left in Kyoto for my refresher Japanese language study. A missionary from the Swedish Baptist group has invited me to stay with her at Lake Nojiri, one of the cooler places where missionaries often go to escape the heat. She rented a cabin for the month of July. She is alone and wants a companion. I thought I would go the last two weeks of July, which is still part of my study time. Even though I won't have a teacher, I can spend that time studying by myself in a cool place, rather than sweltering in Kyoto where I would get less done. Following that, I plan to spend 10 days in Karuizawa, attending the annual missionary conference. Lorraine Fleischman has invited me to stay with her, so the Lord has certainly opened the way for my summer plans without any problem whatsoever.

I went to Ise last Monday to help Clem Auch interview seven baptismal candidates. Clem and Sylvia are now in charge of the Ise Church. It was a joy to hear the clear testimony of some, but others seemed to be rather hazy in their replies. I feel that I may be discouraging some by refusing them for baptism and yet, you also know that if they are baptized without complete assurance of salvation, it will only pose problems for them personally and also for the church. I came away feeling that, perhaps, I was not resolute enough, for we finally approved all who asked for baptism, although there were still some doubts in my mind. I pray that the Holy Spirit will teach them what is still unclear and that they may be obedient to the Lord in what they do comprehend.

One of those requesting baptism is a girl just out of high school, Miss Yokota, who gave a very clear testimony of salvation and also expressed a desire to go into the Lord's service, if He should so lead. I was thinking of asking her to live with me for a year, helping in the home and, at the same time, becoming established in her Christian faith. She is a niece of the woman who was persecuted by her relatives for not worshipping the ancestors.

Robbed at Night

August 28, 1958

The Moores were in language school. Fred was saving up money to buy a motor-bike and had put the money in his steel file case in their bedroom where the baby slept. One morning when I got up, I noticed something strange about my sitting room. The wastebasket which had been beside my desk was on the desk, and the red purse I always put in my bedroom closet at night was on the sofa. Thinking this very curious, I looked inside my purse and discovered that my wallet was missing. I realized then that someone had been in my bedroom while I had slept soundly, not hearing a sound. When I told the Moores about it, Fred looked in the file case for his money only to discover that it was gone too. I did not have much money in my wallet, but Fred had a sizeable amount in the file case. We figured out how the burglar had gotten in. There was a veranda around the outside of our second-floor rooms. There was also a long ladder secured to the side of the house, which was tall enough to reach the veranda. Apparently the burglar had used the ladder to climb up to the veranda and entered through the unlocked window in my sitting room. The Moores had been up that night tending to the baby, but they did not hear anything either. The police were notified and they found a pair of my slipper socks which had been in the bedroom tossed away in the garden. Apparently he had worn them to conceal his own footprints. It appeared that it had been done by an insider who knew the house very well. He was later apprehended but the money was never recovered.

September 24, 1958

I have had two very happy experiences in the past two weeks. Last Saturday, a young lady named Miss Kato, who is soon to be married, declared her faith in Christ as the true God and her personal Savior and Lord here in my home. She had attended my English Bible Class in Ise during her college days, but it was merely to gain knowledge. However, when she planned to marry a teacher at a Methodist Mission school, she realized that she, too, should become a Christian. I asked her plainly, last week, about her present belief and she gave her consent to all the major points. My concern for her is that she will be drawn away from the evangelical faith after marriage, because the school where her fiancé teaches is very liberal.

Last Monday night the neighbor lady came over and told me that she had wanted to believe in God for some time but could not believe that God really existed. She was about to separate from her husband last spring, due to problems in the home. Now she feels that God has changed her way of thinking and she is able to believe in Him. She listened eagerly as I went over the plan of salvation. She, too, gave consent to it and before returning home, prayed to the Lord, asking for forgiveness. My prayer is that her faith will grow and that it may be evidenced in her home, so that her husband may also be won to Christ.

There have been disappointments for me too. The priest's son is now in college in Osaka. He is living in a Buddhist temple and is helping with the work of the temple. At the temple, he received room and board and a part time job. To leave the temple would mean he could not continue his education. His father had a stroke last spring and for a time, it seemed he might die. That would mean that he would be responsible for the care of his mother and younger brother and sisters. To break ties with the temple might mean cutting off all help for them as well. However, later, I received a postcard from him stating that he wanted to leave the temple, providing he could live in an American home, which would give him an excuse to leave, saying that he wanted to learn English. However, we feel that, unless there is a clear surrender of himself to Christ and a declaration of his intention to sever all relations with the temple, there will be no real help for him, even if we were to find him a lodging place. I sympathize with him in his difficult position. Yet there seems to be little that we can do, except call on him to trust in God and take a clear stand.

After my six months Japanese language refresher course in Kyoto (January through June), I went to Ise to work with Clem and Sylvia Auch who had taken charge of the Ise Church while I was on furlough. They had only six more months before their first furlough was due. Auchs had as their interpreter and helper a young man, Hisashi Murakami, who had been a student at Ritsumeikan University in Kyoto. He lived in a one room, pre-fab house in the back yard of the house the Auchs were renting when they were in language school in Kyoto. Mr. Murakami was eager to learn English. Auchs quickly struck up an acquaintance with him and invited him to attend the Rakuyo Baptist Church which had been started in the home of Walter and Barbara Sukut, where he became a Christian. When Auchs moved to Ise they needed a Japanese helper and asked Mr. Murakami if he would be willing to go with them as their interpreter and helper. He agreed to go for one year and then return to his studies. However, when he saw how difficult it was for the missionaries to communicate Biblical truth adequately with the Japanese, he felt that Japanese should be reaching out to their own people with the gospel message. I remember encouraging him to "labor, not for the meat which perisheth but for that meat which endureth to everlasting life." After much deliberation and prayer, he decided to go to seminary instead of going back to Ritsumeikan University.[7]

October 6, 1958

Unexpectedly, a man came to see me. He came to know Christ in the tuberculosis sanatorium just before I went on furlough. During my absence he left the hospital and is now able to do some work again. He lives in a small town quite some distance from here, where there is no church. I wrote asking if it were possible to hold a meeting in his home sometime. He replied by coming to see me instead. He said that he is trying to share his faith with the people of the village through natural means such as conversation. He does not yet feel inclined to have meetings in his home. We pray that he may be strengthened in his faith, that he may be a strong witness there and also that he may not be ashamed to use his home for a meeting place if the Lord should so

---

[7] After Auchs left Japan, our mission sent Mr. Murakami to the Presbyterian Seminary in Tokyo where he studied two years.

lead. His occupation is that of making stone lanterns and images such as are used in Buddhist temples or gardens. He wanted to carve an image of either Christ or Mary for the church as a token of appreciation but we told him that we felt such images would be a hindrance to some.

Tuesday I visited the Juvenile home for two hours. One hour was spent with about 15 of the girls and the last hour was spent talking with one of them privately. She is in the home for the third time. When she returns to her home she finds it impossible to get along with her parents, so she leaves home and eventually ends up living a life of sin and becoming the prey of worthless fellows. She says she is weak-willed and cannot live an upright life. We pray that she may truly repent now that she is aware of her sin and that she may be strengthened by the Spirit in the inner man to withstand the temptations of the devil.

November 28, 1958

It was really chilly until recently with a few snow flurries but not enough to even cover the ground. When the sun was shining it was nice and warm outside, almost too warm for an overcoat. Indoors, unless the room is on the south, it is quite cool. I kept the gas burner going in my living room most of the day, because it is on the north.

All of my fragile equipment arrived in good condition for which I was very thankful. The tape recorder and record player have been wonderful company for me. I have played the tapes over and over, so I could hear the voices of my family often. I played them for some of my Japanese friends who have come to my house. I don't have a radio any longer. When I was in Ise, I loaned it to a man in the hospital, one of our most devoted Christians. The family is very poor. I had given them a bit of money too, but the wife did not use it to pay back her debts as she promised. When her husband had his operation, she took the radio out of the room and pawned it. I don't know how much she got out of it, but being unable to pay back the loan, the radio was sold. I have not yet talked to her directly. I hardly know what to say when I meet her. She too is a professing Christian. I had complete confidence in this brother but the wife betrayed me.

December 1, 1958

We praise the Lord for helping us in the meetings we held in Ise in November for a week. We decided to not invite a special speaker but to use our own mission personnel. Mr. Murakami, our mission helper in Kyoto, Akasaka Sensei, our pastor in Ise and I each spoke twice during the meetings. We used two Moody Science films, one the first night and one the last night. These brought a full house. It doesn't take very many people to crowd out our little church, only about 75-80. The other nights the attendance was about 50. About 20 made decisions of some kind but only four seemed to be clear on salvation. A great number of young people came. It will be wonderful if we can hold on to them.

For a few months, I served in Ise along with the Akasakas. I did not have a car at the time, so I sometimes rode on the back of Mr. Akasaka's motorcycle, a rather strange sight, I am sure. During my time in Ise, Mr. Akasaka worked mainly with the adults and I worked with the youth and children. We had a very active group of young people that met in my house.

Under Mr. Akasaka's leadership, the church moved to a third location, using another rented building. It became apparent that we needed a permanent home for the church, so Mr. Akasaka drew up plans for the first church building to be located next door to a Shinto Shrine at the foot of a hill called Tokugawayama, not far from where the first mission house was located. The Ise church has now formally signed the papers for a loan of $2500 to build their church. The agreement was that they would raise 20% of the cost of the building and then they could borrow 80% from the mission to be repaid over a ten year period. Last Sunday the groundbreaking ceremony was held and the builders actually started working. They have to complete the building by the end of May, with the dedication planned for June 7th. A week of evangelistic services will follow. Much prayer is still needed to complete the work. It would cost just $3000 to build the church. The mission bought the land and the church people eventually will pay for the building.

March 10, 1959

Mr. Schilke arrived in Japan January 22 and departed on February 25th after five weeks. There were so many things to do while he was here, that we were working full steam. Mr. Schilke visited a number of mission headquarters here in Japan, getting as much information as possible about their policies and work, before coming to our area. He was particularly interested in Baptist work so, in addition to Southern and American Baptist, he visited Swedish and Conservative Baptist fields. I was privileged to take him up north to the Conservative Baptist area just north of Sendai. In winter, it is very cold there. Like everyone else, they only heated the room they were in. At night there was no heat whatsoever in the house. To keep warm at night, you took a hot bath and went into an icy cold bedroom, crawled into a bed consisting of two mats on the straw-matted floor, and covered up with as many heavy quilts as you could bear. Mr. Schilke slept in such a bedroom but in the morning when he came for breakfast, he said, "Why don't you missionaries heat your houses?" They explained, "It is too expensive." This experience gave him a taste of missionary life in Japan that he might never have understood otherwise.

Mr. Schilke reported that two single girls were being considered by the mission for appointment for missionary work in Japan in about one year: Miss Lucille Wipf is a student at NAB Seminary in Sioux Falls, South Dakota, and Joyce Batek is a nurse in St. Joseph, Michigan.

Mr. Schilke spent almost a week in Ise viewing our work. During the day we took him to see the nearby cities where we were planning to expand our work. He also went house and land hunting with us. This was all preparatory to our mission meetings. Finally, we ended up in Kyoto, where we had our annual field committee meeting. The first several days were devoted to ironing out the problems between missionaries. They were trying days but the Lord brought us through with greater appreciation of each other.

One of the big tasks accomplished was the organization of the Mission here on the field. Now we have a secretary-treasurer, appointed by the Home Office, and a five member Field Committee elected out here. This organization must still be approved by the Board of Missions, but Mr. Schilke felt it would be acceptable. I am vice-chairman and head of the Personnel and Education Committee. There are so few of us as yet that almost everyone has an office of some sort.

The placement of missionaries was also an important decision, of course. There was a great deal of discussion and planning but we finally concluded that the Kerns would stay in Kyoto until they go home on furlough after their first term. Then the Moores would take over the church in Kyoto. The Sukuts would stay in Ise and I would move to Tsu to begin a new work, probably with university students. I believe that student work is more geared to a single woman and trust that this is the place the Lord will have me serve for some time to come. I have in mind a kind of student center with possibly a little bookstore, somewhere not too far from the university. We have been to Tsu twice since this decision was made, looking for a house to rent, but have had no luck so far.

April 22, 1959

My realtor hunted for a house in Tsu for about a month. Finally he showed us a house that the owner wanted to sell. After talking with him, he said that we could rent it for a year. It was a real nice house for me in that it had just a bit of a Western flavor. It was located about a ten minute walk from the ocean in an area called Otobe Cho. We rented the house and spent a little time getting acquainted with the city and with our neighbors. The house is comparatively new, about six years old, I think. There are two straw-matted rooms upstairs, which Miss Yokota and I can use for bedrooms. Downstairs there is a large straw-matted room for my study, a fairly large living room, a tiny dining area, a tiny kitchen and bathroom. All downstairs rooms have flooring except for my study. The greatest flaw about the house is the Japanese toilet. It is something like the outhouse we had on our first farm, except that it is attached to the house as another room and the hole is in the floor instead of on a seat.

I don't mind the straw-matted floors in my study and bedrooms, because it makes the floors warmer in the cold winter. The disadvantage of them is that it takes more work to keep the mats clean and setting furniture on them damages them. Also it is a good hiding place for fleas. I had trouble the first two nights with fleas getting into my bed. It is amazing what distress one little flea can cause when it gets inside your pajamas. One was keeping me awake, so I began searching for it. I spotted it but that was all. He was too quick on the jump to catch.

My kitchen is typically Japanese. It has a sink and a couple of shelves. I have ordered some kitchen cabinets to be made, which I hope will arrive soon. They are removable so can be used in the next house as well, so I am sure they will not be a loss. They will cost about

$80.00. The mission plans to buy land and build a house for me here in Tsu, providing the work is promising.

So far I have not attempted to do any evangelism but there have been several people here asking me to teach them English. I hope to begin with an English Bible Class and trust that it will give me some contacts for actual evangelism. There are three Christian students from our church in Ise attending Mie University in Tsu. I am counting on them to help me in my work with students. One of the boys already brought one of his friends over and after helping me with my curtain rods and bookcases, we sat down for a cup of tea and cookies. The Lord led us naturally into a conversation with the friend, who seemed interested in religious things, but he does not yet recognize the existence of God. He seems like a fine young man and is open minded, so I earnestly pray that the Lord may be able to claim him for His own. I hope to begin a children's meeting in my home as soon as we are more settled.

I did not know how to get started with student evangelism. I prayed that God would open a door and show me how to proceed with my mission. It required a time of waiting but God did open a door in a marvelous way. When I worked in Ise we had an English Bible Class for high school students. In the class were two young men who planned to attend the Agricultural College at Mie University in Tsu. As a freshman, one of them went to the university officials to ask permission for me to hold an English Bible Class on the campus. The officials apparently thought it would benefit the students and staff to learn English conversation from a native speaker without charge, so they granted permission for me to have an English Bible Class in one of the classrooms. We gradually drew into the class, not only a large number of students, but also some of the staff members.

English Bible class on campus of Mie University Agricultural College

After just a few classes, some of the students showed real interest in the Bible, as well as in English. This led me to form a Japanese Bible Study Class at my home. We averaged about 4-5 regulars. Among them was Mr. Kazuo Nakamura, the first to become a believer in Christ. Others were Mr. Satoshi Yamamoto, Mr. Yukio Hanazono, Mr. Nakata, and Mr. Masakazu Hasegawa, all of whom eventually became Christians.

My house was becoming too small for all the activity that was going on, so I looked around for a meeting place in the neighborhood that I could rent. To my amazement I found an empty building just a few minutes from my house. We named the building "Tsu Christian Center." The Sunday worship hour and Wednesday night Bible Study and prayer meeting were open to anyone who wished to come, but those who attended were mostly students we had contacted at the Agricultural College.

Tsu Christian Center

I realized that I needed a college-educated co-worker if I were to communicate well with the university students. I was introduced to Miss Atsuko Naruse, who had just graduated from Doshisha University, a Mission School in Kyoto. She had been attending Bible Classes in Kyoto. I offered Miss Naruse the opportunity of working with me in reaching university students for Christ. She agreed to come for one year. She lived in the Tsu Christian Education Center. She loved children too, so she worked with both university students and the children.

I went to Ise to see the Crown Prince and his new bride, Michiko, the first commoner in the royal family. They came on their honeymoon to report their marriage to the imperial ancestors enshrined at the Ise Grand Shrine where the Sun Goddess is worshiped and from whom the emperor is said to have been descended. It is pitiful that ancestor worship is still considered sensible by intelligent, educated people. Belief in one God, Who is the omnipresent, omniscient Creator of the world has not yet been accepted by the majority in Japan.

122

Crown Prince and Princess

The royal couple made a stop at the Outer Shrine near the Ise Station and then proceeded by car to the Inner Shrine some distance away. A great crowd gathered in front of the station to see them. A high platform had been built for them to stand on to greet the people. I stood in the crowd for two hours, hoping to take a photo of them. When the crowd became dense, policemen with megaphones ordered the people to sit down to prevent people from pushing. Part of the crowd did not comply with the orders and began shoving. Soon there was a tumult as people began trampling on old people and children. When the wave of people began moving towards me, I tried to get out of the crowd but was hemmed in on all sides. About 30,000 people were jammed together, a seething mass of humanity without an inch between them. After some struggling, I finally found my way toward the edge of the crowd. I decided to preserve my life rather than see the prince and princess. I stood at the farthest edge of the crowd, content to get a distant view of the couple as they ascended the platform, made their bows and went their way to the special train waiting for them in the station.

Ise Grand Shrine of the Sun Goddess

World Vision is planning a big campaign in Osaka, much like those held by Billy Graham. The basis on which they get support from the churches is a promise that those churches that cooperate will be recommended to the converts, regardless of what kind of churches they are. I, myself, am a little skeptical about that policy, because some of the United Church of Christ churches, and others, are definitely not evangelical.

July 13, 1959

For about two months or more, I have been holding English Bible classes in my home. There were about 30 coming at first, so I divided them into four classes, with two for high school age and two for college age and up. I also have a class for Junior High students in my home on Sunday morning. I spend 30 minutes reading with them from their English textbooks and correcting their pronunciation. Then we have an hour of English Bible. About 20-25 are attending. Many primary school children come to the house to see me and keep asking for a class for them, but I haven't felt able to start it yet. However, I do want to try to have a week of Daily Vacation Bible School for them if possible.

After about a month of straight English, I felt that some students were interested, not only in English, but in the Bible itself, so I began a Japanese Bible Class on Sunday night. There have been 5-8 present at each meeting thus far. Little by little, the attitudes of some have been changing from sheer unbelief to skepticism to considering the possibility that the Bible might be true.

A medical school student told me he planned to be a doctor to help humanity. Recently, since studying the Bible and reading the life of Dr. Schweitzer, he feels there may be more of a need in society than just healing bodies. He is reading the Bible carefully and wants to go to a quiet place to think about it all summer. Another student strongly disagreed when I said there was a moral law in the hearts of all men, which indicated the existence of an absolute God. However, the next week he came to class saying he believed there was a moral law in the world and also an absolute God. Both of these students have applied for young people's camp this summer. We are having our first camp this summer, renting the Mennonite camp-grounds in the Osaka area. Young people from all three of our churches are being invited but, even so, we do not expect more than 15-20. Nevertheless, if there are seeking souls, the number will not be so important. Much prayer is needed for this first attempt at a camp in Japan, because none of us missionaries are really fluent in the language. We will use both English and Japanese.

Last week a high school aged girl, who lives two doors down from me, came to the door carrying a lacquered box which she offered to me. It turned out that the mother of the girl had died a year ago and they were celebrating the anniversary of her death, with probably a Buddhist mass at which various offerings of food are made to the dead. The cakes in the lacquered box were all part of the offering. It seems that it is a custom to share them with the neighbors. I didn't know whether to accept them or not. I hesitated asking whether they were an offering or not. The girl, herself, did not seem to know too much about it but wanted me to accept them, just because it was a custom. I accepted them, but when I took off the cover of the box and saw the paper inside on which the name of the deceased was written I felt I should not have accepted them. When a Buddhist dies, it is believed that he becomes a part of Buddha or godlike being called *hotoke*, so he is given a new Buddhist name. I felt that I must return the cakes so I did, giving them a New Testament, which I had underlined in important places. I do not know how they felt about it but I am praying that they will read the New Testament. I felt a little of what the Japanese people feel when they break with the traditional religions of Japan. It is not easy.

September 22, 1959

One of the boys from the medical school came to see me shortly after camp was over. He is a very earnest seeker but is full of doubts about the truth of the Bible and even about the existence of God. He said that sometimes he feels the desire to be saved so strongly that he feels like crying. However, these doubts prevent him from plunging in and simply believing. After talking with him for several hours, he came to the verge of asking God to forgive his sins. He said that he had begun to feel that there was a God and he also admitted that he was a sinner. As we bowed to pray, he said he was afraid, so he stopped short of becoming a Christian. I felt it would be best not to push him into a decision for which he might not be thoroughly prepared.

Our Sunday schedule is very full. So far my contacts are primarily students, but I definitely feel the necessity of getting into the homes in the community in order that the work may have the permanence that comes from family-attached Christians. I need prayer regarding the direction that my work should take. If I concentrate on students, it cannot become a community church very well. If I do otherwise, I will be following the pattern of the church in Ise, which I do not want to do.

Ise Wan Typhoon

October 2, 1959

Mie Ken was one of the three areas hit hard by the dreadful typhoon called Ise Wan (Bay) Typhoon. All of our missionaries and church people are safe. The big city of Nagoya and the surrounding cities and villages north of us were hit the hardest.

The wind became fierce about 7:00 p.m. My helper, Miss Yokota, said that the sea walls could break and the ocean could flood our area. I never thought it could be that bad, but I decided to move as many of my things upstairs as possible. While we were doing this the windows in the study blew out and glass was flying all over. We closed the French doors to the study, pushed my small sofa in front of them and plunked ourselves down on the sofa as we pushed against the doors to prevent the wind from going through the house. We stayed there several hours and prayed without ceasing. I was tremendously impressed with Miss Yokota's good sense and coolness, as well as her faith and sincere desire to be a witness in her attitude. Instead of losing her head, she sang hymns and thereby, both of us were calmed and encouraged. I felt a little ashamed at my own weak faith, for I sincerely questioned whether we would get through the storm with our lives. We watched anxiously as the water rose in the entrance which was six inches lower than the living room floor.

When it seemed that we could hold out no longer, the wind suddenly shifted from the east to the south and by that we were saved, for there was a large house on the south of us which broke the force of the wind. The water in the entrance rose to floor level and stopped, sparing us flooding on the floor. However, we suffered damage from the rain in that the rain came in through the broken windows and about 90 tiles blew off the roof, causing a great deal of leakage upstairs where we had carried some of our things. Our rugs and straw mats on the floor were all wet. It took four days to dry them out. One of the great blessings to me through this experience was the sympathy extended by those who knew us. About 12 different people came to inquire how things were, primarily students from the Bible Classes. For the first time, I realized how much a little visit and sympathy means in a time of trouble and resolved to do more of it myself.

The day after the storm, two of the students came for the morning worship service, since it was Sunday, but because the house was all topsy-turvy, we did not have a regular meeting. We had dinner together and then we had a testimony meeting. Each one told how the Lord had spoken and helped him through the storm. It was a blessed time. We immediately had to get the roof and windows repaired, at least temporarily.

After the Ise Wan typhoon, our little church group took some care packages to people who lived near the ocean and suffered from flooding. There I met a young woman who had been saved in a Pentecostal church. She began to attend our church but is now in the hospital with a serious heart ailment. She almost died. Later, her brother began to attend also.

I went to see three families with whom we had contact within the city and found that their homes had been flooded almost up to the waist. They lived near the ocean. Can you imagine the fear in their hearts as the water in their homes kept getting deeper and deeper? In this section of the city, the fishing boats that were anchored at the piers, rose with the rise of the water and eventually came crashing into the houses, breaking them to pieces. In Ise, the Mission house was badly damaged too. The interior will have to be re-plastered and practically a whole new roof put on. The garage danced over the car and after a few twists in the wind, fell in a shambles. The homes of several of the church members were practically demolished. Two of them were just little shacks to start with. They were in a slum area where poor widows lived with their children. Yesterday the missionaries met to decide what we could do to help these people. The church was also quite badly damaged. We decided to request $500 emergency relief from the Mission and hoped that it would be given. In the area around Nagoya where the sea walls broke there are still about 1000 or more people stranded on the roof tops. Four thousand people died.

December 1, 1959

I went to Kyoto where the missionary family had a day of fellowship together. We had a typical American Thanksgiving dinner which included turkey and stuffing, cranberry sauce and pumpkin (squash) pie. In the afternoon we took a ride out to one of the beauty spots to see the autumn colors. The tiny-leafed maples in Japan turn a brilliant red in the fall and are just gorgeous. I spent the night in Kyoto and in the morning, returned to Ise with Mrs. Kern and three of the Christian women for a Ladies' Meeting in Ise. It was the first time that the women of both churches got together. The Kyoto women were few in comparison to the fifteen Ise women, but they gave stirring testimonies and challenging remarks concerning rearing children in a Christian home. It was what the Ise women needed, for many of their children do not so much as attend Sunday School.

December 16, 1959

It seems that I have lost a younger brother in Christ, although it may be unbelief to say so. About two months ago, the young man who had been such a help to us here in Tsu in getting permission for me to have an English Bible Class on campus, became irregular in attending the meetings. He is the student from our church in Ise who is now living in Tsu and attending the Agricultural College. At first I thought that he was busy, because he got a part-time job. The job, incidentally, was timekeeper at the nearby boat races, sponsored by the government, but they are the usual type where spectators bet on the winner. I asked him to drop in for a little talk and then I learned that he had decided not to come anymore.

He told me that he had failed in two of the tests he had taken to get a job after graduation. When he went home, his father was very disturbed by that and scolded him severely. He said that he had neglected his studies because he had become a Christian and spent too much time on such things. He began to believe that what his father said was true. His faith, his father said, was merely a sentimental thing, and prayer and the guidance of the Holy Spirit were not real or effective. He said that one must trust in his own strength if he would succeed. Just before Christmas, instead of being joyful, I feel a deep sense of loneliness which I find very difficult to shake. I pray that the Lord may help him to see the reality of the spiritual world and that he may again worship the Lord with us.

I am getting a most unusual Christmas present this year. In fact, it is to arrive this afternoon. A CAR! The Benton Harbor church gave the final amount needed and we received the OK from Mr. Schilke to buy it. It is a Japanese made car, a little station wagon. The bad thing is that I will have to park it out on the street, because the little road leading to my house is too narrow. It is only a foot path. I hope that I may soon have a permanent house to live in instead of a rented one, so that I can do with it as I like.

We are grateful to the Lord for opening the door to have an English Bible Class at the Agricultural College. We have had it about a month now. The attendance has varied considerably from 35 to 10, with a few teachers also attending. The agricultural students do not understand English too well, so it is sometimes questionable how much they get out of it. We are very busy right now, preparing for Christmas.

January 5, 1960

Our Christmas program was nothing to boast about, at least from the way I looked at it. Through a primary school teacher who came to my English Bible Class, we got permission to use the school building. About 100 children attended and a few parents and grandparents. The children gave a little play which told the true meaning of Christmas. Then we showed them slides which again retold the Christmas story, and I gave a little talk at the end. Following this, the adults gathered in one of the school-rooms at 5:30 p.m. for a supper together. We ordered a prepared rice dish from a nearby restaurant, which was delivered to us at the school. We each paid 100 yen (equivalent to about 23 cents). For this we each got a bowl of rice covered with a broth with pieces of chicken, egg and green onions (*oyako domburi*). The bowls were covered so the food was still hot when we ate it. We also received a tangerine, a few cookies and candies, all for 23 cents! The adult program consisted of Christmas carols, Scripture and slides, woven together to present the Christmas message. We also listened to portions of *The Messiah* on tape. About 52 were present, with about 30 being adults.

First Christmas program at Tsu Christian Center – December 1959

March 20, 1960

In the last several weeks, we have had the joy of hearing from the lips of three of the students from the Agricultural College that they believe in Christ as their Savior. All three have been attending the meetings here in my home, and have come regularly even during exam time. One of them will be graduating soon, but we are happy to know that he found Christ before leaving Tsu. Realizing that my Japanese language ability was not adequate to teach these young men in depth, I invited them to attend an Inter Varsity Christian Conference (*Kirisuto Gakusei Kai* - KGK) in Kyoto, where they could hear one or more outstanding Japanese preachers and meet many other university students who were interested in Christianity. Mr. Kazuo Nakamura was deeply impressed by the testimonies of Christian students who had formed student-led KGK groups on their campuses. He returned to Tsu with a desire of forming such a group at Mie University. Mr. Nakamura was the self-appointed leader of the group.

Next Sunday we are having a baptismal service in the Ise Church for Mr. Nakamura, who was saved last year. He is graduating also and wanted to be baptized before he left Tsu. We pray that these seniors may go on with the Lord in their new place of service and that the little group of believers and seekers left behind in Tsu may be used to win many others to Christ.

April 26, 1960

We had a good Inter-Varsity Conference the end of March. Eight young people from Tsu attended. Three of them made decisions for Christ and the others, I am sure, were helped. Three of the Christian students graduated from University and now are in different prefectures working. Two very new Christians are assuming leadership of the Bible Study Group at the Agricultural College. I attend and try to help them a little, so they will not give wrong interpretations to the Scriptures. About five students meet weekly for this Bible Study. The attendance at my house has increased recently. Last Sunday we had six in the morning and eight at night. Of these, only four are professing Christians. I pray that we may lead them to a clear faith in Christ.

**7 students and a staff member from Mie University,
with KGK Director, Mr. Ariga, and me
at an Intervarsity Christian Fellowship Conference**

June 30, 1960

Japan has again been in the limelight, not for a typhoon, but for a political upheaval. This has not had any direct effects on us as missionaries but indirectly we, as Americans, have been affected. It is impossible to go into all the phases of the political situation here and why the visit of President Eisenhower was called off. I imagine that the U.S. newspapers did not give an altogether true picture of the situation, for there was a lot more involved than appeared on the surface. Most American reporters seemed to have decided that it was Communist inspired and represented only a minority of the people. The violent aspects of the opposition to the Security Treaty between the U.S. and Japan were undoubtedly the work of Communists and related left wing Socialists. However, there is a strong feeling among the people as a whole, that there should be no kind of military alliance with any country, because the post-war constitution forbids war as the solution to any problem. They, therefore, want Japan to be a neutral country like Switzerland and lead the way to peace by refusing to have an army, as their present constitution requires. In addition to this, many people felt that the Prime Minister and the Liberal Party, to which he belongs, was not taking into consideration the opinions of the people, but were simply acting independently. Therefore, many people

132

wanted the Prime Minister to resign. The Japanese Constitution is different from ours in that it states that, if it becomes apparent that the government is not expressing the desires of the people, the emperor may dissolve the Diet (Parliament) and call for new elections. The demonstrations occurring all over Japan, and especially on university campuses, were an attempt to prove to the government that the people as a whole were opposed to the Security Treaty and to the methods being used by the Liberal Party. In every university in the country, the student organizations voted to strike. They had almost a week of demonstrations in place of classes. They paraded through the streets carrying placards calling for the banning of the Security Treaty with the U.S. and the resignation of Prime Minister Kishi's government.

Here in Tsu, also, the three universities had strikes and demonstrations. Even the Christians engaged in them whether fully in agreement with the crowd or not, I am not sure. When I talked with some of them, they said that since a majority of the students had voted for the demonstrations, it was expected that all would cooperate in them. To them, this seemed true democracy, and not to cooperate with the group seemed to them to be an undemocratic spirit. We, in America, cannot understand why students in schools must take sides in political issues as a student body. Individually, yes, they can, but not as a group. We would not want everyone to have to agree to a given political view. But here, it seems that in the Labor unions and in the student organizations, the idea exists that, even on political issues, one must fall in line with the opinion of the majority and engage in strikes and demonstrations, even if he does not personally agree. I believe that this is the result of Socialism in Japan. Socialism is generally accepted as a good thing here, although it still does not have a majority in government. It has only 1/3 of the seats. Nevertheless, among educators in particular, and labor unions in most cases, Socialism or even Communism is very strong. Because the universities are the places where tomorrow's leaders are being trained, this trend is quite evident for future Japan.

We moved into our new church meeting place, which we have called the Tsu Christian Center. It is conveniently located in front of a small tram car stop and also a bus stop. Apart from a lot of noise resulting from these stops, the place is well located. We had three days of evangelistic meetings, with almost 40 in attendance each night. Quite a few people raised their hands for salvation, but not all were genuinely saved, I am afraid. The meetings did make the place known in the neighborhood and a few new people have been coming quite regularly as a result.

I have been asked to teach part-time at the Mennonite Bible School in Osaka. Our Mission has been trying to cooperate with them and this may be the first step toward that. Nothing has, as yet, been decided definitely, but if I do go, it will begin in October. I'll have to work hard at my Japanese before then.

August 13, 1960

Beginning in November, I shall be teaching part-time at the Mennonite Bible School in Ikeda City, a suburb of Osaka. I will be teaching Inductive Bible Study and also Teaching Methods. This is a new experience for me. My Japanese is not good enough to do a good job. This was in addition to my duties in Tsu, so I'll have my hands full. I must commute to Osaka by train which takes about two and a half hours one way.

Our summer program has been a rather busy one. We finished four days of young people's camp before I left on vacation. Six out of the thirty-five present raised their hands indicating their desire to become Christians. What thrilled me most of all was the fact that one of the young men from Tsu, Mr. Satoshi Yamamoto, asked one of the missionaries how he could know God's plan for his life. He is at the Agricultural College but he seems inclined toward the Christian ministry. He voluntarily began a Bible Class at a Juvenile Home near his college. He has also been printing tracts and gospel booklets in Braille for the blind. He helped with our DVBS and Junior Camp. We would certainly rejoice, if the Lord should so lead, if he would give himself for the Lord's service.

September 19, 1960

Our two new missionaries, Joyce Batek and Lucille Wipf, arrived September 6th. Mr. Fred Moore and I met them at the ship. They have a lovely apartment waiting for them in a new home built by the mother of a southern Baptist missionary doctor, Dr. Clark. I will not see much of them as long as they are in language school in Kyoto, but it is still nice to know they are there.

We had a busy Sunday but it was a good one. I have just begun a baptismal candidates' class. Four boys from the agricultural college have requested baptism. Two have been actively engaged in Bible classes at the juvenile home near the college. The children are from about 10 to 13 years old. One of the University students has also been going to the blind school, reading to the high school pupils and printing some tracts and gospel booklets in Braille. Mr. Yamamoto is so busy on Sunday that he scarcely has time to rest at all. He has undertaken these activities on his own volition, so this makes us doubly happy. Last night I felt led to caution him about undertaking too much, lest his health suffer and his studies be neglected. It is not often that one has to be anxious in this direction. His enthusiasm and zeal often make me wonder if I am putting forth as much effort as he.

One of the other boys is still not very clear regarding his beliefs and only now have we become aware of it. He has attended church almost every Sunday morning, but God still has not been close and real to him. In fact he has only recently begun to think of God as a personal being whom we know through Christ. The word God in Japanese has so many different connotations in this land that it is no wonder that the Christian concept of God is not immediately grasped. We are trying to help him understand God more clearly and grow stronger in his faith.

Another student is facing serious doubts in regard to Buddhist customs. He is an only child. His father died during the war. According to Buddhist customs, memorial services are held on the anniversary of the death. At these memorial services, prayers and offerings are made to the dead. Of course, a Christian should have no part in them. It places the son in a very difficult position since he is the only child. Not to participate would make him appear very disrespectful of his father. He is studying economics at the University and is consequently deeply involved in socialistic ideas. He is trying to discover how Christianity and socialism fit together, or if they can at all. He is having many such problems all at once and his faith seems to be very weak just now. Another boy who seemed genuinely interested in Christianity and who attended an Inter Varsity Conference in August, only recently declared his complete disregard for the Bible by writing across the front of it "Foolishness!" The enemy is hard at work.

September 28, 1960

The Mennonite Brethren Bible School where I have been teaching is now having term-end exams. Tomorrow is the last day of the school term. The students have a whole month off before the new term begins. It will not be a vacation for me, however, because I have a lot of work to do. I will be teaching four courses again next term. Two of them are new to me, so I must prepare for them in advance, during the month of October. I will be teaching Christian Education in the Local Church, Christian Education of Children, Prayer and English. There will be evangelistic meetings and other special meetings in October, too, so the time will slip by before I know it.

October 17, 1960

I've been feeling a little bit "down in the dumps" the last few weeks, for some reason, and in special need of prayer for myself and also for our work. One cannot do his best work feeling discouraged and it shows up in many unpleasant ways. Until last summer I was quite thrilled about the work here in Tsu but, since then, there have been innumerable problems and disappointments. Some of the students who professed faith in Christ are not growing as we would like to see them grow. Some seem to be afraid of going too deep into this religion and will go only so far. Others have indicated that their understanding of Christianity is still either very, very shallow, or else it is a different kind of belief. Still others, upon finding that their Christian faith conflicts with the beliefs of their families and relatives, feel it is too difficult to walk alone. One of our students who has graduated wrote a letter indicating that he has practically given up his faith, believing it to have been generated by emotional forces rather than his intellect. It seems that the group of regular attendees at our meetings has boiled down to about four with some of the others coming once a week or even less often.

In spite of these discouragements there are things for which we may rejoice. We are looking forward to the baptism of three of the boys from the Agricultural College. These three have been very faithful and have been the core of the group. Two of them have been going to the juvenile home on Sunday afternoon, on their own volition to teach the Bible to the children there. One, also, goes to the Blind School, where he reads Christian books to the students and also prints Christian books in Braille.

136

There are two people at the tuberculosis sanatorium in Tsu who say that they believe in Jesus. One is a crippled girl of high school age and one is a man a little older than I. There are several who have attended the Bible Class there, who are very ill. One has been told that she will not recover. She has a light case of tuberculosis but also a nervous condition which will eventually cause total paralysis of her body. We are praying that the Lord's will may be done regarding her physical body but most of all, that she may understand and accept God's way of salvation.

Tsu is gaily decorated for its four day Fall Festival. There is a big circus at one of the temples and parades and dances going on along the streets. Miss Yokota and I went out to distribute tracts to some of the crowd. We passed out about 300 in less than an hour. Many of the people, seeing a foreign woman with a handful of literature, avoid you but others even came up to ask for the tracts, so perhaps some of the seed will fall on good ground.

November 15, 1960

The big event of recent days was our annual NAB Missionary Conference. It lasted five days and included business, devotions led by all the missionaries, an outside speaker, Glen Johnson, the Presbyterian missionary from Ise, and some times of recreation. We all felt that it was a most worthwhile conference. The spirit of unity that prevailed was one of the big blessings. We decided on many things, including the Mission's decision that I would be going home to the U.S. next spring. I am thinking of going home by way of Europe, so I may not arrive at home until summer.

January 2, 1961

My last letter was rather pessimistic, but since then there have been some encouragements, although I am still concerned about some who have dropped away. One of the students who graduated from the agricultural college had practically given up his faith. He came to Tsu a few days before Christmas and spent most of his time with the church young people. He also attended all of the meetings held during that time. I had a little visit with him and sensed that he was still seeking God and wanted to grow in his spiritual life. A short time after Christmas, I received a wonderful postcard from him. It said, "The Christmas of this year was one of the best I've ever had. For I found a precious teaching in it. First I found that Christians are the members of the family of God, however far they are separated. Second, God will come to us when we go near him. Third, I found this surprising growth of the Tsu Christian Center and the Bible class of the agricultural college. By these things I could once more realize that he is working in his step. And, last I could find the chance to go back to him again." This, to me, was one of my best Christmas presents.

One of the senior boys at the agricultural college, Mr. Yukio Hanazono, has decided to go to Bible school after graduation in the spring. I have encouraged him to attend the Mennonite Brethren Bible School, where I am teaching and so far, at least, he seems content to go there. We rejoice that the Lord has led him and pray that nothing may stand in his way. Toshiko Yokota, who has been my helper in Tsu for over two years, has decided to go to Bible school. She, too, will be going to the Mennonite Brethren Bible School.

With my moving have come other moves. Miss Naruse who has been my coworker in Tsu since last April, has decided to leave our mission and go to work in the Christian Literature Crusade bookstore in Kyoto. She just told me this a few minutes ago and we both had a good cry together about it. The Christian Literature Crusade is a faith work and she feels that she would like to learn to trust the Lord more under that type of mission.

Early in December, we held three days of special evangelistic meetings. The weather was already cold, so the number attending was rather small. However there were some who made decisions. The strange thing about it is that some who made decisions have not come to church since then. I find it hard to understand why a person would not come back if he were moved enough to raise his hand and stay behind for further instruction. Some of those who made decisions were first comers. I often have my doubts about such decisions, because they do not understand well enough for genuine conversions in most instances. The follow-up in some cases is rather difficult, because they were mostly young men and it does not look good to call on them where they live.

Our Christmas planning was done late and in a hurry but, in spite of the rush and scurry, I believe the Lord blessed and used it for His glory. The high school and college students presented a play. We had to rent a public auditorium because our church building is not large enough for such events. We had supper brought in from the restaurant for about 75 people and then had the program. There were about 100 present for the program. The mother of one of the Sunday school children said that she had been moved by the play. The younger brother of one of the college boys who acted in the play asked if he could come to church from now on. It was his first time at a Christian meeting, but he liked the atmosphere. He lives in the country. It takes about 40 minutes by bus to get here but he wants to come. These were two of the little encouragements we've received from our program. The young people sang Christmas carols for the old peoples' home and presented a little gift to each resident. They also presented a program at the juvenile home for ages 10 to 15 and gave them each a little gift. We went out to the tuberculosis sanatorium and showed Christmas slides there also. It was a very busy time but we prayed that it would prove to be a blessing to someone.

January 17, 1961

Our mission began to sponsor a radio broadcast which allowed us to insert our church announcements on the radio once each month. Bible correspondence courses and booklets have been sent to inquirers. Although the letters of inquiry have not been many, some have indicated a desperate search for spiritual help. For these, especially, we feel that the radio broadcasts and follow-up have been very worthwhile.

I was asked by a doctor to teach an English Class for Junior nurses at the tuberculosis sanitarium in Tsu in last April. I am allowed to teach them hymns and Bible stories. I go only twice a month. Because they have not had high school, their understanding of English is very poor. I do not know if they are getting much spiritual help or not, but at least the spirit of Christianity is being expressed and it does give me an entrance into the hospital to speak to the patients. We started a Bible Class for patients there every week. The number attending is only four or five each time, but two of the patients have said they believe in Christ.

When God is at work, the devil is not far away. Our chief concerns right now are for some who have declared their faith in Christ but seem content to give only a wee part of their hearts to Him, lest they be bound or are obligated to give up some of their present activities. We are seeking to guide them into surrender of themselves entirely to Christ as His obedient servants. The other concern I have is that we are not reaching into the community of adults as we ought. Older people do not feel at home in a group with so many young people. We are trying to reach out to the parents of our Sunday School children also.

7

OSAKA BIBLICAL SEMINARY

May 1960

It has long been our desire as a mission that our Bible school and Seminary students could study in a school in our area which would be of like faith. This desire is beginning to see fulfillment. Two of the young people from Tsu dedicated their lives to the Lord's service. Since our mission had already decided to send our students to the Mennonite Brethren Bible School, we felt it could be a further tie between our churches and the school if one of our members was represented on the faculty. The Mennonite Brethren were very gracious in allowing us to participate in their school and at the same time seemed grateful for the contribution which our mission would make to the school. The Baptist General Conference has also loaned a missionary to teach at the school, although they do not as yet have any students in it. Thus the three groups are working together, praying that the Lord may be pleased to bless and use this school in the training of our future church leaders. It is still small and lacking in many ways, but if we can continue to cooperate under God's blessing, there is real hope of building a good school.

April 23, 1961

I have been in my new home in Toyonaka exactly two weeks now, but things are still not in place because I had to have a carpenter come in and build some shelves, etc. which always takes time. I decided to ask Miss Yokota, my former helper in Tsu, who was then a student at the Bible School, to live with me so I would not be alone at night. She is allowed to do two hours of part-time work a day, so she is helping me in the house a little.

I began teaching part-time at the Mennonite Brethren Bible School in November 1960, when I was still in Tsu. At that time I traveled to Osaka three hours on the train, one day a week and taught two subjects.

The Bible School schedule has been arranged so that all of the classes are from Tuesday to Friday, leaving weekends open for church work. Our missionaries felt that it would be best for me not to undertake any Sunday assignments, at least from the beginning, until I

141

get more accustomed to teaching. I am grateful that they felt that way, because I feel I need the weekends to catch up and prepare for the following week of classes. I am teaching four subjects: Inductive Bible Study, Christian Education of Children, Devotional Life and English. English is one hour a day, but the others are two hours a week. I am in charge of the afternoon study hall for two hours.

The NAB Mission Society was $40,000 short of last year's budget. We asked for a new couple for Japan. There was a couple at the NAB Seminary who could come this year, providing the funds were available. In Japan we set up a budget for this year which was $2000 over last year. The cost of living rose 22% during the past two years. We cannot hope to operate on the same budget every year, especially if we wish to expand. The implication was that if we expect our budget to be provided, then we need not expect the appointment of a new couple. Our proposed budget was about $7000, which isn't very much for a group our size in a country like Japan. We are all quite discouraged about this and hope the Board of Missions will have the faith to appoint the new couple and also that our churches will get behind the work, so that we can go forward here.

Mr. Murakami, our seminary student in Tokyo, has been invited by our NAB Seminary in Sioux Falls, SD to study there as an exchange student. He quit the Presbyterian Seminary in Tokyo and is now planning to study English in preparation for going to the States, perhaps this fall. If he goes, it will be for three years. He became engaged while at the seminary in Tokyo to another seminary graduate. In view of his probable study abroad for three years, he felt he should marry before he went, so they were married on Easter Sunday. His wife, Nobuko, has had some experience working in the seminary and also in evangelism. Since I felt the need of a Japanese person to help me get my lessons into Japanese, we decided to ask the Murakamis to live near the Bible School and have Mrs. Murakami help me.

July 9, 1961

I had a little fainting spell in church last Sunday. I'm not sure what caused it, although I think it was connected with my stomach, which had been upset for several days. Someone suggested that the water may have been contaminated after the rains. They had announced that the tap water should not be drunk, but I did not hear the warning. I am a little anemic, too, which didn't help, nor did the heat.

As soon as school is out, I am planning on going to Tokyo for the Asian Baptist Youth Conference (a Baptist World Alliance event). Dr. Schilke recommended that as many of us as possible attend. From there, I plan to go directly to cool Karuizawa for a month, partly for study and partly for vacation. Mr. and Mrs. Murakami are coming to stay in my house while I am away, for which I am grateful because I was worried about leaving it unoccupied for that long. Mr. Murakami has finally been given definite word from the NAB Seminary that he may come for the new school year in the fall. He will study a year at Sioux Falls College and three years at the Seminary. His wife will be alone. I admire them both for being willing to make this great sacrifice for the sake of his future service. Hisashi Murakami is a splendid young man and I am sure he will be an inspiration to many of our American young people.

The little band of believers in Tsu has gone through a tremendous time of testing. One of the students, a baptized believer, was found dead in his boarding house. Investigation revealed that he had taken sleeping pills, although no one can be certain if it was an overdose or intentional death. He left no message behind, although his diary indicated that he was going through some great struggles, the content of which was not clearly revealed. He had been in prayer meeting two days before he died. On his desk were his Bible, Scripture memory cards and his Sunday School teacher's manual, indicating that they were the last things which he had used. A letter, sealed and stamped, indicating that it would be posted, was on his desk. It was a nice letter to his aunt, urging her to subscribe to a Christian magazine. This aunt was somewhat interested in Christianity and he seemed to open his heart to her. His mother had no use for Christianity, whatsoever. His father had died in the war and he had no brothers or sisters, so you can imagine the shock to his mother when she learned of his death. He had told his aunt that he wanted to go to Bible School, although his mother would hear nothing of it. We did not know of his desire before he died, so his death remains a mystery. We asked the mother if we could have a Christian funeral for him but she refused. It was a Buddhist funeral. Miss Yamamoto and I attended the funeral but had no part in it.

September 28, 1961

In our class in Mark, we especially studied the training of the twelve disciples. I have been greatly impressed with the Master's skillful handling of men. Parents know how difficult it is to build character in their children. Training spiritual leaders goes one step beyond building character. The attitude and example of the teacher is the greatest influence in the life of the students and it is that which makes me tremble.

The mission has definitely decided on my going home next spring. I am thinking of going home by way of Europe, so I would not get home until summer. I am thinking of participating in a trip to the Holy Land, which is being sponsored by Wheaton College. Some people may misinterpret this as being extravagance, but I feel it will be a valuable experience for my teaching at the Bible School.

Tonight some people came to see my house, with the thought of buying it. The Mennonites want to sell it, so I may be moving again. Pilgrim life makes me look forward to the city whose builder is God.

October 23, 1961

I've been traveling about from one meeting to another during the past month. The second week in October, four of us NAB missionaries and three of our national workers went to Tokyo for a meeting of Bible-believing Baptists. The two main Baptist groups in Japan are the Northern and Southern Baptists. We fellowshipped a bit with them at the second Asian Baptist Youth Conference in July. However, we don't exactly fit in with them. The little Baptist groups that don't go along with them have gotten together for the second time to seek some basis for fellowship and cooperation if possible. Some of the groups represented are: Conservative Baptists, Baptist General Conference (Swedish Baptists), Bible Baptists, Association of Baptists for World-Wide Evangelism, Baptist Mid-Missions, Canadian Regular Baptists, and Independent Baptists. We decided to print a little Baptist church directory, so that if some of our believers moved to another place they could be channeled into one of these churches. We also discussed forming a marriage bureau to help young people find Christian mates of like faith.

Last Friday I went to Kyoto for a women's meeting. There were only five present but two of them were unbelievers. I trust that something which was said will cause them to seek the Lord more

144

earnestly. One of them is the wife of a famous professor of education at Kyoto University. She lives next door to Mrs. Uchida. Recently she has been suffering from a nervous condition and has been asking Mrs. Uchida about her faith. I was invited by Mrs. Uchida to visit this lady in her home once before. She seems to be open to Christianity, but of course there are many things in the way of a person of this social position.

I will be teaching four subjects at Bible School this fall. Three of them are new for me. One of the Mennonite Brethren missionaries was taken out of the Bible School and put into evangelistic work. That means that his courses had to be divided up among the other teachers. I received Isaiah to teach inductively. What a job! The prophets have always been my weak spot but I ought to learn something, even if the students don't.

November 21, 1961

On November 21 I received an international telegram. My heart went pitipat, wondering who had died. When I opened it I discovered to my great relief and sheer joy that it was a congratulatory message from the Benton Harbor church on the 10th anniversary of my arrival in Japan. I had forgotten the day myself. When I thought that the exact date was remembered by someone else and special prayer was offered on my behalf, I really was overcome. I don't know when I have been so completely surprised and overjoyed.

I spent Thanksgiving at the Sukuts in Kyoto, along with Joyce Batek and Lucille Wipf. We had chicken instead of turkey and sweet potato pie instead of pumpkin pie. We've pretty well forgotten what real pumpkin tastes like. We had cranberry Jell-O salad too. It was nice to be together, but I must confess that even a group that size got to be pretty noisy and I went home with a headache. Maybe living alone has spoiled me, because I am getting rather sensitive to a lot of noise and bustle.

We had a rather exciting meeting of the three education committees of the Mennonites, Baptist General Conference and our mission recently. The topic for discussion was the purchase of land for a joint Bible School. A large plot of land in the neighborhood was available at a fairly reasonable price and it was felt that the deal would have to be made at once before someone else came in and began to dicker on the price, which would automatically give the owners a chance to raise the price. The other two groups have either land or houses which they could sell to get part or all of the money needed for their share, but we had nothing at all to work with. We wondered if we dared even make an offer without first consulting headquarters.

After earnest prayer we felt led to take a step of faith, asking our mission to contribute a certain sum. Only by committing our mission in this way were we able to make the purchase of land. The Mennonite group borrowed money from the bank and the contract was signed. We have not yet heard Dr. Schilke's reaction to this, so we did not want the news to get out to our churches. Ordinarily, such a procedure would be denounced at once, but we prayed that the Missions Board would understand and that our churches would rally to this emergency

December 4, 1961

One of our young Japanese pastors, Mr. Nishizawa, who pastors the Kyoto church, is getting married next Friday. It is the first wedding to take place in the Kyoto church and for many of the Christians, is the first Christian wedding they will witness. They are all excited. Whenever weddings take place of course the Japanese start talking about the single missionaries and try to help them out too. Mrs. Uchida and I had a little visit recently. She suggested that when I go home on furlough, instead of traveling about so much, I settle down in one place to give myself a chance to get acquainted with someone and

146

come back married. I thanked her for her interest and concern but didn't feel that I could make that the main purpose of my furlough. I have always felt that if I seek to be in the place the Lord wants me, that is the safest place, and if marriage is in His plan for me, He will arrange for that. Beyond that, I cannot go.

December, 1961

This past Christmas was an unusual one for me in that I had very little responsibility except to help our Bible School students plan their Christmas banquet and program. Thus I was free to receive more blessing this year than at other times. However, I believe that Jesus' words, "It is more blessed to give than to receive" hold true, even in the matter of giving oneself in service at a time like Christmas. I feel that I missed something by being mainly on the receiving line.

Looking back over the past year, I marvel again at the Lord's leading and enabling. Since I have been teaching full-time at the Bible School, I have taught four or five courses each term, some of which have changed from term to term, which has meant a great deal of preparation for an inexperienced teacher, not to mention the difficulty of doing it in Japanese. However, after eight months of full-time teaching, I feel a bit more confident than before. I still feel that I ought to go back to language school some day.

January 21, 1962

We are pleased to see a growing cooperation between the Mennonite Brethren, Baptist General Conference and our North American Baptist Conference in our Bible School program. We are working towards a permanent basis for equal representation and responsibility by these three groups and also toward the building of a Bible School campus. We are currently meeting in a Mennonite Brethren Church in Ishibashi, Ikeda City. but it will be demolished within a year when a new road comes through. We are praying that a new home for the school may be provided by then. Although the Baptist General Conference still does not have any students at the Bible School, all three groups are contributing teachers. Harry Friesen of the Mennonite Brethren group is serving as president.

Second Furlough

May, 1963

On March 19, 1962 a little group of students and teachers from the Osaka Biblical Seminary, where I had been teaching for the past year, gathered at the Osaka airport to bid me farewell. My year at the Seminary had been a difficult but a most enjoyable one. My journey home enabled me to see something of the mission fields of Asia and Europe. I made stops in Hong Kong, India, The Holy Land, Greece, Italy, Switzerland, Germany and England. Becoming aware of the needs and problems of these other countries helped me to take heart with regard to our own work in Japan. It is easy to think that the place to which the Lord has called you is the hardest place and that your work is making the least progress.

I arrived in the U. S. on July 10 and by August 10 was engaged in summer camp work and deputation in our churches. On this tour I was privileged to visit one of our home mission fields in Canada, namely our native American Indian work. I was impressed with the devotion and patience of our missionaries and teachers there, living so close to their own culture yet so isolated from it as they seek to identify themselves with the people with whom they work. It was a joy for me to visit the Christian Training Institute in Edmonton for the first time, and to see the dedicated faculty working hard with very limited resources to raise the standards so that it may become an accredited school able to give the best training to our young people.

My deputation took me mainly to our churches in the Midwestern part of the U.S. and Canada. Many of these were first time visits. It was a joy to meet former acquaintances from time to time also. It was an encouragement to hear these words, "We have prayed for you for many years. It is good to meet you now in person." I remember especially the prayer of an elderly woman at a women's missionary meeting in one church. As she mentioned the missionaries by name and brought their specific needs to the throne of grace, I could not help but think to myself, "This woman has been keeping up with the work our missionaries are doing and is praying daily for them in a specific way or she would not pray like that." Unfortunately this attitude was not evidenced everywhere.

September 22, 1963

I am now living in an apartment over the garage of a Mennonite Brethren missionary family, the Friesens. Harry Friesen is the president of the Bible School. I am doing my own housework now. The apartment is small and can be cleaned in about an hour. I prefer to do my own work as much as possible because it gives me an opportunity to relax my mind by forcing me to engage in manual labor. Also I think it is better if all one's private affairs are not known. I am now enjoying my gas stove. It is the first time I have had a decent oven. The one I used on my kerosene stove was hard to regulate to get an even temperature.

I spent a week in Nojiri, a missionary resort area north of Tokyo. While I was there, I ordered a box of Western-style pears, like Bartletts, sent to me. The usual Japanese pear is something like a cross between an apple and a Kieffer pear (round, juicy, hard with coarse texture). We can get Bartlett pears in Nojiri, so many of the missionaries have them sent to their homes and can them. I put mine in the refrigerator and ate some every day. There were too many for me to eat so I canned 16 pints. I hope they will turn out well. I also made some bread-and-butter pickles.

After arriving back from Lake Nojiri, I spent the day cleaning my dirty house. The dust seems to have piled up during my absence. I didn't get as much studying done at Lake Nojiri as I had hoped, because living with other people puts you under some social obligations. I found that, if I gave my afternoons to study, that was about as much as I could take without getting weary. My head gave me a little trouble on several occasions, so I know my troubles are not over. My pills ran out, but I didn't notice any difference when I was not taking them. I enjoyed the missionary fellowship at Nojiri. It helped me catch up on some of the happenings and to feel a part of the work here in Japan again.

I have classes only three days of the week. On those days I generally have four hours a day, so I must prepare for them on the other days. I do not have any responsibilities on Sundays. We have completed the first week of school and so far everything has gone along smoothly. I am never satisfied with my preparation. Even so, I have enjoyed the classes and feel that the students have too. There are 23 students in all, just twice as many as when I taught a year and a half ago. That is a good increase. It certainly is thrilling but it will require more adequate facilities. The majority of students are from Mennonite Brethren churches but some are from other groups, in addition to the two Baptist missions that are cooperating. There are seven women and the rest are men students.

Next Friday the students will go on a picnic and are planning a little welcome back for me. They have asked me to give a little talk about my trip home via China, India, the Holy Land, Europe and England. I am using the information gained on the trip through Palestine in my Life of Christ class. It adds interest for the students to hear about present-day Palestine, as well as ancient Palestine.

September 29, 1963

Lucy Wipf travels from Ise to Osaka to teach organ to the Bible school students. She stays overnight with me because she can't teach all who want to learn in one day. It is nice to have someone to chat with and to have meals with, although I find it a little hard to get my work done with someone around. I feel as if I should visit with them and before I know it, an hour has slipped away. Lucy stayed two nights this past week, because we were having a school picnic on Friday and she wanted to attend. We went to Mino Park, not far from here, where there are beautiful Japanese maple trees. They are still green but the leaves will be turning brilliant red. This is one of the few places in Japan where you can find wild monkeys in the woods. They are temperamental and if you try to touch them or if you stare at them for a long time, they sometimes get angry and can attack you. They say there is a whole tribe of them, with a boss at the top, and various social ranks that are strictly guarded.

Richard and Frances Mayforth are on their way to Japan now and should be arriving next Saturday. They were studying Japanese in Hawaii before coming to Japan. This was a new experiment by the mission to see which was more effective, studying in Japan surrounded by Japanese or studying in Hawaii, surrounded by English-speaking people. Mayforths will be living in Kobe which is about one hour from Ikeda and also from Kyoto. None of our missionaries will be close enough to them to be of much help, but at least they will know some Japanese by the time they get here. They will continue their language study in Kobe. We are all looking forward to their coming. I plan to go to meet their ship, if at all possible.

October 15, 1963

I have been in Ise for the weekend. Joyce Batek, who is carrying on work in Matsusaka which the Sukuts began, invited me to speak at the Sunday evening meeting. Our Field Council, made up of our Japanese workers and five missionaries, will meet on Tuesday, so I am spending almost half of the week here. Every week finds me busier, it seems. This weekend, away from home and school, has taken me away from my usual responsibilities, so I have been filling in time playing the organ, reading, and visiting with the two girls. When I get back, I will have to buckle down.

Joyce made pizza for lunch yesterday since it was Lucy's birthday and, in the evening, we thought of going out to a special restaurant in Matsusaka for *sukiyaki*. When we discovered that it would cost almost $3.00 each, we gave up the idea and decided to fix our own at home. This restaurant specializes in Kobe beef, the best in Japan. We were told that the beef comes from cows that are fed beer to tenderize the meat and also that the cows are massaged to marble the fat with the lean meat. No wonder it is expensive! Our homemade *sukiyaki* wasn't as fancy as the restaurant type, but we enjoyed it and had more than we could eat.

Richard and Frances Mayforth and family arrived in Japan safely a week ago. I went to meet them at the ship in Kobe, along with some of our other missionaries. They have two children. The youngest is just three months old. It was quite a chore for Fran, especially, to pack and move out here, so shortly after the birth of the baby. They are living in Kobe, where they will attend Japanese language school. Dick (Richard) started language school this week and, as soon as they get their house settled and find a maid, Fran will start.

The Mission has been looking for a new meeting place for the church in Matsusaka, because the building we have been using has been sold and must be vacated soon. There seems to be nothing suitable available at present. Pastor Akasaka in Ise came up with the idea of buying an old, broken down bus and converting it into a meeting place. It might be a problem finding a place to park it but it might serve temporarily.

November 10, 1963

I was invited to the Mayforths for supper last Monday. I saw a pie in the kitchen that looked almost the color of chocolate pudding, but it looked dry rather than moist. I asked Fran what kind of pie it was. She said it is the pie that "I told the maid to put into the oven five minutes, but she understood that it was stay in until 5:00 p.m." (4 ½ hours). It was a pumpkin pie. It wasn't really burned, just thoroughly dried out. We ate it anyway. Their maid is an elderly woman who cannot read even Japanese, which is very unusual in Japan. At least they have someone to stay with the children when Fran goes to language school.

It was a relief to learn that the Baptist General Conference finally voted to continue cooperation with the Mennonite Brethren and our NAB Mission after the three year trial period. Now we plan to proceed with building a school campus of our own. We are using a Mennonite Brethren Church in Ikeda for classrooms and various other rented buildings in the neighborhood for other purposes, but we need a campus of our own to hold things together and to give us the needed space as the student body increases. We are praying that the necessary funds will come in. We are also trying to find Japanese teachers, but this is extremely difficult. One young man who recently received his Master's degree in theology at Dallas Seminary is being interviewed. He has indicated that he would rather teach in a secular school, to be a witness there.

November 24, 1963

The shocking news of President Kennedy's death reached us here on Saturday morning at about 6:30 a.m. Our two Japan Baptist Conference students and I were having our early morning prayer meeting when Harry Friesen, who lived next door, knocked on the door, saying that he had just heard on the radio that President Kennedy had been assassinated. Later in the afternoon, Miss Yokota brought an extra edition Japanese newspaper which had just come off the press. There were pictures of the president's car going to the hospital. President Kennedy was very popular in Japan. The fact that an assassination of a president could occur in a democratic country like America seemed to shock all the Japanese.

We have just three weeks of school before the term ends. I have enjoyed teaching Christian Education of Children more than any other course. Next term I will be teaching Christian Education of Adults. This is the weak spot in our Japanese churches. We have mostly young people attending and find it difficult to reach the middle aged or older. I went to visit the Sunday School class of one of my students this afternoon. The class meets in the home of a Christian lady who teaches art and brush writing. The boy who is in my C.E. class also teaches English and Mathematics at this home on Saturday and Sunday. About 200 pupils come there. However, only about 15 attend Sunday School. The teacher says she has the pupils write simple Bible verses for practice in brush writing, such as: "Children obey your parents," "Be kind one to another," etc. She said that at first she was afraid to do it because she thought she might lose some pupils if she introduced anything religious, but apparently she has not. The children take home what they have written. Of course she chooses the verses that are not likely to give offense.

December 30, 1963

There is just one day left of the old year and everyone is getting ready for the New Year. I won't be doing anything special for New Years. When I was in church work, I automatically got involved somewhat, because you take the opportunity to visit the church people and others during this extended holiday. At the Bible School the students are gone and I am quite isolated from Japanese homes. It makes me feel a bit lonely at times, but right now I need the quiet to get ready for the new school term, which starts next week. I have arranged to go to the Mayforths on January 2nd and take them around a little to see how Japan celebrates New Years. They live 1 ½ hours away by train from me, which isn't so much, but we see very little of each other. If I don't make an effort to visit them during vacation, I probably won't see them for a long time. It was our plan to get all our missionaries together for Christmas in Ise and then to have our Annual Missionary Conference at a Japanese inn for two days. At the last minute, Mayforths called us saying that they were not fully recovered from the flu and did not think it wise to take the children out. We called off the conference, but the rest of us did get together to celebrate Christmas, at least. We were sorry that our newest missionaries had to have such a lonely first Christmas in Japan, but there wasn't much we could do about it.

Last Sunday morning I went to Tsu for a homecoming gathering of university students in Tsu. Two of the students who were saved in Tsu planned this little reunion of those who were connected with the Tsu Christian Center during their student days, but are now scattered all over. Four of the young men were from my time in Tsu. It was good to see them again and to hear from them, at least a little of their witness for Christ in the places where they are now working.

Mrs. Murakami is getting rather excited about going to America to be with her husband. Her husband sent several tapes to the churches and to the missionaries for Christmas. His English has improved so much that he makes very few mistakes. We missionaries made a tape in return for him, but we did it all in English. We were the ones to be ashamed of our Japanese.

January, 1964

Since my return to Japan last July, I have been in good health, especially in recent months. Though times of exhaustion come when the work piles up, under ordinary circumstances, I feel a sense of well being with joy and contentment at being in the place where I am. I sometimes feel that angels have come and ministered to me, so remarkable is the change.

As missionary teachers we are constantly made aware of our inadequacy with regard to language and cultural background. Occasionally I have the satisfying experience of reading a word of appreciation from a student at the end of an assignment such as this: "I was experiencing a personal problem along the very lines of the assignment you gave, so it has helped me to find a solution from the Scripture." On another occasion I was pleased to have a student ask me at lunch time to elaborate on what I had said in class about the call of God to Christian service. She said, "I came to Bible School to study the Bible but did not have a clear call to any particular work. Since then I have yielded by life to Christ completely and am willing to do whatever He asks of me. How can you be sure that God has chosen you for special service?" It is at times like this that you feel you are really fulfilling your responsibility as a teacher and guide.

February 2, 1964

The past week has been uneventful except for a few complaints which have come my way from our students. The fact that missionaries are in places of leadership, both in our churches and in our Bible School, means that we are the ones that do the teaching and training, whereas the Japanese, as newer Christians, are generally in positions of learning and being trained. It is easy to see how these feelings can arise. If they were under Japanese leadership, they would probably feel a certain amount of regulation and control too, but it would be considered natural for those in such positions of leadership. Because the leaders are foreigners, it is interpreted as foreign domination and suppression. I am sure there are areas where our attitudes are not always as Christian as they should be and need to be corrected.

April, 1964

Today was Buddha's birthday. A missionary friend, Pauline, invited me to go with her to a Buddhist temple to observe the celebration. We were a little late and missed out on the first half which was strictly religious but got there for the last half which was cultural. The temple teaches many things other than religion, for example: English, Organ, Japanese Music, Japanese folk dancing, Flower Arrangement, Tea Ceremony, etc. Just before we left the priest presented us with a Buddhist rosary as a gift. Pauline then invited Miss Sugimoto and her friend to come to her house for supper. After supper we listened to part of *The Messiah*. As we did so, we had the opportunity to explain the words, especially of the Hallelujah Chorus – "King of Kings and Lord of Lords,"[8] and of the resurrection part, "I Know That My Redeemer Liveth." At first the girls thought that Christianity was very much like Buddhism but when we explained the difference between reincarnation and resurrection, they began to see the difference. The priest's daughter had never read any of the Bible. We gave her a New Testament and the other girl, who had attended a Christian Junior High school, accepted a Gospel of John which she said she would read. She had received a little instruction from the Bible in school but had forgotten most of it. How we pray that God's Word may speak to their hearts and convince them that Jesus Christ is indeed the Savior!

May 24, 1964

Our school term is already half over and the students are beginning to think of all the term papers and exams that lie ahead of them. The teachers too are thinking about summer and making their plans. I will have one summer assignment, namely teaching a young

---

[8] Handel, G. F. *The Messiah*, 1912.

155

people's class at our family camp. I don't know the details yet, but know I will enjoy doing it. However, being out of church work I feel a little lost too, especially not having much contact with unbelievers now. I am planning to spend about three weeks at Lake Nojiri. I have rented a cottage from a Norwegian missionary couple who are now on furlough. It is very primitive, however, and sometimes I wonder whether the inconvenience outbalances the comfort of coolness. I still enjoy being there, because it is a wonderful opportunity to be with other missionaries from all over Japan.

Next Sunday I go to Matsusaka to speak. Lucy Wipf asked if I would come once a month to help her out. She still finds it a little difficult to prepare a message in Japanese every week. I would really like to be able to attend one of our churches every Sunday and have some small responsibility there. I feel as if I am teaching only theory and not practicing what I teach.

The Moores will be moving to the Kobe or Osaka area sometime soon. They have been in Kyoto working with the Kyoto Church. Fred will be teaching at the Bible School. This means that the Moores, the Mayforths and I will be out of touch with our churches. I think we need to start a church in this area very soon, but I haven't been able to convince anyone else yet.

June 1964

I spent a wonderful day in Tsu on June 7 witnessing the baptism of seven people: a father and his seventeen-year-old son, a kindergarten teacher, two nurses and two high school girls. We rejoice over the addition of several adults to the group of believers in Tsu. The work in Tsu began as a student work, but we felt the need for adults from the community to be added to give stability and financial strength. Gradually the church is putting down its roots and hopes to build perhaps this year.

On June 16 we bade farewell to Mrs. Murakami who has gone to the States to join her husband for his final year of study at the Seminary in Sioux Falls, SD. She will be missed by us all, especially at Tsu where she has served with the Kerns for the past two years. Mr. Kern, our secretary-treasurer, having many responsibilities other than his station work, has been overloaded and has been ordered by the doctor to cut down. Our seminary student, Mr. Hanazono, helps on weekends and Miss Yokota from Matsusaka comes to help with the

Sunday School, but even so it is not adequate. We pray that workers who can help may be raised up amongst the believers in Tsu.

September, 1964

School officially opens September 15, next Tuesday, but the students were asked to return a day early to clean up the school and dorms. Since moving the school from the Mennonite Brethren Church to the Friesen residence, there has only been a depositing of the school equipment in the building. Nothing is properly arranged and everything must be cleaned up, including the yard.

I will be teaching seven hours this term. My three courses are: "Life of Christ," "Inductive Bible Study," and "Teaching Methods." I have taught these courses before, so I have my notes in fair order, but each time I teach them, I feel the need to reorganize them. With the extra little responsibilities of the library, student counseling, etc. I should be kept busy. I was given the title of Dean of Women, since both of the other women teachers were in the States. However, I hardly know what this responsibility entails and don't feel qualified for the job. Now that Elaine Nordstrom is back, she is likely to get the job after she gets re-acclimated to the school. She took a few courses in counseling at Fuller Seminary and has a real interest in it.

Tomorrow I will go to Kyoto. Sukuts have invited me to dinner. It is the first time for me to be in their home since they returned to Japan. The Mission's plan for them is to begin a new church plant in the Kyoto area, so the Rakuyo Baptist Church will have a sister church to fellowship with. In the meantime, they are helping a bit in the Rakuyo Church with English Bible Classes and Women's work. The Kyoto church has some good young people in it, but adults are few.

November 7, 1964

The big event here in Japan was the Olympics which have come and gone. I enjoyed watching the opening and closing ceremonies, as well as a few of the athletic events on TV. My neighbor has a TV so she let me watch with her. Some of the seminary students asked me which team I cheered for, the United States or Japan. That put me on the spot. I rooted for the United States, although it sounds a bit disloyal to Japan to say so. I am saving up all the gifts that have been sent to me for Christmas and birthdays, etc. to purchase a TV.

I spent last weekend in Mie Prefecture. I visited the Tsu Church Sunday morning and spoke at the Matsusaka Church Sunday evening. I hadn't seen Meraleen Kern for six months or more. She is now expecting their second child. Their only child, Timmy, is seven years old. He had hoped and prayed for a brother or sister for so long, but had given up, I guess, because when he was told that a baby was coming into the family, he couldn't believe it was true. Sukuts have invited Mayforths, Moores and me to their house for Thanksgiving. All our missionaries gather together for Christmas, but for Thanksgiving we usually divide up into two groups, one in Mie Prefecture and one in the Kyoto/Osaka area.

January 1, 1965

Lucy Wipf invited me to Matsusaka to speak twice. I have two messages to prepare. I spent Christmas day house hunting because I will have to move out of my Mennonite Brethren apartment over Friesen's garage the end of February, when the Mennonite Brethren missionary who lived here returns from the U.S. I am not yet sure what my living arrangements will be. We have a mission house, purchased for me by our mission, but it is now being used for the Seminary Women's dorm. It is very suitable for this purpose and, of course, the school would like to keep on using it. The new school term opens January 5th and then I shall be busy again every day. I will be teaching a new course, "Christian Education of Youth," which will require considerable work. As yet, I have done almost nothing on it.

February 21, 1965

We have just one month left of the winter term at the Osaka Biblical Seminary. New students are beginning to make applications to enter. We have two fine young men, seniors in university, who are planning to enter Seminary next spring. One, I believe, will definitely come to our school. The other has not made a final decision as to where to attend.

We recently invited the pastors of the three cooperating missions (NAB, Mennonite Brethren and Baptist General Conference) to meet with the teachers and board members of OBS. We were encouraged to see their interest and hope to incorporate many of their suggestions in our new curriculum, starting next April. Other missions and churches have been showing interest in our school also, although we have made no special efforts to advertise it. We feel that the school is gradually being strengthened and are encouraged to believe that there is a real need in this area for such a school. Please continue to pray for us as teachers. So much depends on the teaching done, as to whether or not future church leaders will be effectively used of God.

March 15, 1965

We have been concerned about several students who have indicated their desire to drop out of seminary at the end of this year. One of the boys said his father wants him to come home and help in the family drug store. He says he does not really feel a call to the Christian ministry and would like to do as his father says. One of the girls said she feels she should drop out because her mother is sick and is unable to look after the house and younger brothers and sisters adequately. She said she does not feel a call to Christian service either. Another girl's father is living alone and she feels she should live at home with him and commute to school, an hour and a half away. She would probably have to take a lighter load of classes to do this. Then just yesterday, the girl who helps us in the house said she had received a letter from her sister asking her to come home and take care of their mother since she is living alone, or will be, when the older sister goes to work in Yokohama. It seems that the devil is hard at work to pull these students out of seminary and eventually away from full-time Christian service. It is hard for the students, because they want to be a good testimony to their non-Christian families by being helpful to them. If they must do so at the cost of turning aside from their call, it is indeed a victory for the devil.

Applications from those desiring to enter the school are supposed to be in by March 15. Thus far there are only three that we know of for sure. Our entering class last year was 12, so it will be quite a let-down if there are not more. We had hoped to have a young couple enter this spring, but he wrote saying that his employer would not release him at this time. He is doing experimental work for the government and they say he has an obligation to finish his work. He is already about 27 years old. We pray that he may not be side-tracked.

Our one and only full-time Japanese teacher, Mr. Kitano, has been asked to become a part-time teacher, since he is now about 66 and past the usual age for retirement. He took this as an offense. Also it means a reduction in his salary. Consequently he has said that he wants only responsibility for classes from now on and does not wish to be given any other responsibility. It is exactly in the other areas where he is most needed, since there is no other full-time Japanese teacher who can attend to the many little things that really require a Japanese rather than a missionary. We are praying that God may send us a full-time Japanese teacher soon in view of Mr. Kitano's present attitude.

Ed and Meraleen Kern will be going home on furlough this summer. We are hoping that the Murakamis will get back to Japan from the U.S. earlier than they planned, which was in September, so there would be someone in charge of the work in Tsu. The mission decided that Joyce Batek should go to Tsu after language school to do hospital and student evangelism. Sukuts wanted her to come to Kyoto to help them, but the majority felt that Tsu was the best place for her. We will now have to find housing for her.

April 18, 1965

The new school term opens on April 20th. Twelve new students have enrolled. Two are college graduates, both from our own JBC churches. Three of them have not completed high school. The rest are high school graduates. We now have three separate courses for these different levels, although many of the classes are together. We are very happy about having two of our young men at the Seminary. We may have another next year. One of the young men from Tsu, our very first convert there, has written saying he would like to enter Seminary. He has been living in Tokyo and is now a member of a Baptist Church there, but his loyalty is still with us. It is still a struggle for him to give up his work.

The Mission purchased a new house for Elaine Nordstrom and me to live in. It is located in a very nice residential neighborhood. A construction company built 40 houses in this area and ours is one of them. They are all different and very interesting. In the U.S. they would probably all be built similarly. It is a one story, modern house with a large room in the middle for kitchen, dining room and living room, which we share. On either side of the large room are two small rooms. I have the two rooms on the south, facing a little garden and Elaine has the two rooms on the north, facing the street. This allows each of us to have private rooms for bedrooms and studies. We are having a carpenter build a kitchen cabinet with a counter top and shelves and drawers in the closets which were built to store Japanese sleeping mats and quilts. Our laundry room is really outside, but it has been enclosed with plastic sheeting, so we will at least be protected from the rain. Of course, it will be cold in winter but that is one of the inconveniences of Japanese houses, even the new ones. We had a little storage shed placed in the back yard for our trunks and drums and still have a tiny bit of yard left for a few shrubs, grass, flowers and a clothesline.

Our house is near the area of the city that is famous for cherry blossoms. They are in full bloom today, so Elaine and I took a little ride up the hill to see them, after church.

One of our JBC seminary students, Mr. Yukio Hanazono, was married to a Mennonite Brethren girl. They are now in the city of Matsusaka in Mie Prefecture, working with Lucille Wipf. I went to Matsusaka to speak for their Good Friday service and visited the Hanazonos in their new home. They are not yet settled, but seemed to be happy with their home. Their wedding was a very happy occasion for all, because it definitely was a case of mutual love for each other and, in addition to the approval and blessing of all concerned, both families and churches and seminary, was evident. We trust that they will be used of the Lord to build up the work in Matsusaka. Mr. and Mrs. Richard Mayforth (Fran) will be going to Matsusaka in the fall to work with them. It is a special joy to me to see Mr. Hanazono going out into the Lord's work after four years of training at the seminary, because he was led to the Lord during my time of student work in Tsu. So it is, in a special sense, my first fruits being dedicated to the Lord.

May 8, 1965

Last weekend I was away from early Saturday morning until late Monday evening, so I got behind in many things. We had a Sunday School Teachers' Conference and a Deeper Life Conference. Thirteen young people who are either teaching Sunday School or may be teaching in the near future came from all four of our churches. Many of them are young Christians themselves, so they are hardly qualified to teach. We trust that the Lord will bless our efforts in training them and their efforts in teaching. We also had a Deeper Life Conference on Sunday and Monday. The guests were from all four churches. The out of town guests all stayed in the mission house, which is unoccupied right now. We spread out thick mats on the floor and got over 20 people into the house. Of course, there is no furniture in it now. This cut the cost way down, since the people had to pay only their travel and food. We had a good conference and the people really seemed to enjoy the fellowship with the other church people.

Walter Sukut asked me to help in the Kyoto church's Sunday School, especially with teacher training. Last night we had a meeting with 6 young people of the church who have offered to help with the Sunday School in some capacity. We hope to have a special meeting in two weeks to draw children to the church and then, we hope, to be able to again divide up into classes according to ages. The morning worship service was held out of doors today. We walked to a lovely hill overlooking the city and worshipped there.

July 18, 1965

My companions on a trip to Hokkaido were four girls from the Conservative Baptist Mission. We took in some of the lovely scenery, mountains, volcanoes, hot springs, etc. In order to do this, we had to keep moving most of the time, so it was a bit tiring, especially since the trains were very crowded and we had to stand part of the time. People in the U.S. will never appreciate what a blessing it is to be able to get on a train and find a seat. Sometimes we had to stand in line an hour ahead of departure time, hoping to get a seat.

August 18, 1965

On my way back from Hokkaido, I stopped at Karuizawa, a mountain resort town, where missionaries from all over Japan gather for a Deeper Life Conference. One of the speakers was David McKee from Ireland. It was a real blessing. I was especially impressed again with my need for a personal walk with the Lord, above all else. It was good to renew friendships with missionary friends and to make new friends. I had not been to Karuizawa for three years, so there were many whom I did not know. Those of us who have been in Japan fourteen years are beginning to feel like the old timers we saw when we first came here. I wish that I could feel that I was a wise, experienced missionary. Perhaps I am richer in experiences, but am not sure how much wiser I am for having had them.

After returning home from my vacation in Hokkaido and Karuizawa, I went to Tomoshibi Camp for four days. It was held in Mie Prefecture, on the ocean. It was for youth from Junior High and up. We averaged about thirty campers each day. The majority had some connection with our churches and had made some kind of a decision regarding Christ previously. There were also a few new people. Five young people responded to the call to dedicate their lives to Christ for service. Seven stayed to talk with the evangelist about salvation. We cannot be sure if these were truly born again, but at least it indicates a desire to believe.

I had five girls in my tent. At the beginning of camp, none of them could pray. In fact none declared themselves to be Christians, although three had been going to church quite regularly. Little by little, I could feel the Holy Spirit working. Before camp was over, one girl gave a testimony of her joy in having been able, first to believe in God, then in the resurrection of Christ and finally in the second coming of Christ. The night before camp closed, she asked about the meaning of baptism and later declared she was willing to be baptized, even if it meant opposition from her family, as she was sure it would. The last night, all four girls prayed, although some were still seeking assurance of salvation.

Autumn, 1965

Last week our Seminary faculty and student body went on a two-day retreat. It was the first time we had done something like this. We felt the need for more fellowship between students and teachers, especially in view of some of the problems which arose during the summer. I believe that all of us learned to appreciate one another more. One of the students said that now he felt like calling the teachers *Kyodai* (Brother), instead of *Sensei* (teacher). This gives an indication of the effect the retreat had on some of the students. One evening was largely recreational. Each class presented a little skit. The first year students imitated their teachers. Fortunately for me, I am not teaching any first year students now, so I escaped the painful experience. On the other hand, I was curious to know what characteristics in me they would have chosen to laugh at. Perhaps my turn will come later.

The Mayforths have completed language study in Kobe and will now be moving to Matsusaka, where they will be working with Pastor and Mrs. Hanazono. I think it will be a real adjustment for them to move to a rather isolated area, at least as far as contacts with other Americans or missionaries is concerned.

A city-wide evangelistic campaign has been going on in Kyoto for the past week. A large public auditorium was rented and quite a number of evangelical churches cooperated in the effort. There were about 1000 to 1500 present each night. It was reported in church this morning that there were about 24 people who had been taken to the meetings by Christians from our church and that a number of them had made first time decisions for Christ. Others indicated that they wished to study the Bible or attend church. There were quite a few new people in church today as a result. There is much work to be done in the way of follow-up personal work, visitation, etc. before these 24 can be really led to faith in Christ.

December 6, 1965

Seminary classes are over for the fall term. It is exam week for the students. Both students and faculty are preparing a musical Christmas program for December 10. We are inviting outsiders from the local churches as well. There will be a special supper and a gift exchange among the students preceding the program. This is to give them a little chance for a happy fellowship time with each other.

My next Christmas celebration was the Sunday School program presented by the children of the Kyoto Church. The program consisted of several little plays and pageants which I had written. With the help of Joyce Batek and several of the young people, we managed to get through it quite successfully. In fact, Walter Sukut said he thought it was the best children's program they had ever had in the church. We were especially pleased that so many non-Christian parents came. We had it in the evening and of course the little children cannot come at night by themselves, so that brought out the parents . We had the Christmas story given in slides and on tape also, so they had the chance to hear the real Christmas message as well as see their children participate. I trust that we may see some fruit from these contacts later on.

Elaine and I invited four of the neighbor ladies in for a little Christmas tea. There were others we would have liked to invite also, because we have six houses almost directly surrounding our house, but we didn't have room for any more in our living room. We chose the four with whom we have been most intimate and who have been especially considerate of us. We were a bit taken aback and embarrassed when they walked in carrying big gifts. Three of the ladies went together to buy a huge basket of beautiful fresh fruit, which we estimated must have cost close to $3.00. The other lady brought a lovely set of tea cups. We told them we wanted to celebrate Christmas with them, so I suppose that meant "present" to them. They told us it was the first time they had been entertained in a foreigner's home, so I suppose they didn't quite know what to expect or what was proper. You can never out-give a Japanese person, so you simply acquiesce and accept their gifts. We explained that we always offer a prayer of thanks before partaking of our food and they graciously cooperated, although none are Christians. The daughter of one lady has attended a nearby Christian church. Our conversation was not particularly religious, just centering around things of common interest to us all, but it did break the ice between us and helped us to become better acquainted. We discovered that they didn't really know each other very well either, since all of them have moved into this new housing area within the past two years. We sent a few cookies home with them for the children and enclosed a Christmas tract which we trust will be read and give a witness.

January 16, 1966

Toshiko Yokota, the girl who worked with me in Tsu and who recently graduated from our Seminary has become unofficially engaged to one of our first year students, Tomokuni Aoki. He was a student at the Agricultural College in Tsu and Miss Yokota was helping in the Tsu church after graduation, so they became friends there. The Seminary does not like first year students to become engaged, but it seems that in this case, it was unavoidable, because another fellow had proposed to Miss Yokota. When she told this to Mr. Aoki, he felt the need to make his claim then and there, since he had not yet made his intentions known to her. He still has three years of study left.

I took a Sunday off from going to the Kyoto Church because the weekend was full of other unexpected things. Elaine Nordstrom, Joyce Batek, Blanche Becker and I took Friday night off for an evening of relaxation. Blanche stayed overnight. We saw her off Saturday morning and did a little shopping. Tomorrow we have a Field Council most of the day and after that Kerns are coming over for supper. They have not yet been to our house, so I wanted them to come. They are due for furlough this summer, so this will probably be the last chance to have them here. Their furlough date is still undecided, because we have been waiting for definite word regarding the return of Mr. and Mrs. Hisashi Murakami from the U.S. They will probably be taking the Kern's place in Tsu when they get back. We heard that they were expecting a baby in June and their return would probably be delayed until fall. Mr. Murakami said that he studies until about 3:00 a.m. at night. I hope he isn't making himself sick before he graduates. Japanese students often ruin their health by over doing.

February 6, 1966

I have been enjoying my study in preparation for teaching Genesis. I have been reading Ramm's book on *The Christian View of Science and the Scriptures*. It has been sitting on my shelf for many years but I have never really delved into it very deeply. I am trying to come to some conclusion in my own mind about how to interpret the Creation account. I should have done this a lot sooner but never really had the pressure put on me to do so.

Next week we will be having a discussion at our women students fellowship on the subject of boy-girl relationships. We were divided into three groups with each taking a different subject for discussion. My group is presenting the subject of "Proposals and Engagements." We will be discussing such things as "Love Marriages" and "Arranged Marriages," the pros and cons of each. I was told that today in Japan marriages are about half and half.

Mr. and Mrs. Yukio Hanazono had a baby girl. Hanazonos are pastoring the church in Matsusaka City in Mie Prefecture. Mr. Hanazono is one of the boys who came to know the Lord while I was doing student evangelism in Tsu. He graduated from Mie Agricultural College and then attended Osaka Biblical Seminary. Mr. Hanazono asked me to be the "go-between" for him and his wife at their wedding, but I declined thinking that a Japanese couple would fill the bill better than I. In any case, because I have had rather close ties to this couple, I almost feel like a grandmother to the new baby.

March 4, 1966

We had a very interesting chapel service the week before exams. The students were in charge. When Elaine Nordstrom taught the Poetical Books of the Bible, she had the class write the main message of the book of Job in play form. The students presented this in chapel as a kind of radio play, no acting, just reading the parts effectively. It was quite well done. At the end of the play, Miss Okuda, the girl without hands and feet who is a special student at the Seminary, gave her testimony. She said that her family lived in Manchuria after Japan had taken it over. At the end of the war after Japan's defeat, Japanese living in Manchuria had to return to Japan as refugees. When the Okuda family returned to Japan, she was just an infant about two years old. The Japanese were herded together, almost like cattle, in freight cars and freighter ships. In this process of transportation, because of the cold, the little baby's hands and feet were frozen. Sometime later, back in Japan, they were amputated. Someone offered to buy the little deformed girl to display as a freak, but her mother did not consent. However, her mother hardly let her out of the house because of her deformity. She had almost no schooling. She wondered why God, if there was a God, had allowed such a thing to happen to her.

Some neighborhood children discovered her and asked her parents for permission to take her to Sunday School at a Mennonite Brethren Church. They carried her on their backs. Eventually she came to believe in Christ as her Savior and her whole attitude changed and hope sprang up in her heart. She was provided with artificial feet and legs from her knees down. Her arms extended to just below the elbow. She learned to walk and to use the stumps of her arms to do amazing things. By grasping a pen with both arms, she was able to write and do almost everything the other students did. It was such a touching story as she stood there before us with her handicapped body and such a real application of the message of the book of Job regarding how God can bring good out of suffering, that there was hardly a dry eye in the whole room. How often we complain over our lot, when we ought to be giving thanks to God continually.

We had our graduation service Saturday night. There were four graduates, two men and two women. There are also four new students entering this year, so the number of students will remain the same. Last year we had twelve students enter, so it seemed a bit of a let-down, in a way, but if we had had twelve this year, we might not have been able to accommodate them all. Our new school building is being delayed, due to rising costs. The plans are completed and the contractors made bids on them, but they all exceeded the allotted funds, so now there must be more revisions and more consultation with the Home Mission Boards of the three missions.

Kerns will be going home in July. Joyce Batek will probably be going to Tsu sometime this summer and Lucy Wipf will be returning to Japan the end of August. The plans are for her to live in my house while I am gone and attend language school for six months. This would save the mission rent.

It is only three months until I leave Japan so I need to make definite furlough plans. I am waiting for the Board of Missions to approve my plans when they meet the end of April. I am considering spending one term at the Southern Baptist Seminary in Fort Worth, Texas. They have an excellent Religious Education Department.

April 17, 1966

Elaine and I were invited to a wedding a week ago. The bride was a member of the Mennonite Brethren Church in Ikeda and also served as one of the part-time teachers at the Seminary. She taught psychology and organ. Her father was president of Osaka University. She came to our house once a week to help me grade papers. Elaine and I were asked to sing a duet at the wedding reception. The guests were given a box of sandwiches, a pudding-cake desert, wedding cake, an orange, a cup of tea and a large box to take home. When I opened the box, I was amazed to find a beautiful glass vase, which must have cost several dollars. This was the first time I had ever received a gift like that for attending a wedding. We felt a little ashamed at the small gift we had taken to the wedding.

We had our Annual Workers' Conference this past week for three days. There were ten of us present altogether: our two Japanese pastors (Akasaka, Nishizawa), our two Seminary students (Aoki, Arita), Miss Yokota, our four missionaries and myself. The theme of the Conference was "The Organization and Authority of Baptist Churches." Our study all came out of the Bible, so we weren't using the word "Baptist" very much, having decided that if we followed the Biblical pattern, that was all we wanted. We had a rather lively discussion regarding whether or not all believers have equal authority.

June 12, 1966

I just received a letter from Dr. Schilke today saying that I could get in one term of study as I had planned. This means that I will be in the States until about the end of March. However, I am afraid the months will be so full that there will be little time for real relaxation and fellowship. I have applied to Southwestern Baptist Seminary in Fort Worth, Texas. If I am accepted, I will be there from August 29-Dec. 22. I have been asked to do some deputation on weekends and perhaps take a few days off from school for some missionary conferences in the fall. I will probably be doing deputation most of January and February.

July 22, 1966

I wanted to visit my father's only living brother, Adam Miller, who lived in East Germany, so I planned to go home via Russia. I had heard from a missionary that this was an economical way to go.

Three missionary friends saw me off from Yokohama: Elaine Nordstrom, Peggy (Winter) Kitamura and Mary Johnson. The Russian ship I was to travel on had accommodations for about 250 people. We had lovely weather and a very smooth voyage of two and a half days to the port city of Nahadka.

There were only a few people at the port of Nahadka to meet the ship. We were taken on a tour of the city by bus but there was not much to see. We visited a graveyard for Japanese soldiers. Most of the ship's passengers were Japanese, so it was of interest to them. Then we were taken directly to the train by bus. It was a very special train reserved for foreigners only, headed for the city of Khabarovsk. I had a sleeper unit with two bunks all to myself. Soon after I occupied my compartment, an attendant knocked on my door and asked if I was missing anything. I said I didn't think so. He then showed me my purse which he had found in the restroom. I was flabbergasted, as I realized that I had carelessly forgotten my purse when I left the restroom. My purse contained all my valuable papers, my passport, and all of my money. This is the worst blunder I made in all of my travels. The Lord saved me from the serious consequences that could have resulted had the wrong person found my purse. We were taken on a tour of Khabarovsk, a very large city, and saw the river which serves as the boundary between Russia and China. Little fenced-in gardens around the houses were carefully tended. I was told that these are private and the growers can raise whatever they wish there and even sell any surplus they may have.

I took a two engine propeller plane from Khabarovsk to Moscow. The airport in Moscow is very new and beautiful. It is far out from the city and is surrounded by a forest of birch trees. It took an hour by bus to get from the airport to the city. I stayed at a special hotel for foreign tourists. Our meals were paid for with coupons which we bought in Japan. This was very troubling and I am sure we got cheated, not knowing exactly what the cost of the meals was. I took two tours: one of the city and one of the Kremlin. Our guides were students from the University of Moscow. They spoke good English.

I was able to go inside the tomb of Lenin. It is a dimly lit vault with guards stationed inside and out. You are not allowed to speak inside the tomb. Lenin's body is marvelously preserved and looks as if he had died yesterday. It lies on a raised platform under a canopy and is lit up in such a way that the light seems to be coming from within him. It is very impressive. One of the Americans began talking on the way out and a guard hissed "Shhhhh." Some Americans are really foolish in their behavior.

In the evening I went to the circus by myself. There was a small skating rink in the center. All of the performers were on skates, even when doing acts on the trapeze. They were very skillful. The bears on skates really stole the show. The bears even played ice hockey. We were free to take pictures in Russia, providing they had nothing to do with military installations, airports, or train stations.

The train from Moscow to Hanover, Germany took over 33 hours. Passports were checked at three borders from Moscow to Hanover, even in the middle of the night, which was a bit scary. I was not permitted to stay with relatives in their home. I could only stay at a hotel, so I gave up my plan to visit Uncle Adam. My German was not so good and if I got into trouble I would not be able to explain myself.

From Edinburgh I flew on Irish Airlines to Ireland where we had to lay over for one hour to refuel. We were told to get off the plane and look around in the airport shops, which I did. However, I looked a little too long and when I went to check about getting back on the plane to New York, I was told "Oh, that plane has already taken off!" I was told that all they could do was put me on stand-by for the next vacant seat on a plane to New York. They said that nearly all the airlines were on strike so there were only a few planes flying and some passengers had already been waiting at the airport several days. I did not know what to do because I did not have much money left for a hotel room. They said that since I was flying on Irish Airlines, the airline would put me up at a hotel one night, even though I was at fault for missing my plane. The next day I saw the stewardess in the phone booth a lot of the time. Then I noticed that a small group of four people were told to get their suitcases and a short time later they left the hotel. I thought that if those people could get a plane, maybe I could too, so I followed the stewardess around and told her my sad story of being away from my family for many years and I needed to get home soon. Finally, after some time, she beckoned to me and said, "Go get your suitcase. You're going." She had routed me to Canada instead of New York and from Canada to New York. I did not care if it was a roundabout route, as long as I got across the ocean, I would find a way to get to New York.

I had asked Edwin to meet me in New York, if possible, because I never had a family member meet me when I returned to the U.S. He was pastoring a church in Wilmington, Delaware at that time. He agreed to meet me. At that time, Hisashi Murakami had enrolled at Eastern Baptist Seminary in Pennsylvania to get his Master's degree in Theology after attending NAB Seminary in Sioux Falls. My brother was taking classes at Eastern also so he suggested that Mr. Murakami go with him to meet me at the airport in New York. When they got there, they discovered that I was not on the plane from Ireland as I had said. Later I was able to phone them and tell them that I would be arriving the next day from Canada. I really did not expect anyone to meet me the second time, but Edwin was there, by himself. What a relief that was to see him there! Missing my plane when most of the major airlines were on strike was one of the biggest mistakes I made during all my travels.

March 1967

This furlough has been shorter than usual, just nine months. I arrived in the U.S. on August 2 and will be returning by plane from San Francisco on March 27. I spent most of August visiting with my family. I was at the Southwestern Baptist Theological Seminary in Fort Worth, Texas for one semester of study to take some refresher courses in the field of Christian Education to help me in my teaching responsibilities at the Osaka Biblical Seminary. It was good to get some fresh ideas and to become acquainted with some of the new books and Christian education materials.

The two months of January and February were spent mostly in deputation in our North American Baptist churches. It was good to renew acquaintances with many former friends and also to visit some of our churches for the first time. It is always a joy to see new churches being established and growing.

March 31, 1967

It was so nice to see my sister and family in Tacoma for three days over Easter. I spoke in two of our churches while I was there. I was happy to learn that one of the churches has Negroes from the community attending it. My sister and brother-in-law's church has wonderful facilities. All they need now are more people. Edgar is challenged by the possibilities. Lill seems a little overwhelmed by the responsibilities. While I was there, a couple from the church took us out to a lovely Japanese restaurant, where we had four different Japanese dishes. The rooms were very similar to those of a restaurant in Japan, so it helped Ed and Lill realize what it is like here.

At Osaka Airport, I was greeted by three missionary friends and five Seminary students. Since then I have been busy every day getting settled. Today was graduation at the Seminary. Seven young people graduated. We will miss them, but we rejoice that they will be joining the ranks of Christian workers. The new Seminary Office and Classroom building is wonderful. Plans are now underway for Unit II: a dormitory/dining hall building. School begins in two weeks.

May 1, 1967

I returned to Japan in time for graduation at the Osaka Biblical Seminary. There were four weddings involving students during April. I attended all of them. Two of our own young people got married, Mr. Aoki, a third year student, and Miss Yokota, who had graduated from OBS and was helping in our church in Tsu. When it appeared that the Sukuts might be going home this year, it was felt that the Aokis should be permitted to marry and that Mr. Aoki would begin working as a student pastor in the Kyoto Church.

The new school term opened April 17th. Nine new students entered, one of whom is from our church in Tsu, Miss Nakai, who just graduated from Teachers' College. I am teaching three courses: "Pedagogy," "Christian Education of Adults" and "English."

The Sukuts had planned to stay in Japan until next year but, just this past week, Mrs. Sukut had a chest x-ray taken which showed clouding of the lungs. The conclusion was that, since the nature of the disease was uncertain, it was necessary for her to return to the States immediately. Walt has also had problems and so have some of the children. We are praying for the entire Sukut family and Barbara in particular.

Since I do not yet have any church responsibilities on Sunday, I have been going to visit various churches. Last Sunday I went to Tsu for a baptismal service. Five young people were baptized, two high school students and three college students. This was Pastor Murakami's first baptism, so I was sure it was especially thrilling to him. He invited me to come down for it and I was glad I did. It was a real blessing to me also. There is always something new and fresh about a beginning church which the older churches tend to lose. The baptism was held at the river in a nearby town. They even had communion afterwards by the river.

There are a lot of changes taking place with regard to the relationship of the mission to the churches. A lot of important things were discussed during the time Dr. Schilke was here and decisions made. Perhaps I will understand after a while, but some of the decisions seem to me to be premature. We will wait and pray for the Lord's leading.

June 18, 1967

Yesterday was a lonely day for us in Japan and especially for the Kyoto Church, because we said goodby to the Sukut family. Mrs. Sukut returned to the States about six weeks ago, but the family stayed on long enough for the children to complete the school year. The doctors diagnosed her case as a lung disease that resembles tuberculosis in many ways but is not as life threatening. Barbara is not in the hospital now but is staying with a friend in Minnesota and is receiving the necessary treatment. We do not know how long this will be necessary.

Sukuts were advised by the doctor not to return to Japan, so they have sold all of their household goods. This always involves a great loss. It will be expensive to set up housekeeping in the States. They need prayer regarding these material needs as well as for Barbara that she may be restored to health as quickly as possible. Sukuts would very much like to return to Japan, if the Lord should so lead later.

There is no missionary to take the Sukuts' place in Kyoto now. We do have a third year seminary student, Mr. Aoki, who was married in April, and is going to serve as student pastor. The Lord has wonderfully led in providing the Aokis for this crucial time. He is a college graduate and has an attractive personality, many leadership qualities, and a sincere love for the Lord and his work. Mrs. Aoki worked with me in Tsu for two years before coming to the Seminary. She graduated two years ago and has been helping in our church in Tsu. Mr. Aoki's first responsibility is still his study at OBS, so he cannot yet devote a great deal of time to the church. Wonderfully, the Lord has provided some capable men in the church who will be able to assume much of the responsibility and perhaps preach once a month. I will also be continuing the English Bible classes at the church.

There were about fifty people who came to the train station to see the Sukuts off. Right after that, we returned to the church to get ready for the first night of a series of special evangelistic meetings. There were several new people attending. We pray that there may be some definite decisions made this week. The responsibility of carrying on the work will undoubtedly strengthen the believers and take their minds off of their own loneliness. We can see the Lord's leading and trust Him to make it all work together for good.

June 18, 1967

We were happy to hear that a new couple was appointed for Japan at the last Board of Missions meeting in April. They are Wilfred and Jeannine Weick, graduates of our NAB Seminary who have been serving in one of our NAB churches in Minnesota. They have two small children. They are planning to arrive in Japan the end of August in time to begin language school in September. They will be living in Kyoto, attending the language school there. They will also be able to attend our church in Kyoto. We thank God for answering prayer in regard to new workers.

Summer, 1967

During a four day Senior Youth Camp held at Lake Biwa, with an average attendance of 25, three first time decisions for salvation were made and one for baptism. The three-day Junior Camp, held at an ocean camp-site in Mie Ken, was attended by about twenty-five campers, over half of whom had never been to church or Sunday School before. None of the three girls in my tent knew anything about God, Christ, or the Bible. During morning devotions, I spoke about the true God and during evening devotions about Jesus Christ.

174

We praised the Lord when we received word that the Billy Graham Crusade would pay travel and lodging expenses for seminary students attending the Pastors' Conference, conducted during the Tokyo Crusade. We quickly decided to dismiss classes and attend this four day School of Evangelism. We felt it would be a wonderful learning experience exceeding that of an ordinary week at the Seminary. It was a thrill to see between 15,000 and 18,000 people attending the meetings each night and to witness 500 to 1000 people step forward each night to indicate some decision. Over 40,000 attended in the Korakuen Stadium the last Sunday afternoon. There was to be a half hour TV broadcast in some cities, but there was no sponsor for Osaka. The Pastors' Conference was very challenging and helpful. We pray that the effects of these meetings may continue to exert an influence for good on all of the churches in Japan, even those which did not cooperate at this time.

May 3, 1968

We recently had a Day of Prayer at the Seminary. Classes were dismissed all day to enable us to have a quiet time with the Lord and to share with others in the study of God's Word and prayer. Our Scripture passage for the day was Philippians chapter 2 and our theme was "The Mind of Christ." I personally experienced a real blessing as I studied this chapter, in which Paul states that he is planning to send Timothy to Philippi to minister to the church there and to report to Paul on their affairs. Concerning Timothy, Paul says, "I have no man like-minded, who will *naturally* care for your state, just as a mother naturally cares for her children." I had to confess that I had failed to care for some whom I have had the privilege of guiding spiritually, but who were now in other cities. Among them is a young couple living in a city where there is no church. I felt that they were strong Christians and would be able to maintain their own faith nonetheless and even be able to hold a Christian service in their own home. Satan has been at work and both of them seem to have hit rock bottom spiritually. I received an emergency call two weeks ago to the effect that both of them were about to lose their faith completely. Their home life, too, is in serious trouble. We are praying for this couple that they may be restored to fellowship with the Lord, first of all, and then reconciled to each other. Pray for me also that I may be of some help, even from a distance.

Last weekend the Christians from our four churches gathered together for a few days of fellowship around God's Word at our annual Deeper Life Conference in Ise. The church was almost full for most of the meetings. It was a special joy to see some of the early believers of the Ise Church still taking the leadership in the church. One of the widows testified to the joy she had recently of seeing her second child married to a Christian mate.

Friday I dropped in on the Moores for a little visit. The Weicks were there from Kyoto too, and before the evening was over Lucille Wipf dropped in also. Pat Moore is getting along fairly well with walking after her stroke, but still cannot use her right arm at all. She is getting massages, but progress is very slow. She is attempting to do some of her work with her left hand, but isn't too effective.

Prayer is needed for our young student pastor and his wife in Kyoto. Mr. Aoki found it very exhausting and time consuming to commute from Kyoto every day, so since last term he has been staying in the dorm and going home on weekends. His wife is expecting in August. She is alone four days of the week. The work of the church, naturally, cannot be done too well under these circumstances. He will graduate next spring, Lord willing, so it means two more terms of school after this one.

Mr. Aoki had been teaching a baptismal class for three people, two adult women and a high school girl, but just recently all three of them decided that they were not yet sure of their faith and wanted to put baptism off. Needless to say, this was very discouraging to Mr. Aoki.

July, 1968

It is the rainy season here and, with the construction work going on in the new dorm, our school grounds are anything but lovely, with mud and wood and gravel, etc. all around. In the midst of this, the new four-story dorm-dining hall is nearing completion, at least on the outside. The women teachers were permitted the privilege of choosing colors for the tile in bathroom and kitchen, flooring, etc., so we feel we have a part in it too. We are planning to dedicate the new building, Lord willing, September 23rd.

September 14, 1968

This summer I reflected on the work of a Japanese Christian scholar, Uchimura Kanzo, who is said by some to have done more to present the Christian gospel to the Japanese in enduring form than any other individual. He lived from 1861-1930. Sunday after Sunday between 600-800 gathered in Tokyo to listen to his sermons and biblical lectures. Among his followers are two presidents of Tokyo University, a Chief Justice of the Supreme Court, two distinguished Ministers of Education, three ambassadors, three prominent scientists and many in the arts, professions and business. His complete works consists of 20 volumes. The sales of these books indicate that the interest in his writing is as great today as it was immediately after his death.

Several years ago a high school boy discovered one of Uchimura's books in the bookstore. He was so intrigued by it he bought the entire set and read them all. One day a friend invited him to come to the English Bible class I was teaching in Kyoto. He stopped attending after several lessons. He later wrote saying the reason was that he was teaching English to a group of children Sunday morning. He invited me to attend a party for them and then I learned that he had a real interest in the Bible itself, not only English. He asked to talk with me about the Bible so I gladly arranged a time for him to come. After explaining salvation to him, I sensed that he either already believed or else was on the verge of believing. When I asked him if he was ready to accept Christ, he hesitated a bit and said "I wonder what my family would think." He returned home thinking seriously about it. I gave him *Peace with God* by Billy Graham and several weeks later received a letter saying: "The other day I read *Peace with God*. I thought seriously of God and was determined to turn Christian. I would like to make a special study of theology. I want to know how to be a pastor."

You can imagine my joy. It was my privilege to recognize ripened fruit and pluck it. Now the reproduction cycle must begin. I must help him become a soul-winner. We are praying for his family, for his friends in the Bible class and the university.

Dormitory dedication, Osaka Biblical Seminary where Florence taught for 13 years.

The new dormitory of the Osaka Biblical Seminary was completed and dedicated on September 23rd. It was truly a day of rejoicing, because an urgent need has been met.

The day before dedication, a Christian business man from Canada visited the dormitory. Seeing that the lounge had not yet been provided with furniture, he inquired how much it would cost. The building committee chairman said, "About $400." On the way to the train station, the businessman said, "Get the furniture and send me the bill." What a wonderful provision that was!

As part of the dedication program, we invited young people from the churches related to OBS to come for a visit to the Seminary. We conducted a class and a chapel hour in typical fashion to let them get a taste of life and study here. A challenge for Christian service was given during the chapel hour by a graduate of the Seminary. At noon we served lunch in two shifts to about 150 people in our new dining hall. We trust that the Lord will use this introduction to call others into his service and to study at OBS

April 2, 1969

The Osaka Biblical Seminary graduation service was held March 23 with two of our North American Baptist students as the only graduates. Mr. Aoki will now be serving full time in his ministry in Kyoto. Mr. Arita will be going to work with the Kerns in Tsu. A home has been found for him and this will also be the meeting place for the church, from the beginning at least.

The new school year begins April 14. There are six new students entering, four men and two women. One of the incoming students is a young lady from our church in Ise. Her mother is a believer of one of the Japanese religions and was strongly opposed to her daughter's going to seminary. She told her not to expect to find a room for her after she goes to seminary. Another of the students, a young man, met such opposition from his family that he had to leave home and come to live at the seminary a month ahead of time. Please pray for these young people who are often suffering from real conflicts in their minds and a sense of guilt for having gone contrary to their parents' wishes.

The Matsusaka Church dedicated their new building on January 15th. It is a tiny but attractive church, limited in size due to the limited financial resources of the little group of believers. We are grateful to the Lord for the way that the pastor has been strengthened and inspired in recent months as a result of this new effort by the church. We are praying that the little group there may multiply and that the church will be a real witness in that city.

May 13, 1969

A week ago our four churches gathered together at Tsu for our Deeper Life Conference. Rev. Hattori, one of Japan's best spiritual leaders and radio preacher, was our speaker. He spoke about the things which contributed to church growth. He also gave his personal testimony one morning which touched the hearts of two young college girls. It was my privilege to speak to them and lead them to make a commitment of their lives to Christ.

July 23, 1969

Several weeks ago our Kyoto church held special evangelistic meetings. Among those attending for the first time was a freshman from the nearby technical university. He attended my English Bible class the following Sunday and declared plainly before the other students that he wanted to become a Christian and yet at the same time he did not want to because he had for the past three years studied and adopted a philosophy of existentialism which he did not want to give up. I had lunch with him after church and listened to his reasons for not wanting to become a Christian. Basically there were two: 1) He did not wish to appear to be a weakling who had to seek refuge in religion and call on God for help instead of relying on his own strength. 2) He knew that his family was opposed to his becoming a Christian and he feared their reaction. I tried to point out that some of the world's greatest men have been Christians and that he should let nothing stand between him and God, not even his family. During the week I received a telephone call from the pastor saying that he had made his decision to follow Christ.

Last Sunday another university student was baptized. He had attended our church when in junior high school but had dropped away. He spent one year in the States as an exchange student while in high school and stayed with a family who took him to the Hollywood Presbyterian church every Sunday. He returned to Japan but did not decide to become a Christian until a group of *Sokka Gakkai* (a new vigorous Buddhist sect) pressured him to join them. Almost in self defense, he declared himself a Christian and returned to our church to ask for baptism. God led him in mysterious ways over a long period of time to take a stand for Christ. We are praying that he may come to know what it means to be a true disciple of Christ.

November 17, 1969

The atmosphere in Japan is becoming increasingly tense as 1970 approaches. The big issues around which everything else seems to revolve are the Japan-U.S. Security Treaty which expires in 1970, the reversion of Okinawa to Japan without U.S. nuclear bases, the Vietnam war, and the university disputes. The radical students have been conducting a kind of guerrilla warfare in the streets, opposing Prime Minister Sato's visit to Washington to discuss the Okinawa problem. One church in Osaka was burned recently. We are praying that Christians in Japan may have wisdom to know how to act as responsible citizens and that they will not become so deeply involved in the social problems that they forget the true mission of the church.

March 30, 1970

March 22 was graduation day. Four young men received diplomas on the completion of a five year theological course and four young women for the three-year Christian education course. With the opening of the new school year on April 10, two new young women students will enter. We regret that there were no men applicants this year. I will be very busy next term teaching three courses, plus getting ready for furlough.

The Moore's are planning to begin worship services in their home in Ikeda starting in April since we have not been able to find any other meeting place. I plan to attend also and perhaps to help in some way.

June 1970

There is just a little over a month of school left and then the Baptist World Alliance Christian Education Conference will be held in Tokyo from July 7-10, followed by the regular BWA sessions from July 13-19. After that I will be heading home on July 19 with the NAB tour group from the U.S. I plan to arrive home July 23 and will be home just a week, before going to Canada for the Triennial Conference.

December 14, 1970

August 15th was the big event of the year for the Miller family. The occasion was Mom and Dad's Golden Wedding Anniversary. Our family was all together for the first time in 13 years. It was a wonderful time of reminiscing with relatives and old friends. We are grateful that both Mom and Dad have been well, even though they were still farming this last summer and working as hard as ever. The farm is up for sale now.

August and Clara Miller's 50th Anniversary - 1970
Florence, Evelyn, Edwin, Lillian, Sherrill

August and Clara Miller's
Golden Wedding Anniversary

April 19, 1971

Just about a week before I was to leave home to return to Japan, my mother had a heart attack and has been in the hospital for almost a month now. She made a good recovery during the first 10 days, but had a setback and had to go back to intensive care the second time after being out only about four days. She will require much rest at home. In view of this, I felt that I had to request a leave of absence to care for her. I expect to be home until the end of August and then another decision will have to be made. We as a family are very much aware of the Lord's hand over mother and praise Him for His mercy in sparing her life.

October 20, 1971

It is about a month and a half since I returned to Japan. I had almost three weeks to get settled and prepare for the opening of school.

School opened September 20th. Our enrollment is down to 17 students now. Two of our fourth year students left this summer for study in the States. One of them, Mr. Yukio Fujie, is from our church in Tsu and is now at our NAB Seminary in Sioux Falls. I am teaching "Christian Education of Children," "Christian Education of Adults" and a "Christian Education Seminar this term."

January 27, 1972

The future of the Seminary is still hanging in the balance. The Mennonite Brethren want to withdraw from the Seminary. If they do, the Baptist General Conference may do so also. Sometimes we are encouraged and at other times it seems we just do not have the finances, personnel, etc. that are needed to keep going. The next month will be a critical one, because I think the committees now working on the plans will have investigated all the possibilities quite thoroughly and something definite will be decided. Prayer is needed very much at this time. Because of all the uncertainty, the atmosphere at school is something like a clock that is running down.

My housemate of over six years, Elaine Nordstrom, of the Baptist General Conference, moved out the early part of December and returned to the States for furlough. About a week after she left, Miss LaVerna Mehlhaff, one of our NAB short-termers, moved in. She will be in Japan for two years. She teaches English in various places, mostly in the evening. Two weeks ago, we were invited to Ise by two of our single missionary ladies, Lucy Wipf and Luci DeBoer for a birthday party for me. They had a cake with *lots* of candles. They have only a two-room apartment, so we wondered how we would find room to sleep four people. We pushed the furniture into the corners, clearing enough floor space to spread out the sleeping mats and went to sleep.

December, 1972

I am working on a play, which 12 young Japanese will give in the U.S. and Canada from July through August in 1973. I have written the script based on the true story of a Japanese family. The wife became a Christian and endured a lot of persecution from her husband but eventually he was won to Christ. It will help our American churches appreciate the difficulties faced by those who choose to follow Christ and also the joy that comes when they are enabled by Christ to become witnesses for him to others. Our drama and music group will sing, give testimonies, show flower arrangements and the tea ceremony. I know they will be a blessing and a challenge to their audiences.

March 6, 1973

The play practice of the *Young Ambassadors from Japan* is going ahead. It will be a busy but interesting experience, to present our program in the States and Canada for two months this summer. We are praying for all the group members--10 Japanese and 4 Americans (3 short-termers will serve as drivers). We will travel by car most of the way.

April 25, 1973

The school term opened last week with a three-day retreat at a conference grounds near here. There are only six students this year. I think there was a good spirit at the retreat and pray that it will continue.

August 1973

It was a privilege for me to have the *Young Ambassadors from Japan* present their program in my home church, Napier Parkview Baptist Church in Benton Harbor. On Friday I wanted to show the group some of the sights of the area, so I called the Benton Harbor Open Air Fruit Market so see if I could bring the young people there to observe the farmers bringing in their loads of fruit and selling them to the buyers who then ship the produce to Chicago and other cities. The market master consented, so I took them to the market, where normally only farmers and buyers were permitted to enter. We stood on one of the loading platforms while the market master explained to the group how the market operated. When he finished, I said to him, "Did you ever meet my father, a farmer by the name of August Miller, who brought his produce here?" His mouth dropped open and he said, "August Miller! He was our neighbor!" Only then did we recognize each other. We had been in country grade school together for several years but had not seen each other for about 35 – 40 years.

When I told my father how expensive cantaloupes were in Japan, he bought a bushel of them and set them in front of the young people in our back yard and said, "Help yourselves. Eat all you want." And they did.

After the *Young Ambassadors* had presented their program in my home church, we traveled to Pittsburgh, Pennsylvania for our next presentation. Soon after our arrival there, I received a phone call from my brother saying that Dad had had a heart attack and had died soon after being taken to the hospital. Fortunately, my sister, Lillian, and her husband, Edgar Wesner, were with my mother when it happened so mother was not alone. Of course, I immediately made plans to return home for the funeral and turned my responsibilities over to others on the team. How grateful I was to be able to attend his funeral and to help mother adjust to his absence.

Interlude September 1973-April 1976

It was a huge shock to my mother to lose Dad so suddenly, so I knew I had to take time out to be with her. However, I did return to the drama group in Wichita, Kansas in order to be a part of the program they gave at the Triennial Conference and then to go with them as far as California on their way back to Japan. Following our last presentation in Anaheim, I accompanied the group to the airport in Los Angeles and saw them off on their plane to Japan. Then I boarded my plane going in the opposite direction to Benton Harbor. Before my plane even took off, I fell asleep because I was utterly exhausted. When I awakened during take-off, I looked around to see my little flock and count heads, but I could see none of them. I had forgotten that I said "Goodbye" and sent them home a few hours earlier.

Back in Benton Harbor, I sensed that my mother needed someone to be with her for a while. I asked Dr. Schilke if I could take a leave of absence. Permission was granted. I did not know how long I would be needed but it turned out to be about two and a half years. I knew that I needed to find some kind of employment during my leave of absence but it was not easy to find a suitable job. Then a member of my church suggested that I might serve the church as a Director of Christian Education for the duration of my leave of absence. The church voted to employ me in that position for almost two years.

Return to Japan

My return date was set for January 1976, but an unexpected event occurred. I had a physical exam by a physician in my church, in preparation for going back. He pressed on my abdomen and said, "I think I feel something hard." He ordered an x-ray, but nothing showed up on it. He asked me to come back in November. This time he had dye put into the kidneys to enhance the x-rays and a tumor was found in my right kidney. The urologist said that most kidney tumors were malignant and so it would be advisable to remove the entire kidney.

After the surgery, I was told that the tumor was about the size of an egg and that it had been encapsulated. By removing the kidney, there was no danger of it spreading. I did go back to work at the church when I was strong enough to do so and then received permission to go back to Japan in April 1976. How grateful I was that I had been detained long enough to make that second exam necessary.

I was thrilled to hear that my 77 year old mother wanted to accompany me on my trip back to Japan for a month's visit. We left Benton Harbor on May 11, 1976 and spent a few days in Tacoma, Washington with my sister, Lillian, and husband, Edgar. Then we made a two day stopover in Honolulu to catch our breath and do a little sightseeing. She was overwhelmed with its beauty and said, "It is just like the Garden of Eden." We arrived in Japan on May 20th.

I returned to my former home in Ikeda, which had been rented out in my absence. It was about a fifteen minute walk from the Ikeda train station so it meant that Mom and I had to walk that distance a number of times when we took the train to visit various places. My mother enjoyed meeting many of the people I had been working with, both missionaries and Japanese.

Dissolution of the Osaka Biblical Seminary

One of the sad things I encountered upon my return to Japan, was the dissolution of the Osaka Biblical Seminary while I was in the States. I knew that serious problems existed with regards to cooperation between the three missions that established the school (Mennonite Brethren, Baptist General Conference and North American Baptist Mission), but I never thought that the school would be disbanded. The problem seemed to originate with the Mennonite Brethren Japanese pastors who were among the first to graduate from the school when it was solely Mennonite Brethren. Then the M.B. Mission went along with them in feeling that the two Baptist groups were not as conservative in their interpretation of Scripture as they were. Then the Baptist General Conference began to reconsider their cooperation, saying that their strongest churches and leaders were in the Tokyo area and would prefer to have their Seminary students study in Tokyo. Our mission was not strong enough to carry the load by ourselves.

After many difficult discussions, it was agreed to disband OBS and to allow the Mennonite Brethren Mission to retain ownership of one third of the property and the remaining two thirds would be sold and the two Baptist missions would receive their portion in money. This meant that the main classroom and administration building would have to be demolished so that the land could be sold to a developer who wanted to build a lot of homes on the property. I had been teaching there for thirteen years and Fred Moore had served there as president and teacher also. Pastor Hisashi Murakami had also been teaching there. A number of our Japan Baptist Conference young people had been trained to be pastors and Christian workers there. It was a great loss to our mission and to our JBC churches. For me personally, it was a very painful experience, having given so much of myself to the school and to the students, but we had to accept it and go on, and I had to find another avenue of service. When we no longer had seminary students going back to the churches on weekends to help with the work and to inspire other young people to give themselves to full-time Christian ministry, the flow of young people to Bible School and Seminary began to dry up, much to our dismay. This resulted in a shortage of Japanese pastors for the churches which the missionaries were starting, a detriment to our entire mission work.

8

IKEDA TO RETIREMENT

July 1976

This week we had our Annual Missionary Conference with all of our missionaries together for three days. We had a Southern Baptist missionary as our guest speaker. It was a time for fellowship and inspiration and relaxation. There were nineteen present in all. A good time was had by all.

February 4, 1977

On New Year's Eve, we ate noodles, a Japanese tradition. Because the noodles are long, it is a symbolic way of wishing everyone to live a long life. On New Year's Day, there was a worship service at the church. Almost all Japanese go to visit a shrine or temple on the first day of the New Year to pray for good fortune. After the morning service, everyone was served a thick red bean soup with a roasted rice cake in it.

On January 11th, the Ikeda Church held a *sukiyaki* party at my home. This is the day when all who have become 20 years old are recognized as adults and are honored in some way. There were ten present. I was especially happy that Tadashi, the younger brother of Mr. Yamamoto in Kamigori, and his wife were present. They came to the Christmas evangelistic meeting also. Mrs. Yamamoto is especially open and seeking. I hope to talk with her again soon.

I just finished a private English class with Dr. Iida, a pediatrician. I enjoy talking with him about health matters, especially because I sometimes get good advice (free). He says he has no religious beliefs but he certainly is conscious of people's psychological needs and seems to be quite open to spiritual things. He consented to study the Bible along with English, so we are able to discuss religious things quite easily.

October 5, 1977

I was asked to speak at a Sunday School Teachers' Seminar in Kyoto. This is hanging over my head and yet, I can't seem to get down to preparing for it. This past week has been exceptionally busy for me.

Just about the time I began to feel that I had to say "no" if any more requests came, I received a registered letter from Canada. I looked at the return address but there was no name. So I tore it open and tried to discover who sent it but I couldn't read the writing. Finally, after reading the letter, I realized where it came from. One of our first short term missionaries had dropped out of the program and gone to live with a Japanese family. Later I heard that she had married the son of the Japanese family with whom she had been living. They are now living in Canada. She is working on her Masters degree in education and her husband is in Bible College. I don't know if he was a Christian when she married him, but apparently he is now. She said they were blessed spiritually in Canada. She also said that they had received a sum of money unexpectedly, and that they wanted to give one tenth of it to the Lord. After praying about it, they decided to send me $40.00. I was flabbergasted to hear from them and on top of that, to receive such a generous gift. She used stationery that had written on it the words: "God's standards are completely different--When you think you are at the end of your resources, He gives new tasks and new strength." These were just the words that I needed.

A few hours later, Mrs. Seki, a Christian woman who seldom goes to church, dropped in to tell me that she had just learned that there was a lump in her breast requiring surgery. She seemed very anxious about it, so I shared with her my experience with kidney cancer and also the words on the stationery. It seemed to be a help to her also.

December 1977

Our mission needs prayer for the financial needs of our work. Japan is now being called "The Land of the Rising Yen," instead of "The Land of the Rising Sun." The value of the yen rose 20% last year, making the prices of everything very high, especially land. We must have land for five infant churches and money to loan them for buildings. The tiny congregations cannot carry the burden alone.

June 22, 1978

It is time to *REJOICE*! The seed sown in a doctor's heart has sprouted and is growing. Thank you, if you have helped water the seed with your prayers and tears. "They that sow in tears, shall reap with joy." Dr. Iida had requested me to pray for the quadruplets he was attending. Not long after this, we had a Bible lesson on the ten lepers whom Jesus healed, but of whom only one returned to give thanks. I don't know if the message of the lesson prompted it or not, but he wrote out a prayer of thanks, which he read in my presence. A number of experiences led him to want to give thanks. His wife, who had cancer surgery, is getting along well. Both of his children passed their entrance examinations for a higher school and the quadruplets all went home from the hospital in good health. As he read his first real prayer, my heart was bursting with joy, because I knew that God, too, and the angels in heaven, were rejoicing over this one who had come to put his trust in Him.

Dr. Iida had indicated his desire to attend church, so I invited him to attend ours. He has been coming almost every Sunday and has even been taking part in some unusual ways. Last Sunday we took our Sunday School children on a picnic. He volunteered to go with us and help us, even though his wife and children were at home. He is now studying the Bible with Pastor Fujie twice a month, so he only comes to my house every other week. I am happy to see him becoming a part of our church fellowship. We pray for his continued spiritual growth and for his wife and children. They have not yet attended with him or shown any interest. Pray, too, that Dr. Iida may find an older Christian with whom to fellowship.

It is time to *WEEP*! May I ask you to join me in weeping and praying for some who have been drifting away from the Lord. Sometimes the seed must be watered with tears. I must confess that I have not done this often, but when I have, it has been productive. After counseling with a young couple, whose marriage was going on the rocks and who were about to give up their faith, I left their house in despair. I was too down-hearted to even say "Goodbye." The wife spoke of suicide and the husband seemed to have surrendered himself to the devil, asking the devil to destroy their marriage. As I got into the bus, tears were coursing down my cheeks uncontrollably, as I prayed, "O Lord, I can do nothing for them. I turn them over to you. Deal with them as you see best."

It was not long after this that I was invited to their home. Things had changed. The atmosphere in the home was peaceful. Husband and wife were communicating with each other. Amazingly, the husband said, "I would like to do evangelism in this town." Today there is a little church in that town as the result of the vision and efforts of that Christian couple. I have never discovered what it was that changed the tide of events in that home. In my own heart, I feel that the tears that flowed in the bus and the prayer abandoning them to the Lord may have had something to do with it.

July 3, 1979
My six-month furlough is drawing to a close. I plan to leave Benton Harbor for the Triennial Conference on July 9th. Following the Conference, I will remain in Bismarck, North Dakota, for a Missionary Workshop and then go to Anaheim for my final speaking engagement at Sunkist Baptist Church, stopping at the Grand Canyon on the way. I plan to leave Anaheim on July 24th, stop in Honolulu for two days, and arrive back in Osaka on July 27th. It will be nice to see all the people I was working with there.

Since my furlough was short, my speaking engagements were fewer than usual. I did visit all my supporting churches except one, and participated in a number of missionary conferences. I visited churches in North Dakota, Kansas, Colorado, New Jersey, Michigan, Illinois, Wisconsin, Ohio Alberta and California. It was interesting to visit several churches I had never been to before, since they have taken on some of my support recently.

On June 22, our family all gathered at my eldest sister, Evelyn Chaddock's home in Wheaton, Illinois for a family reunion. My brother, Edwin and family came from Delaware to Wheaton for their daughter, Beth's graduation from Wheaton College. My sister, Lillian Wesner and husband, Edgar, came from Portland, Oregon on a vacation. So we all converged on the Chaddocks. My brother-in-law, Dale Chaddock, was already very ill with amyotrophic lateral sclerosis, but he was able to join in for the reunion. Just a week later, he was called home to be with the Lord. How thankful I was to be with my sister and family during this time of bereavement!

A physical exam resulted in several unexpected little problems, but nothing too serious. An angiogram showed no obstructions in the arteries, good valves, but my heart may not be pumping as much blood as it should. I am taking medication to improve that situation.

Beginning at Ikeda

September 27, 1979

When I arrived back in Ikeda, I was greeted with the news that Mrs. Iida, wife of the pediatrician, Dr. Iida, was very ill in the hospital with cancer. On September 8th she passed away. We were so thankful that a month before she died, she declared her faith in Christ and expressed a desire to be baptized. She was too weak even for bedside baptism, but at least she and her husband had the assurance that they would be together in the presence of the Lord. Mrs. Iida's funeral was the first Christian funeral for the little Ikeda Church. We had to rent the Mennonite Brethren church in order to accommodate the 350 people who attended. Many professors from Osaka University and many doctors from the Osaka University Hospital where Dr. Iida works, were present. Dr. Iida's Christian faith was openly declared to all these people at the funeral. We are praying that he will now be a courageous witness for Christ at the university and at the hospital.

Since September my classes have resumed. I am again teaching three English Bible Classes for women, one at the church and two at the Y.M.C.A. The pastor of the Ikeda Church wanted me to have all my classes at the church, so I have none at my house now. I was asked by the pastor to take the junior high and high school English classes at the church. I have thirty minutes of Bible in English with each class, following one hour of English conversation. I am praying that I can persuade some in the English classes to attend the Sunday School class. I am also supposed to be helping train Sunday School teachers, but my first love is the Women's Bible Classes. We are praying that some of these ladies may come to know Christ and unite with the church.

Last weekend, we conducted an English Bible Camp for about 30 people from all of our churches. The purpose was to practice English and listen to Bible teaching. An outstanding Japanese pastor brought two evangelistic messages and about five responded to the invitation. Pray that these campers will be encouraged to study the Bible in their churches. Some had never opened a Bible before.

January 30, 1980

I am praying for a young man who is seeking for God whom I met in the waiting room of the hospital. He spoke to me in English and told me his English name was "Oscar." He asked me if I could communicate adequately with the doctors in Japanese. I thought it was considerate of him to inquire, because this is a real problem for many foreigners. After assuring him that I could, he told me that he had had a brain tumor removed two years earlier. I told him about my cancer operation involving the removal of one kidney in 1973 and the great peace I felt from giving myself over to my Heavenly Father, who cares for me, in prayer before the surgery. He said that he had prayed to his god, too, before surgery. I asked him to whom he prayed. He said, "It really doesn't matter, does it?" I replied, "Oh yes, it does. Suppose that you had a fire and you dialed the fire department for help, but you had the wrong number. How much help would you get?" Then I told him about my God, the Creator of the universe, who made us and knew how to help us in our times of need. I then invited him to attend our Christmas program at church, which was soon to take place. He came and brought his wife, much to my surprise. She had attended a Christian kindergarten and has had a little exposure to the Bible.

About two weeks later, "Oscar" called, asking if he could visit me. I thought he just wanted to speak English with me. After awhile, he opened his brief case and took out a book which explains very simply some of the important parts of the New Testament. He said he had been reading it, but needed help in understanding the Bible. He asked me if I could help him. I could hardly believe my ears. It is so seldom that people come asking for Bible Study. I was on cloud nine for the rest of the evening as I presented the gospel to him as simply as I could. Last Monday evening, he came again and we have arranged to have a regular weekly Bible Study together. I am praying that I will be led of the Holy Spirit in teaching him and that the Holy Spirit will enlighten his mind and heart to understand and accept the truth.

There were originally nine members in my Bible class at the church, but two have dropped out to take part-time jobs. This leaves seven, but even these do not attend every week. One of them, the only single lady, has been going through a period of deep depression. She was a high school English teacher for many years but had to give up her job, because of emotional problems. She is now teaching at an evening school, but even this seems to be too much for her to cope with. She has attended the English Bible Class for many years but she is afraid to make a clear decision for Christ. None of her family are Christians. She is easily moved emotionally and is very sensitive, but at the same time, she is easily hurt and tends towards self-pity, feeling that she has been cheated because she is not married and does not have a family as most people do. She came to the class recently for the first time after a long absence. We are praying that we can help her put her trust in Christ and that her emotional life will become more stable and happy.

A group of high school students have been attending the church since December. They came to the special evangelistic meeting with a radio preacher on the Lutheran Hour. Two of them had listened to the broadcast and were taking the Bible correspondence course that was offered to listeners. The radio office had informed them of the meeting, so they came. There were about 8 who came and 5-6 are continuing to come on Sunday mornings, which has really boosted our attendance. We decided to begin a high school Bible Study group one Sunday afternoon a month. We will be studying the book of Mark for one year. None of them are yet Christians.

Dr. Iida's family is making a good adjustment to the loss of the wife and mother. Dr. Iida comes to church as often as his work permits. His high school age son comes quite often too, sometimes by himself.

June 11, 1980

Last weekend was very special. The Billy Graham music team was in Osaka and had concerts in preparation for the October Crusade. The missionaries of Osaka area were invited to a breakfast with the team at one of the nicest hotels. Next week-end I will participate in our English Camp, one day and overnight. "Oscar" and his wife will go with me. "Oscar" is the man whom I met in the hospital, who had had brain tumor surgery. He has studied the Bible with me every Tuesday evening. I pray that they will come to believe in Christ. Both are very interested.

October 12, 1980

It was good to welcome back Bill and Luci Lengefeld at the end of August and to welcome a new short-termer, Karin Klettke from Kitchener, Ontario. Lengefelds are attending Japanese Language School in Kyoto for one year before going to Tsu to begin the English Language Institute at the new Center building.

Our General Missions Secretary, the Rev. Fred Folkerts, came to Japan for a two week visit, the first part of September. It was his first visit to Japan, so we were all eager for him to observe our work first-hand and to meet our pastors, missionaries and other church leaders. The first week was spent visiting missionaries and churches. The second week was spent at various meetings, including the dedication of the new Japan Baptist Conference Center building. In the Center are offices for the Japan Baptist Conference, the NAB Mission and the Student Center. There are rooms for conferences and guests as well as rooms for English and Bible classes. There are also dormitory rooms for a few college students to rent. Living quarters for the Stollers, who manage the building, are also in this building. Pray for them as they seek to do evangelism among the university students.

We have been rejoicing over two young men who were recently baptized and became members of the Ikeda Church. One is a college student and one is a high school student. Both are very sincere and are attending church faithfully as well as witnessing to their fellow students. A high school girl and a middle-aged woman are also believers but face opposition from their families. They are waiting for an opportune time to be baptized. Pray that this day will come soon.

Tonight is the last night of the Billy Graham Crusade here in Osaka. Already thousands have responded to the invitation to accept Christ. I was pleased that seven ladies from my English Bible classes attended the Ladies' Meeting. We pray that the churches will adequately follow up on the decisions.

May 18, 1981

Recently I have been taking a backward look to see how the Lord led me, our other workers, and our Christians here in Japan during the past three decades. In November, it will be just thirty years since I arrived in Japan and our mission work began. On May 3rd and 4th our Japan Baptist churches held their annual Deeper Life Conference and one hour was given to a celebration of the thirtieth anniversary. I was asked to prepare a set of slides to review the development of our work. The Japan Baptist Conference gave each of the missionary units a gift of a wall clock which appropriately reminds us of the time spent in Japan. It will be a cherished remembrance of these many years of ministry and the rich experiences I have been privileged to have.

Several weeks ago, a phone call came from one of my English Bible Class students. I knew that her husband was very sick. He had been operated on in January, but had only recently come home. However, the doctors told her that he did not have long to live. Her husband thinks he will recover. Here in Japan, doctors and family members almost never tell the patient if his illness is terminal. She told only her mother and her husband's brother, but the burden was getting too heavy for her and she wanted to share it with someone, so she called me. I offered to visit her. We talked together and I shared some Bible passages with her. This seemed to help, so I asked her to come to my house once a week.

Today she came to our morning worship service for the first time, of her own accord. She has a daughter in Junior High and a son in fourth grade. She says that she wants to die with, or before her husband dies, but because of her children, she cannot. We pray that she may find hope to live by committing everything into God's hands.

We continue to pray for our Ikeda Church. The attendance has been growing gradually. We average about 25, but there is still a lack of unity and there seems to be a lack of confidence in the leadership on the part of some. This group seems to form a clique and others feel left out.

May 18, 1981

There are a number of comings and goings among missionary personnel. April 7th brought Lucy Wipf back to Japan. Pastor Aoki will graduate with a Master of Divinity degree from our NAB Seminary on May 24th and will return to Japan May 28th. His family is counting the days. Woykes will come back to Japan July 1st. Weicks and the short termers, Jan Willeke and Arlynn Friesen, will go back to the States in July. We have just heard that the new short termers will be joining us in the summer. Stollers are also going on furlough this summer. They and Lengefelds are expecting additions to their families in the fall.

January 5, 1982

As a result of our recruiting students for the English Classes at the church, two new men were added to my Sunday evening class, making a nice group of four. They tend to be atheistic materialists who believe in evolution rather than a Creator. I discuss all kinds of topics with them for one hour, followed by an hour of English Bible. I don't know what thoughts go on in their minds as we read the Bible, but I keep praying that the Holy Spirit will use the Sword of God's Word to pierce their hearts and convict of the truth. When I asked one man what gave meaning to his life, he said, "Doing my best." When I asked him how he knew what was best, he replied, "I rely on my own judgment." This is so typical of many people here, especially men. This man is a very brilliant PhD, doing research on cancer drugs. At times I think I see a crack in his armor, where the Holy Spirit could gain entrance. His wife is in my English class at the YMCA.

I will be due for a six month furlough around March. Our senior pastor in Japan, Rev. Akasaka, may be going to visit the U.S. for a few months, and I may be doing some deputation with him. His son, Izumi, who plans to be a pastor, is now studying at Michigan State University for one year. I plan to attend the Triennial Conference in Niagara Falls.

January 19, 1983

The Wednesday night Bible Study group seems to be meeting a need in the lives of some who do not come on Sunday. The young people in the church are very active. Six or seven attend regularly. They print a little paper quarterly and are trying to encourage the Junior High group, which grew from one to five within one month, making them very happy. The elementary school department of the Sunday School is very small. We need a Japanese woman helper who will make contact with the homes and play with the children. We are praying for such a person to be supplied.

The lady whose husband died last spring is now teaching English in her home and is very busy. She has been studying the Bible with me in Japanese and wants to attend my English Bible Class at church again. Pray that she may come to true faith and not merely gain Bible knowledge. She has indicated that it is hard for her to become a Christian, due to her Buddhist upbringing. She feels obligated to worship at the Buddhist altar in her home, where she believes her deceased husband's spirit is enshrined.

March 30, 1983

Our little church in Ikeda has found some respite from the turmoil through which it was going. Unfortunately, the respite came from one person's leaving the church. We hope it will not be

198

permanently. Right now, the young people are the most faithful and active. A college girl is planning to be baptized in May, even though her parents are very opposed to it. She has not yet told them of her decision. She has asked us to pray for her, because she knows it will be difficult to tell her father.

Dr. Iida and I visited the young widow of Dr. Kai who died of lung cancer last fall. It was the first visit to her after the funeral. Her father-in-law asked us to introduce her to a good church in her area, since Dr. Kai had shown interest in Christianity before his death. Shortly before Dr. Kai's death, Dr. Iida and I visited him in the hospital. Dr. Kai was a young pediatrician, working under Dr. Iida at the Osaka University Hospital.

We had given him a New Testament, which his wife took apart and gave him a few pages at a time to read, because he was too weak to hold the entire book. When we walked into Dr. Kai's room, his wife informed us that he had read the entire New Testament in a few days, so eager was he for something to sustain him as he faced death. We learned that Mrs. Kai had attended a Protestant Sunday School for a short time in her childhood. This Thursday we will visit her again and introduce her to the pastor and a lay woman from a church near her home. We are praying that it will be a church that will be suited to her and her three children.

May 5, 1983

On April 29th I had a visitor with a great burden on his heart. He is a spiritual son of mine who had great potential and at one time was greatly used of the Lord, but like Sampson, allowed a woman to drain off his spiritual energy and dishonor the Lord. He has shown evidence of genuine repentance but the problems he has created still surround him and weigh him down. He wanted to confess his sin to me and to request prayer for guidance for the future.

On May 2nd and 3rd our churches came together for the Annual Deeper Life Conference at a hotel near Lake Biwa. About 130 people, including children, attended. Our guest speaker was the radio preacher of the Lutheran Hour. He has the ability to lead people to make decisions. He is also a warm-hearted pastor who takes interest in individuals. He is in great demand, so we felt fortunate to have him. I was glad that a young lady from our Ikeda Church could attend one day. She has not been attending Sunday Services recently but she said she was glad she went. She drifted away from church when she began to doubt the existence of God because her prayer for a marriage partner had not yet been answered and she is in her forties.

August 21, 1983

I just went to a new doctor who is trying to discover the cause of my headaches. He gave me new medication and told me to refrain from fermented foods (cheese, yogurt, soy sauce, etc.). He also told me my cholesterol count is higher than the previous one, which was already high, so I must stay away from fatty foods. I need to learn how to cook vegetable dishes, lean chicken and fish dishes.

My fall classes have begun. I inherited some from short-termer Cherie Lake, so I am very busy with twenty teaching hours per week and about thirty five students at church and about 15 at the YMCA. I am excited that some of Cherie's students are eager to study the Bible.

February 3, 1984

It seems as if I can see a little cloud rising up out of the sea, a sign that God is beginning to answer our prayers for growth in our church. For almost two years, we were afraid to invite people, because the atmosphere of the church was not conducive to evangelism. Now, people are communicating with each other and seem to enjoy coming, so we felt it was time to reach out. November 13th was designated as "Evangelism Worship Sunday." Everyone was encouraged to invite at least one person. The need for this was felt by the lay people and they were the ones that took the responsibility for planning it. This was a new spirit. I really doubted that any new people would come, but to my surprise, there were seven. Some may have come out of obligation, but at least the Christians made an effort to invite others. As I expected, none of my students came, since they are mostly housewives and find it difficult to come on Sundays when their husbands are home.

In December we planned a Christmas meeting for women on a weekday morning, when housewives could come out easily. The ladies of the church offered to make a curry rice lunch following the meeting. We were pleased that eight of my English Class ladies came, plus eight church ladies.

On December 25th we planned our second Evangelistic Worship Service. It was easier to invite people this time, since it was

Christmas Day. Our little church was packed with 29 people, many of whom I had never seen before. A time of fellowship was provided after church with tea and cookies. In the evening we had our Christmas program, presented by the Sunday School children and youth group. Again we had almost 30 people. I was happy to see three parents of the children and some friends of the young people.

April 6, 1984

Alan and Judy Steier arrived back in Japan as career missionaries, after four years in the States. Alan was in Japan as an NAB short-term missionary for two years and Judy was a secretary with another mission for one year. They were married in the States and Alan completed his seminary training at Bethel and NAB seminaries. They now have a three month old baby, Jennifer. They will be in language school two years. It is nice to have some young missionaries replace those who have resigned. Actually, we only have two families in church planting, so they are very much needed. We could use another couple easily for that work.

We requested five short-term missionaries this year, because all of our short-termers are scheduled to return to the States this summer. We need one teacher for missionary children in Tsu, where Lengefelds and Stollers are. Jonathan Stoller, who is in first grade, is studying under his parents' tutorship now.

July 6, 1984

We just finished two weeks of Continuing Education for pastors and missionaries with Dr. Ted Faszer from NAB Seminary in Sioux Falls. He brought his wife and two daughters with him. He spoke on Christian Education and Nurture. I read Richard Foster's book, *Celebration of Discipline*, dealing with development of the spiritual life and gave a report on it. I thought it was a very good book, worth reading.

Next week is our Annual Summer Missionary Conference for our NAB missionaries. We will again go to the little village of Goza on the bay south of Ise where we will spend three days. This year we will have TEAM missionaries, Stan and Mary Barthold, come to speak to us from their experience of planting churches. We will also have a little time to relax together. After the conference, two of our short termers will be leaving for the States, Tanell Gerloff and Val Mikul. They will spend one night with me before leaving from Osaka.

September 13, 1984

My classes have all begun again. I have lost some students and gained a few. I keep praying that God will give me wisdom to better know how to teach the Bible so that there will be more decisions to follow Christ. One lady who quit in order to work said she was sorry she had to stop coming, because she was just becoming interested in the Bible. I will try to keep up contact with her personally in some way.

This coming Saturday is a holiday, "Respect for the Aged Day." I have planned to take Kenelee Proctor, one of our new short-termers who teaches missionary children, around Osaka, so she will be able to find her way by herself when she has business or wants to go shopping, etc. I have to preach this Sunday, too, so I must prepare a message.

October 3, 1984

Tonight I called "Oscar," the man who had two brain tumor operations. It was the first time I talked with him since the second operation. I had heard that his speech was badly impaired and that it was difficult for him to speak, so I was surprised when he answered the phone. It is true that his speech is slow and his words don't always come to him, but I could understand him clearly. I wanted to congratulate him on his baptism. He and his wife were baptized a week ago. They have two small children. The youngest was one year old today.

Pastor Fujie and I decided to try something new to see if we could build a bridge between my English Bible Class students and the church. Whenever there is a 5th class in the month, he will come and lead the Bible Study in Japanese. Last Sunday evening he came to my class at 7:00 p.m., so I excused myself and went to a missionary fellowship and prayer group in the neighborhood. It was the first time for this too. There were only six of us present this time, but I'm sure there will be more from the area next time. I plan to have the fellowship at my house in December. We all feel the need for a little fellowship outside our own church now and then.

202

We held our JBC Leadership and Workers' Conference in Tsu from Sept. 23-26th. The Leadership Conference is for lay leaders and pastors and missionaries. The Workers' Conference is for pastors and missionaries, but does not include the wives. Edwin Kern spoke to us about Church Growth. His family is now in Tsu, filling in at the Tsu English Center for Lengefelds, who are on furlough for one year. Ed will be visiting all our churches to observe and make suggestions for growth. We hope it will be helpful.

I had returned to Japan on August 19th on the same plane as the four new short-term missionaries. Immediately after arrival in Japan, we had two weeks of orientation for them, which included Japanese language study, observation and practice in teaching English, lectures on Japan, field trips to a Buddhist temple, Shinto Shrine, auto factory, pearl farm, etc. It was a very busy, exhausting time, but now we are all settled in our respective places of work. Kenelee Proctor is teaching missionary children in Ikoma, where the two Woyke children study. April Schauer is teaching Jonathan Stoller in Tsu and is teaching some English classes also. Robert Moss is teaching English in Tsu and Marlene Ginter is teaching English in Matsusaka

I have resumed my English Bible classes at the Ikeda Christian Church, at the YMCA and at my home. I have lost some students and gained some new ones. A Ladies' Luncheon will be held at the Royal Hotel on October 8th. One thousand ladies usually attend this. Four ladies from our church are planning to attend. October 28th is a family picnic in the park for my Sunday evening class, which is mostly men. The pastor's family is planning to attend too, to get acquainted with them and their families. The brother of one of the men, a newspaper reporter, was killed in an auto accident recently. His heart seems tender and open to spiritual things right now.

December 8, 1984

There are many Christmas meetings being planned. The list is long and looking at it almost makes me tired already: Dec. 11 – YMCA Christmas. I am the main speaker. Dec. 16 – Children and young people's Christmas at our church. The children are preparing a drama of the first Christmas. The young people made a set of slides by photographing pictures from a story book about Zacchaeus. Dec. 19 – Women's Christmas. The church ladies will prepare curry rice and serve decorated Christmas cake. My English Class ladies are invited too. Dec. 22 – the main church event will be Sunday Christmas worship in the morning and an adult program in the afternoon. Dec. 25 – Prayer meeting followed by fellowship over a bowl of sweet red bean soup.

Missionary Christmas meetings are: Dec. 24, Area meeting for our JBC pastors and NAB missionaries with a potluck supper. Dec 25, Christmas dinner at the Woykes. Dec 27-28 – NAB Missionary Christmas at the Center in Tsu.

I have begun teaching English at a Junior High School every other Friday for three hours in the morning. I was asked to teach pronunciation and conversation. It is the first time for me to teach in a public school in Japan, so it will be rather interesting. I have already observed that the students are very noisy. I'm not sure yet whose responsibility it is to keep the students quiet, the Japanese teacher or myself. I don't know how much noise is permissible, but at least I want to hear what the students are saying.

January 1985

I just celebrated my 60th birthday on January 14. In Japan the 60th birthday is a special event. Mrs. Yamamoto and Mrs. Aoki, the wife of our pastor in Kyoto (both women worked with me in Ise and Tsu) and Mrs. Sekoguchi, an aunt of Mrs. Aoki, who became a Christian in Ise in the early days, came to my house to celebrate my birthday and to renew fellowship with each other. We went out to a little restaurant and had a Japanese meal that is cooked in a large pan in front of you. It contains a broth into which the guests add the vegetables, fish, shrimp, oysters, etc. and finally big fat noodles and little rice cakes.

On Tuesday, January 15th, the church young people came to my house to celebrate the "adulthood" of the young people who became 20 years old. They prepared a stew using white sauce and bacon and vegetables. It was very good. There were twelve of us at two tables so it was a little crowded, but it was nice to have my house used for such a purpose.

March 4, 1985

At our last members' meeting, we welcomed five new members, three who were recently baptized and two who transferred their membership. It was good to hear their desires and suggestions for further growth. Another young man has requested baptism. He has just graduated from college with a teacher's certificate, but he needs a job in order to stay in the Ikeda church. Otherwise he will have to return to his parents' home where his faith may be stifled.

The eight Japan Baptist Conference churches reported eighteen baptisms in 1984. Four years ago, a goal was set of doubling our membership in ten years. Seventy-six persons were baptized in four years, which corresponds to our goal of a 10% increase each year. The percentage of active members went up over 5% but the actual membership increased only 2%, due to deaths, erasures and transfers.

The Japan Baptist Conference voted to buy a piece of land for a new church in Higashi Muko in Kyoto. The church there has been blessed of the Lord and the congregation of thirty to forty people can no longer be contained in the small meeting place. The land is selling at half price and is much larger than we expected to find in a crowded residential area.

April 16, 1985

I have decided to go on a three week tour of China with Elaine Nordstrom before going home on furlough and have cancelled my plans for the triennial conference in Anaheim. My plans are to leave Japan on July 17 and return directly from China to Seattle on August 6th. I would spend a few days with Wesners in Tacoma and leave on August 9th for Chicago. I suggested to Mom that she might like to go to Tacoma to be with Lill for several weeks and fly back home with me.

June 17, 1985

From Tuesday evening to Friday evening I was in Tsu attending a Continuing Education Seminar for our JBC pastors and NAB missionaries. This year a Norwegian missionary and two pastors from the Christian Advent mission joined us. Ed Kern has been leading the seminar on the subject of Theology of Missions. We are supposed to do a lot of reading and also write some reports but I'm not sure how much I can do. It is hard to study when there are so many people around. Someone is always talking.

Last Sunday the Tsu church celebrated its 20th anniversary since the church building was constructed. All the missionaries who worked in the church were invited to come. I was asked to give a testimony, since I was the first missionary in Tsu and started the work. Ed Kern gave the message. A lunch was served following the service. The church was full with about 80 people present. Some were out-of-town guests who came back for the reunion. Several of the students who became Christians during my time were there. Two of them I had not seen for about 27 years. The church's head deacon presented plans for the new church building which they hope to build in 3-4 years. They have a large vision and want to build a home for the aged near the church.

After my Trip to China and my Furlough in the U.S.

March 14, 1986

I arrived back in Osaka after a beautiful flight on Japan Airlines. My departure from Benton Harbor was a very hurried one, because time ran out. I don't know how we could have managed without Evelyn and Edwin. Edwin did a tremendous amount of work in the basement and in getting mom's furniture moved to Wilmington, Delaware, where mom will be staying from now on. I felt badly that I had to leave mom without any quiet time with her. When I got on the plane at Ross Field, the tears started to flow, partly at the thought that it might be the last time that I would see mom, and partly regrets over the lack of time I spent with mom during the busy days of packing, the irritation which sometimes crept in as I tried to attend to many details in a short time, and a very poor farewell. I wondered how she and Evie felt as they locked the door to the house and pulled out of the driveway at 1778 Colfax Ave. I pray that the Lord will make up to mom any loss she may feel by providing her with many special events and bringing her into contact with many new friends who will love her as her old friends have. It was hard to tell mom that we children were concerned for her health and safety because she was 87 years old and had fallen quite a few times, and felt it would be best if she went to live with Edwin and Mary. After some persuasion, she graciously consented to accept Ed and Mary's offer to care for her.

I spoke at the Magnolia Baptist Church in Anaheim Sunday morning. The present pastor seems to be a good man but I sense that the church did not know very much about our NAB mission work. I spoke at the Sunkist Baptist Church in Anaheim in the evening. I was given the full time, since they are a supporting church. Some pastors seem to feel that if the missionary has been given a place to stay and meals and transportation are provided, that is all that needs to be done. I really appreciate it when pastors take a little time to talk with missionaries, more than just a greeting. I feel that the pastor-missionary relationship is very important when a church takes on support of a missionary.

My house in Ikeda was just as I left it. It was cold inside. I turned on the electric pad under my bed sheet and crawled in bed about 11 p.m. using only the blankets which were on my bed. During the night I got so cold I got up and put my coat over me, but it slipped off. In the morning I knew that I was coming down with a cold. It was full-blown the next day so I stayed indoors as much as possible since it was cold and rainy and took a little extra rest. I had to make some adjustments getting used to living alone again after being with mom seven months and being able to talk on the phone to other family members. Also, it is an adjustment being back in Japan, where I am still an alien, in spite of having lived here 34 years.

The first Sunday after my return to Japan, the church had a welcome back *sukiyaki* party for me. There were about twenty people in the morning service, but only about twelve stayed for the meal. It was a very good meal with a lot of food left over. I bought some of the meat because they wanted to get rid of it, so I am again cooking with soy sauce and eating rice.

Pastor Fujie and I discussed what the church might like me to do this term. He said that the church people wanted me to plan more fellowship with them, because some of them feel they hardly know me. These are the ones who are in Fujie Sensei's classes which I do not attend. We only meet each other at church services and then it's just a friendly greeting. He also said that I could have a Japanese Bible study class for new people. I will try to recruit students for it from my English classes and other contacts. I will, of course, continue some of the English Bible classes which I had before. I met with our Japan Baptist Conference executive committee also and my work was discussed there. The result was that they feel I should stay in Ikeda and cooperate with the church as best I can and try to help it grow.

I met with my Thursday English Bible class twice. Fujie Sensei took over this class in my absence. He taught both English and Bible as I did, but he did the Bible lesson in Japanese. I was hoping that, since the ladies had become accustomed to Bible study in Japanese, that I could continue it in Japanese, but when I asked them which they preferred, they said English. There are four regular members in this class now, but I hope that two former students will come back to it. I called the ladies in my Monday English Bible class to see if I could change the day since we are supposed to leave Monday open for mission committee meetings, etc. They agreed to come on Friday. There are four ladies in this class, too. The other classes have not yet been decided. I want to keep quite a bit of free time so I can visit people personally and plan some fellowship luncheons. At the same time, I want to keep busy enough with my classes that my students can have as much exposure to the Bible as possible.

I visited the Matsusaka Church last Sunday evening. This church has been without a pastor since Pastor Hanazono resigned in 1978. Murakami Sensei goes there on Sunday evening and once during the week. He has been training the laypeople to assume responsibility and as a result, the church has been growing. There were about 25 present last Sunday. There are several young couples who attend with their children. This is very encouraging. Lucy Wipf lives in the church and helps here and there, plus her work of teaching English at the Center in Tsu. In September she will move to Tsu and take Ron and Joan Stollers' place, doing student evangelism as well as teaching English classes. The Tsu Church is planning to relocate and build within the next year. It will be a rather large church. They have about 90 members now. The Higashi Muko Machi Church which was built in Kyoto last year can seat 200 people, but so far they have only about 50 attending. They have a lot of room to grow.

While I was in Tsu I was invited to a little birthday party for Marlene Ginter, one of our short-term missionaries. I got to see four of the short termers. Later I spent the night with Lengefelds and the next day I had lunch with Stollers. Next week I will have supper with Steiers who are in language school in Kobe and perhaps I can meet Leah Kramer, the newest short-termer, too. I would like to do these extra things before my schedule becomes full.

April 3, 1986

Three weeks have passed since I arrived back in Japan. I'm gradually getting back into contact with people, both missionaries and Japanese. Last Wednesday our Sunday school children had a picnic in the park. They wanted to go by car, so Pastor Fujie and I both drove.

208

There were nine children in all, two of them only four years old. The children found a little artificial stream of water near the place where we settled down. They took off their shoes and socks and waded in the water. It was a nice day but the water was cold, so I worried that the children would catch cold, but Pastor Fujie and another man who is the head of a church kindergarten were along and they did not object. We had a Good Friday service on Friday evening with a meditation on the death of Jesus. Easter Sunday morning we had a rather ordinary church service with an Easter message. Two of the ladies boiled eggs to give to the Sunday school children and church people. I offered to color them on Saturday. It added a little festivity to the event. We ate them after the Sunday a.m. service with tea and rice crackers. Easter lilies were given to everyone before they went home. I don't know who paid for them. They are quite expensive.

Easter Sunday evening I went to an inter-denominational Easter Rally held at a Christian girls' college. It was a very good meeting with a fine evangelist. The Salvation Army band played and a testimony was given by Mrs. Ueda (Okuda San), who was a special student at our Osaka Biblical Seminary some years before. She is the one who lost both arms and feet from frostbite when her mother brought her back to Japan from Manchuria after Japan was defeated in the war. She is married now and has two children. I was eager to see her again and hear her story. Five of our church young people also went to the meeting. I was glad they went.

Fujie's daughter, Yurika, nine years old, wanted to spend the night at my house so I agreed. Her little brother, aged four, wanted to stay too. I had them both for supper and overnight. I made potato pancakes because Yurika likes them. I spread a mat for them in my bedroom. In the morning I heard Hiroki whimpering. I found him lying at Yurika's feet, totally uncovered and shivering from the cold. I guess I am not a very good "mama" because I did not get up during the night to check on them.

The church people went flower viewing to see the cherry blossoms after church on April 13. We had a picnic lunch in a little park with a lot of cherry blossoms. Then they walked to my neighborhood which also has many cherry trees in front of every house, so it looks like a cherry blossom tunnel. Then they came to my house for Kool-Aid and cookies. Some of the other ladies who used to come are not coming to church right now. Our congregation is very young. There are about 20 people attending on Sunday morning.

I teach a 30 minute junior high English class Sunday morning. There is a Japanese Sunday school class for them following. Last Sunday there were just girls present. One high school boy used to be in the class but he felt overwhelmed by so many girls and he left. He is the only male high school student, so he feels lonely. I hope we can get some high school students to come on Sunday.

May 25, 1986

The other day I stood looking over the shaded garden of lavender irises with their green sword-like leaves protruding from watery hilts and sighed at the breath-taking beauty. After taking in the beauty of the scene, my five English students and I proceeded to the center of the compound where the main shrine stood. Three of the ladies went up the steps to the large, slotted offering box and threw in their coins. Then they pulled the long fat rope which jangled a bell and they bowed before the statueless shrine. I was a bit shocked and even hurt that one lady did this, because she has studied the Bible with me for many years. I sat beside her on the train and shared with her how God had wonderfully answered my prayers for a renter for mother's house, just before my departure. She then told me that she, too, had been seeing God's hand at work in her family with regard to her children. I was happy to hear that, and yet she has not yet been able to disassociate herself from the shrines and temples which are so much a part of Japanese life. Through studying the Bible, the students become God conscious, but it seems so hard for them to conceive of Christ as God, not just a man, and when I speak of God, they think of gods in nature or their ancestors.

June 16, 1986

I was encouraged recently when a student invited me to her home one afternoon. We spent the whole time talking about the Bible. She said she wanted to follow Jesus, but did not think she could give up ancestor worship. I told her not to let that stand in her way of believing in Christ, but to walk in the light as God gives it to her. She read a book I gave her about the fundamentals of Christianity and is now listening to English tapes on the life of Jesus. I am praying that she will have the faith and courage to take a stand for Christ.

210

Last Wednesday we had a ladies mini-luncheon at church. It was not well attended, however. I called many of my former students, but either they were busy or were not interested. Five of my contacts came as well as one lady from the church. I was grateful that two of those who did come feel a need in their lives and showed some interest in coming again.

June 28, 1986

I returned from Tsu after completing two weeks of continuing theological education for pastors and missionaries led by Dr. Gordon Harris, from the NAB Seminary in Sioux Falls. We studied Old Testament with units on the authority of the OT, family life in the OT, social issues such as ecology and war, aging, death and dying, etc. We had to read some books and write several short papers on Bible passages. It was very interesting and helpful, because the churches in Japan do not use the Old Testament very much.

August 2, 1986

Lucy Wipf and I plan to take a short trip with Lea Kraemer to the Japan Sea to spend one night in a Japanese inn. Since she is the only short-termer in Japan now, we felt we should do something with her this summer. Two of the short-termers who left will be getting married. April Schauer will marry Dr. Rodney Zimmerman, a missionary doctor to Cameroon. After one year in the U.S. they will go to Cameroon together, quite a change from Japan. We are expecting four new short-termers on August 30th. Two will teach missionary children and the others will teach English.

October 6, 1986

Knowing that I was soon to retire from my work in Japan, Dr. Iida, a pediatrician who is a member of our church and to whom I taught English Bible privately before he came to church, asked me to give a series of talks about my life as a missionary in Japan on Sunday afternoons. I was reluctant to do this, because I do not like to talk about myself and prefer to teach God's Word, but I consented and will try to do it in such a way that Christ will receive the glory. I didn't know where to begin but decided to start with my childhood and youth and how I felt God's call to missionary service in Japan.

I invited my former and present English students and the church people invited some to come also. There were about 32 present at this first meeting. Our little sanctuary was filled. That was very encouraging but I wondered what the reactions of the listeners were.

Mrs. Ishibe, a student in my Thursday English Bible class, called me one day and asked about the state of the dead according to the Bible. I asked her to read several Bible passages on the phone and after doing so she said, "Then Buddhism is wrong." I was glad that she made that statement and I could agree with it.

November 3, 1986

I held a new Japanese Bible study for three ladies on Wednesday morning. One is a Christian from another church, one is a former English Bible class student and the third is a lady who lives in my neighborhood. She does not yet believe in God and has never studied the Bible. She invited us to her home for lunch and to the second Bible study. She is lonely and desires fellowship more than the Bible, but I hope we can deepen her interest in spiritual things. I hope we can meet at least once a month.

November 28, 1986

Official Japanese "Thanks to Labor Day" is on November 23rd, which was Sunday but I celebrated American Thanksgiving on Monday with NAB Missionaries from the Kyoto-Osaka area. Woykes, Clausens, Lea Kraemer and Cathy Jennings came to my house for a turkey dinner and all the trimmings. I prepared the turkey and hot vegetables and the others brought the rest. We were nine people in all. The Woyke children are now almost adults, so everyone came with a big appetite. Unfortunately I was busy most of the time so I didn't really get to visit as much as I would have liked, but it was still nice to have everyone come and be my family for that special day.

Last Sunday afternoon I gave my second biographical talk about my life as a missionary in Japan. Each time I prepare, it seems the talks get longer. I always feel a lot of tension while I am preparing, wondering if what I am writing is going to be meaningful to the listeners. One night I had a dream in which it was time for the meeting to begin, but I was not ready. There was so much fussing around getting myself and the room ready that the people who came gradually left. I was really troubled by that dream, because it seemed so prophetic. There were about 27 people which was pretty good for a holiday weekend when many people had family plans. I was especially glad to see two men from my Sunday evening class there. The response of the people has been quite positive so far.

Practice for the Sunday School Christmas program has begun. Mr. Satoh, a teacher of handicapped children, is directing the elementary children's play this year, so I don't have much responsibility, except to help with costuming. All the church people will help with decorating the church this Sunday.

January 6, 1987

Last Sunday, January 4th, our pastor and family returned to his parents' home to be with his relatives, so I spoke at the morning worship services. After tea-time, we had a time of sharing, looking back over the past year and ahead to our plans for the new year.

December 17th was a day of rejoicing for the Ikeda Church as we travelled to Kyoto for the baptism of Mrs. Tamaki (our church has no baptistry). Mrs. Tamaki was not a Christian when she married her husband who was in seminary. He became a pastor of a United Church, but things did not go well with a non-Christian wife, so he became the head of a Christian kindergarten. Gradually his wife came to understand Christianity and wanted to be baptized. They lived near our church so they attended it for almost two years. Soon they will again pastor a church, so she will only be a member of our church a few months.

For about five days, the Japanese people have been enjoying the New Year's holidays and are in a festive mood. No sooner was Christmas over than the New Year's decorations of pine, bamboo and plum branches appeared at the entrances of most of the shops and over the doors of the houses. On the front grille of the cars was placed a decoration of straw rope, fernlike leaves, an orange and zig-zag paper resembling lightning that is intended to ward off evil. Everyone is busy cleaning their houses and gardens, buying year end gifts for those who have done favors for them in the past year, making and addressing New Year's cards with the animal of the year according to the zodiac (the rabbit this year) and attending parties to forget the old year. New Year's Eve and New Year's Day saw millions of people, almost everyone, going to the shrines and temples to pray for a good new year and to buy good-luck charms for specific blessings like health, prosperity, success in studies, work, marriage, children, etc.

January 7, 1987

I felt very discouraged after my English Bible Class today. I asked one of the ladies who has studied with me for about ten years what she believed about Christ. She said she believed that there was such a person, but she does not presently feel the need to be a Christian. She said she studies the Bible for the spiritual uplift it gives her. What will it take to cause her to see her need? Will it take a serious illness or a death?

English Bible Class at Ikeda Church

January 22, 1987

I have been encouraged by the attendance at my classes recently. One class at the YMCA (Old Testament) now has twelve students who come quite regularly. The New Testament class gained one, making four. My Thursday English Bible Class at church now has eight. The Japanese Bible Class which I have been wanting to hold on a regular basis has begun every Wednesday morning. I invited a number of former students who I thought showed interest. Even though they cannot come every week, the class will always be open to them. I am hoping that we can have 5-6 regulars. This class takes on a different atmosphere, because, only if they are interested in the Bible will they come to it. I pray that God's Spirit will use His Word to bring conviction of sin and the need of a Savior.

Last Sunday we had a guest speaker at our church, an 80-year-old pediatrician from a Christian hospital in Kobe. He said that in Japan, pediatricians were not allowed to treat newly born babies, because that was the realm of the obstetrician. However, he felt that the obstetrician's way of looking at a child was very different from that of a pediatrician. The obstetrician thinks first about the mother and may sacrifice the life of the child to save the mother. A pediatrician values the life of the infant as much as that of the mother and feels obligated to save the life of the infant also. Therefore, pediatricians should be permitted to examine newborn children and to keep records on them from birth. This he does in his hospital. When the child reaches fifteen and tends to become rebellious and wonders about the purpose of life, he invites them to come to see him. He talks with them about the meaning and value of life and gives them a Bible. He also gives them a figurine of "The Thinker" by Rodin and tells them to be thinkers also.

Next Sunday I will be giving my third biographical talk at church. This time it will be about my first two years in Japan, adjusting to the country and learning the language. Lorraine Fleischman will be coming from Tokyo to share her testimony. She will talk about her relationship with me also. We lived together for one year when we were in language school in Tokyo.

March 7, 1987

I have felt rather tired this week. Pastor Fujie spent most of the week at the Presbyterian Hospital participating in the Counseling Program for terminal patients. He asked me to lead prayer meeting and one of his Bible study groups. From March 23-April 4 the Fujie family will go to Hawaii. During that time, I must fill in for him at many of his Bible studies and regular church services.

My Bible classes are going quite well as far as attendance is concerned but I have not been able to see decisions made for Christ, nor do these people attend church services. I did have a good conversation with one lady as we had lunch together. She lives about an hour and a half away but has just recently decided to come to class after a long absence.

June 1, 1987

Since April, I have been going to the Tsu Church on the second Sunday of the month to teach a class in Bible Study Methods. We are using the book of Ruth as a text. The first class had 30 and the second had 36. There will be five sessions in all. The ages of the students range from the 20's to the 70's. It amazes me that the senior citizens seem to have done the most study. Perhaps they have the most time. At the Tsu church, I met Mrs. Morikawa who told me that she had studied English with me in Ise when she was in high school over 30 years ago. Now she is married and lives in Tsu where she is attending Luci Lengefeld's English Bible Class.

We just finished a two week seminar for pastors and missionaries on "The Spiritual Life" led by Dr. Stephen Brachlow from our NAB Seminary. It was good because it was very personal. We read *Augustine's Confessions*; *Life of Antony*, one of the desert fathers who lived alone over twenty years in meditation and prayer; *The Celebration of Discipline* by a Quaker, Richard Foster; and *Life Together* by Bonhoeffer. We were asked to do journaling, writing about our lives, thoughts and feelings. It turned out to be a good way to open us up, so we could share with each other, revealing ourselves more fully than we had done before. We had a long period of quiet and meditation and fasting for one meal the last day. I sat by the ocean for two hours under a pine tree, contemplating the attributes of God seen in His handiwork of sea and sky, and other things around me. It was very enjoyable and meaningful.

September 12, 1987

I arrived back in Osaka safely following my brief trip to the States. Mrs. Wada and her son, both students of mine, and Mrs. Fujie were at the Osaka airport to meet me. Mrs. Wada and Mrs. Ishibe, both students, had purchased some groceries to get me started and had even made sandwiches and a container of soup, so I didn't have to cook the first day except for breakfast.

Tomorrow I will start teaching Sunday School and my Sunday evening English Bible class. Monday I will go to Tsu for our Leadership Conference for deacons and the Workers' Conference for

216

pastors and missionaries. It will end on Thursday. Thursday afternoon, Alma Henderson, former missionary to Cameroon, will arrive from China for about five days.

My little garden had gone to weeds about eight inches high. It took me several hours to get it cut by hand with my grass shears. I ended up with a big blister on my thumb.

October 3, 1987

Our leadership conference for deacons was good. We had a guest speaker who spoke to my heart, so I'm sure he did to others too. This was followed by the Workers' Conference for pastors and missionaries. We had no speaker for this. Instead we hashed over our plans for our work in the next ten years and tried to set some goals for them. The NAB Conference wants to send money and personnel where the results are greater. We are all feeling the pressure to produce, or else! Only the Holy Spirit of God can bring forth fruit.

A young lady, recently divorced, will be baptized next Sunday. Her parents went through a bankruptcy recently, so she has had some bitter experiences. God used them to lead her to put her faith in Christ.

November 2, 1987

Leighton Ford and his team held special meetings for young people for three nights in Osaka. The meetings were geared mostly to Christian youth, challenging them to engage in world-wide evangelism. I went to the meetings only one day. When I went to get my car, I discovered that the parking lot had closed, so I had to go home by public transportation and go back the next morning to get my car. Live and learn!

One of my missionary friends and I went to see a movie entitled "Kenny." It was about a young boy who has a body only to his waist. The lower part of his body was deformed and not functioning, so it was amputated. Now he walks with his hands and a skateboard. He can do almost everything other children do. He goes to school also. He is now an actor, making movies as well. It was a good movie.

November 24, 1987

I attended the dedication service of the new Ise Church, which is very large and beautiful. It can seat about 100 people. At the dedication it was filled, but many who came were guests. We pray that it may one day be filled with members.

This week, I will have two Thanksgiving dinners with two ladies' classes at my house. The Thursday dinner for nine is potluck style. I will bake pumpkin pie. The Friday dinner for six is fully my responsibility. I will make a roasted chicken and all the trimmings. November 23 was our NAB area missionaries' Thanksgiving at the Woykes. Sharon, a former home economics teacher, always has everything done to perfection. She prepared the turkey and hot veggies. I brought a fresh fruit platter which everyone seemed to enjoy.

December 4 is the first Christmas celebration for me this year. It is for missionaries of all denominations who live in the Osaka area.

At our church, we are making preparations for our Christmas program. The number of children in Sunday School is very small and irregular in attendance, so it is hard to plan anything. Ladies from my English classes will be singing at least one Christmas song. My Bible classes at the YMCA are well attended right now. I am using Japanese along with English to help the beginners understand the Bible.

December 7, 1987

Before Thanksgiving I went shopping at the Foreign Grocery Store in Kobe where we can buy foreign goods, not available anywhere else. I spent $150.00. Since then I have been using my "goodies" for special events such as Thanksgiving and Christmas. At my Friday Thanksgiving dinner I served roasted, stuffed chicken with cranberry sauce and pumpkin pie. The stuffing, cranberry sauce and pumpkin pie were new to my guests. For the December 4 Osaka area Missionary Christmas held at a large Korean church, I took some of my newly purchased dill pickles and Mom's velvet custard pie. For the bi-monthly NAB Osaka/Kyoto pastors and missionaries' prayer meeting and potluck dinner, I took some canned American green peas and made a gingerbread cake. It may sound as if I have been partying all the time, but I have been carrying on all my classes as usual.

When the Thursday English Bible Class came to my house for Thanksgiving, I asked each person to say what they were thankful for. Mrs. Kawamoto said that next to meeting her husband, she was thankful for meeting me, because she came to know the Bible through me and through it, to lay a spiritual foundation for her life. A lady who

218

comes to the English Bible class on Thursday and the Japanese Bible Class on Wednesday had her fiftieth birthday, so she and I went out to celebrate. During lunch she voiced some doubts about the existence of God and the person of Christ. After talking with her awhile, she seemed to gain some assurance, because she wrote me a note saying that when she drove back home, she repeated to herself three times, "God exists" and "Jesus is the Son of God." I hope this was a confession of her faith and not just an attempt to squelch her doubts.

January 31, 1988

I gave my seventh biographical talk on January 31 with about 23 present. There were about 7-8 ladies from my Bible classes in attendance. I think the interest is waning so it may be time to stop, even though I won't have completed my story.

February 29, 1988

A week ago we had a *sukiyaki* party after the morning service at church with about seven participating. The purpose was mainly for fellowship and enjoyment, so I think that purpose was accomplished, but oh, how I long to see a breakthrough and to sense the power of God bringing conviction of sin and transforming lives!

I was feeling very discouraged and lonely this past week. I called a Mennonite Brethren missionary with whom I taught at the Osaka Biblical Seminary. She told me about their church, which has two Sunday morning worship services and a branch Sunday afternoon church. She said the church just keeps on growing. She also said they have a large number of young people entering the M.B. Bible School this spring, making 18 in all. After listening to her, I felt as if I was not accomplishing anything, because, although my students show interest in studying the Bible, they do not come to the church services and none of them has yet openly declared themselves to be a Christian.

April 14, 1988

Mom fell and broke her hip. My brother, Edwin, and Mary in Wilmington, Delaware have a split-level home with several steps leading from the first floor to the second floor where the bedrooms and bathroom are located. It seems that she was carrying something in her hand, which may have contributed to her fall down the steps. Her hip was repaired and she was getting rehabilitation at a nursing home. She was practicing walking, using the parallel bars.

My cholesterol was 303 in 1985, 280 last fall and at my last check up two weeks ago, it was 267. I am trying to lower it even more by diet and exercise. My headaches have been more severe recently and I have been feeling rather tired. I took one week off from classes as a spring break, but I filled the week with more activities than I should have.

A week ago our missionaries and pastors from the Kyoto/Osaka area had a prayer meeting and fellowship time. Monday evening I went to Tsu and spent the night with Lengefelds. The train was crowded and I could not get a seat, so I had to wait for the next train, an hour later. On Tuesday our mission had a business meeting most of the day. I spent a little time working in the Center library and spent the night with Lucy Wipf. Wednesday I worked in the library all day and returned to Ikeda late in the evening, a three-hour train trip. Thursday morning my English Bible Class planned to go cherry blossom viewing. The weather was rainy and the blossoms were not out, so we watched a video at church, "Joseph" and then went out to lunch together.

The day after Miss Yamamoto and I returned from our trip to Shikoku to see the new Seto Bridge, I had to be at church at 8:30 a.m. because it was the first day of my new term for English classes. I had handbills advertising the classes printed and inserted into three Japanese newspapers, which was rather costly, but so far the only result was that four ladies who studied with me before and stopped when I went on furlough, decided to begin again.

On Monday two of our short-termers came to Ikeda to see me. I took them cherry blossom viewing, to the waterfall in Mino Park, to a temple and to a park to see old Japanese houses. Now I am back in my regular class schedule.

April 16, 1988

Spring was late in arriving this year but Easter Sunday was a beautiful day. After the Sunday morning service, we took one of the lovely bouquets of lilies from the church and went to the church grave-site where there is a mausoleum for ashes. The tombstone was washed off with water and the flowers placed in front of it. We sang hymns and listened to a brief talk by the pastor. Prayer was offered for the family of Dr. Iida, whose wife died eight years ago and whose ashes are interred in the mausoleum. The words, "I am the Resurrection and the Life" are inscribed on the mausoleum. Many churches in Japan go to the cemetery at Easter to hold memorial services and to meditate on the hope of the resurrection.

Two ladies for whom I have been praying have recently been attending Sunday morning worship services at the Ikeda Church. Mrs. Wada came to my English Bible Class at the YMCA for several years and then, about a year ago, began to attend my English Bible Class at church, as well as the Japanese Bible class at my home. Mrs. Michiko Ishibe attended both the English Bible class at church and the Japanese Bible Class in my home. Last Sunday she and her high school-aged daughter came to the Sunday morning service. She said she enjoyed it and would like to come again, whenever she can. I am praying that both of these ladies and their families may come to believe in Christ.

I was hurrying to catch my train at the station near my home when I fell forward, right in front of the station. I landed on my knees and left hand. At first I could hardly move. Some of the station men came and helped me up. I skinned both of my knees, tore my shoe strap and sprained my hand. At first I wanted to go back home, but I was on my way to our JBC Deeper Life Conference at which I was supposed to give my testimony. I had reserved a seat on the train and I knew it would be hard to get another seat, because it was a three-day holiday and the trains were very crowded. I forced myself to get on the train, but I felt woozy so I crouched in the corner of one of the train cars with my bags. No one offered me a seat, so I had to stand for a half hour before transferring to another train with reserved seats.

I spent one day in Tsu working in the library and then rode with Lucy Wipf to the Conference. I shared a room with four ladies older than myself. The conference was two days long and was held in the middle of a recreation area, which was very large, so we had to walk quite a distance between buildings. There were 190 people present, including children. Our speaker came from the Evangelical Free Church.

June 4, 1988

Last night I put a tape into my tape recorder to find out what was on it, since it was not labeled. It happened to be a tape made by the Millers who were in Wilmington last Thanksgiving, which included Mom, Ed, Mary and Evie. It was so good to hear Mom's voice. Her mind, too, was normal and she even sang parts of two songs, one of which was "Safe in the Arms of Jesus." I was glad that I was able to talk to Mom directly the day before her stroke and learn that she was walking with a walker and was in a clear state of mind. That was a special gift from the Lord and will be my last happy memory of her. I made a tape on which I bade Mom a fond farewell, in the dim hope that she might still be able to hear and comprehend what I said to her. It is probably best that the Lord take her home to Himself soon. I know that she did not want to linger on.

I was to give my last biographical talk on June 5 but I postponed it indefinitely in view of Mom's critical condition. Some of my students seemed disappointed that it would be my last talk. I tried to include Scripture pertaining to my experiences and prayed that it would speak to the listeners.

July 14, 1988

Tom Johnson, from the NAB Seminary, spoke at the Continuing Education Conference in Tsu on the four gospels, pointing out their unique characteristics. He spent two nights at my house and spoke at the Ikeda Church. The next week was our NAB Missionary Conference at a Japanese inn on the ocean.

August 3, 1988

I have just arrived in cool Karuizawa where I usually come every summer to attend missionary conferences. One is a Deeper Life Conference (like Keswick) and the other is the Japan Evangelical Missionary Association (JEMA), which has speakers more geared to actual missionary work in Japan.

Oswald Sanders from New Zealand is our speaker for the Deeper Life Conference. I just bought some of his books which I hope to read while I am here. I am sharing a room with a single missionary my age from the TEAM mission. We have known each other for many years but seldom see each other, even though we live only about two hours apart by train.

Yesterday, after the meeting, I had lunch with some of the younger girls whom I met here. There is a nice bakery that sells sandwiches, so we ate them for lunch. Then we browsed in some of the shops. On my way back to the TEAM Center where I am staying, I got lost. I walked and walked and arrived very exhausted.

August 17, 1988

I met one of our new short-termers, Robert Joy, last Sunday. He will be working with Stollers in Tsu, assisting with the student work there. He is from our NAB church in Alpena, Michigan. He seems to be a fine young fellow. He has worked five years before coming to Japan, so he is mature. Linda Kieswether will be arriving soon to teach the five missionary children in Tsu (Stoller and Lengefeld children).

September 1, 1988

This summer I started taking painting lessons, something I have wanted to learn as a means of taking home with me a little of the Japanese culture for my retirement. I will then have eight months of furlough and deputation, ending January 1990. These painting lessons have sharpened my powers of observation, changing my outlook, teaching me spiritual truths, as well as developing new skills.

I went to my first class with my sketchbook and watercolors, feeling like a first grader starting school. The first thing the teacher did was to show me many volumes of prints of famous paintings. She then asked me to choose one to copy. I thought, "Why doesn't she give me something simple to start with, instead of masterpieces to look at?" Later I came to realize that one secret of becoming an artist is to train the eye by viewing works of the masters, before trying to develop painting skills. Already I had learned an important spiritual lesson too. We must keep our eyes on Jesus, if we want to become like the Master, instead of on people who will disappoint us. After my first attempt to paint mountains, clouds, water and buildings, I realized how difficult it is to produce realistic three dimensional effects. Now, as I walk or ride the trains, I find myself carefully observing things around me, thinking how I could reproduce them with paint and brush. It is as if I am looking through new glasses.

September 16, 1988

With the death of my mother, it seems that the earthly comforter has gone and I am compelled to look up to the Comforter whom Jesus sent in His place, namely, the Holy Spirit.

I stopped in Tokyo to have supper with eight people who had been related to the Tsu Church while I was doing student work there. Two of the women I had not seen for twenty-five years. One of the men is working for the Government Fishery Department and wants to go to Bangladesh as an occupational missionary as soon as the door opens. He said he had been inspired to do this through seeing missionaries in Japan. As we shared about our lives and work, I thanked God that, although there are difficult times, God has kept them and is using them where they are.

November 17, 1988

I am sitting by my gas heater with a wool afghan over my knees. Outside the weather is sunny and brisk. Brightly colored maple trees and colorful chrysanthemums can be seen in many gardens. In a few places orange persimmons are hanging on the trees. Gardeners are busy manicuring the shrubs and hedges. Rice straw is drying on racks in dried-up paddy fields. It is autumn in Japan.

On October 23rd, a special meeting was held in our church with a young Christian social worker from the slum area of Osaka as speaker. She has been working as a nurse among the day laborers and homeless people for nine years. At first, she was not accepted by them, because of her youth and her difference in background, but by listening to their problems, they began to believe she really cared about them. When she tried to help those with tuberculosis get into the hospital, they said they preferred to die and end their miserable lives. No one seemed interested in her witness as a Christian, but one day a man said to her, "I'm not so interested in you, but I would like to know about the God Who caused you to come here and Who kept you here for so long." She was able to give him a Bible and lead him to believe in Christ. How wonderful it would be if people around me could see Christ in me and want to know Him too!

In contrast to this report of the poor, I recently received an invitation to supper with a member of the Upper House of the Diet (Japanese Parliament), Mr. Tomio Kawakami, and his family. His wife, Kyoko, came to my English class in Ise when she was a university student thirty-five years ago. After university, she married Mr. Kawakami, whose father was the founder of the Japan Socialist Party. They were celebrating their 30th wedding anniversary with their two daughters at a Chinese restaurant in a hotel. I learned that his great grandfather was a samurai who persecuted the hidden Christians when Christianity was banned in Japan, but his grandfather became a bishop in the Methodist Church. His father also became a Christian and was called the Cross Chairman of the Socialist Party because, as a politician, he openly spoke about Christ. He was a Christian also, making three generations of Christians in his family. Before the meal, he offered a prayer of thanks. At the end of the meal, the parents gave their daughters copies of the newest translation of the Japanese Bible and gave their granddaughter a children's hymnal. I was pleased to see that the family was practicing their faith in daily life. He said there were a small number of Christians in the Diet, who meet for prayer before the sessions.

It was a pleasure to have Carol Potratz, a former short-term missionary, visit Japan for two weeks. As a result of her renewing acquaintance with her former students, Mrs. Kenjo began to come to my Friday Bible Class.

Mrs. Ishibe and I have been taking painting lessons from Mrs. Komura, who sometimes invites us to have lunch with her. She seems interested in religious things, reads the Bible and admires Christ, but has never attended a Christian church. I believe she is a seeker after truth but she doesn't want to be bound by one religion. I pray that I may make good use of my contacts with her to witness of Christ.

November 20th is Dedication Day for the new Tsu Church. I am praying for Pastor Murakami and his wife and that the building will contribute to a large ingathering of souls.

I have been asked to give the message at the Ikeda Church's Christmas program on December 25th. Pray for the guidance of the Holy Spirit and good attendance, especially of my students and contacts.

The value of the dollar has again dropped considerably in recent days (123 yen per dollar), reducing the purchasing power of the missions offerings. Greater contributions will be needed to maintain the present level of work. We are praying that the budget will be met in 1988.

I will be returning to the States permanently in May, 1989. I will visit supporting churches until December 1989 and retire in January 1990. I will then be living in the home of my parents in Benton Harbor, Michigan, which I purchased when my mother passed away.

February 20, 1989

Scarcely had the New Year begun, when news came on January 7th that the ailing emperor had passed away. Even though he was 87 years old and had been ill for more than a year, his death came as a shock to many. Some said they thought the emperor would never die. The majority of the people felt very sad, especially the older people who had lived through his 62 year reign, having experienced both the tragic war years and the peaceful, prosperous years that followed later. On the other hand, some who suffered very much and lost many members of their family in the war, felt that the emperor should have at least apologized to the people. The people of Okinawa, where one person out of three died, and the people of Nagasaki and Hiroshima, in particular, felt that the emperor should have acknowledged some responsibility for their sufferings. The question of the emperor's responsibility for the war remains unanswered and most Japanese prefer to let it remain thus.

With the close of the *Showa* era, the people want to forget much of the past and look ahead to the new era named *Heisei* (Achieving Peace) under the reign of the new emperor, Akihito. Some of the opposition political parties and some religious groups, including Christians, fear that the present government is seeking to turn the country back to pre-war values, including the deification of the emperor. The ceremony, equivalent to the coronation of the new emperor, will take place next year and will follow the same traditions of the past, which symbolizes the entrance of the emperor into the womb of the Sun Goddess and his birth as a deity.

I went to my painting lesson in the morning and was able to have lunch with my teacher, Mrs. Komura, and Mrs. Ishibe and her daughter, Junko, at a famous noodle shop in Ikeda. I will really miss the noodle shops when I go back to the U.S. My teacher presented me with a lovely frame for my first oil painting. The painting takes on greater value in a nice frame. My last picture will be done in pastels. It is almost finished. I hope that I can find a teacher to help me when I get back to the U.S.

NAB Executive Director John Binder and Missions Director Ron Salzman were in Japan for about one week. They spent one night at my house and attended our mid-week service. They visited all of our churches and met with all of our pastors and missionaries. They were present at the annual business meeting of our JBC churches also. I think they were quite favorably impressed at seeing the churches in action and the growth that has taken place since they were here last. They brought the good news that our mission budget for last year was met.

One of my students who has started to attend Sunday morning services is a very earnest seeker. She comes to an English Bible Class and a Japanese Bible class also. Now she wants to have some private time with me. We are doing one of the most difficult parts of the Bible in my Japanese Bible Class: Romans chapters 1-8. After doing chapter six, she said after class, "Now I really understand. It helped me very much." I am praying for her and her two daughters who now come to Sunday School.

May 1989

The months of March and April were a whirlwind of activity as I prepared to conclude my ministry in Japan. I had to sort out the things I wanted to take back to the U.S. and dispose of things I would leave behind. There were many, many farewell meetings and parties to attend. One of the last meetings was the Japan Baptist Conference Annual Deeper Life Conference in Ise. I was asked to speak at one of the sessions. Since we were gathered together in the area where Mr. Mikimoto invented the process of artificially culturing pearls and where many pearl farms were located in the nearby ocean, I chose to speak about "The Pearl of Great Price." I interpreted the pearl of great price as the Good News of salvation that comes through the death and resurrection of Christ and is received through faith in Him as our Savior. The pearl oyster is an excellent illustration of how salvation is achieved. The pearl is harvested only through the death of the oyster that produced it. In the parable which Jesus told in Matthew 13:45-46, a pearl merchant who sought for beautiful pearls found one that exceeded all others in beauty. He desired to have it but it was very costly. Because he valued it so much, he was willing to sell all his possessions to purchase it. Jesus said that the Kingdom of Heaven and all it represents is like that pearl, worth everything you might have to give up to obtain.

This was the message I wanted to leave with those who were present at the Conference. Later, one of the young people gave me a gift from all the young people who were there. It was a silver pin of a flying dove with a pearl in its beak. To me it spoke of God's messengers who carry the Good News (gospel) to those who had never heard it, a message of peace with God through faith in the death and resurrection of Christ. I was reminded of Romans 11:13-15: "Whoever calls upon the Lord shall be saved. How then shall they call on Him in whom they have not believed? And how shall they believe in Him of whom they have not heard? And how shall they hear without a preacher? And how shall they preach, unless they are sent? As it is written, 'How beautiful are the feet of those who preach the gospel of peace, who bring glad tidings of good things.'"

It was a message something like this that came to me as a first year student at the Moody Bible Institute when I heard Amy Carmichael's dream of a long procession of blind people marching toward a precipice and perishing because there was no one to warn them of the danger. And then she saw another group of people sitting in a circle on the grass, singing and laughing, making daisy chains, unaware and unconcerned about the perishing. I felt the Holy Spirit speak loudly to me as if I were one of those in the circle enjoying the fellowship of Christian students and the instruction of many excellent Bible teachers but not being very concerned about those who were in spiritual darkness, never having heard of their lost condition or of the Savior whom God had sent to save them from perdition. I felt compelled to respond to the call with a promise to God that I would go somewhere where the name of Jesus was not well known.

When my class graduated from Moody in December 1945, we chose as our motto, "Witnesses Unto Me", based on Acts 1:8. Just before Jesus returned to heaven He gave His disciples His last command, "You shall be witnesses unto me." I helped to make the banner with these words written on a large cross. I also wrote a song entitled, "His Witnesses" that was chosen as our class song and which we sang at our graduation ceremony. It was a reminder to us that this was to be the responsibility of all who have been blessed to know Christ as Savior and to be His followers.

His Witnesses

Florence J. Miller

D. Ruth Nunn

1. The glo-ry of God in the heav-ens is seen, His knowl-edge in
2. How ho-ly, how just, and how right-eous is He, The law and the
3. Oh, let us be faith-ful, for on-ly thro' us Lost sin-ners may

day and night; The vis-i-ble things of cre-a-tion dis-close
heav'ns de-clare; The mes-sage of life thro' His own pre-cious Son
know and see That Je-sus has died to a-tone for their sin;

His wis-dom, His pow'r and might.
The ran-somed a-lone may bear.
His wit-ness-es we must be.

CHORUS

What a mes-sage we have! What a

task to ful-fill! Christ's wit-ness-es are we; We will go in His

strength to the ut-ter-most parts, His wit-ness-es we will be.

9

REFLECTIONS IN RETIREMENT

August 20, 2011

As I look back over the years since our mission began work in Japan in 1951 and the missionaries who have had a part in it, I am convinced that each one has left some footprint behind. Some have served much longer than others but even those whose stay has been brief have touched somebody's life. Their influence may not have been realized until many years later, when seeds that were sown and lay dormant sprang to life and bore fruit.

In spite of many struggles and failures, God has blessed our labors and granted us fruit that will endure for eternity. Each soul drawn to Christ as Savior is precious in God's sight. Although there has not always been perfect harmony, there has been cooperation that has allowed the efforts of both NAB and JBC to produce results beyond what could have been accomplished, had we not worked together for 60 years.

As one of the first NAB missionaries in Japan, I helped to lay the foundation for the Ise Baptist Church and the Tsu Christian Center with a focus on university student evangelism, which developed into the Tsu Shinmachi Christian Church and later the Tsu Toyogaoka Christian Church. As the need for trained national workers became evident, I was led to help in the establishment of the Osaka Biblical Seminary, a cooperative school between three missions and their respective Japanese church associations (Mennonite Brethren, Baptist General Conference and North American Baptists). When that cooperation broke down after thirteen years, we had to find other means of training national Christian workers. While teaching at the Osaka Biblical Seminary, I also served in various capacities in JBC churches where help was needed. I remained in Ikeda teaching English and Japanese Bible classes and participating actively in the life of the Ikeda Christian Church until my retirement in 1989 after 38 years of service.

Following my retirement, I returned to my home town of Benton Harbor, Michigan. I was privileged to return to Japan for ten short terms in our JBC churches, one of which was serving in the

Kongo Bible Church for six months during the Woykes' home assignment in the States.

Florence speaking at Kongo Church

ABOUT THE AUTHOR
Florence Miller

Florence Jane Miller was born on January 14, 1925, the fourth child and third daughter of August and Clara Miller, in Benton Harbor, Michigan. Her father was born in Poland of German parents. He immigrated to America as a young man, shortly before WWI. Her mother was born in Benton Harbor, Michigan, of German ancestry. They were hardworking fruit growers and instilled in their children the Christian faith to which both of them were devoted.

At the young age of eleven, Florence responded to the invitation to receive Christ as her personal Savior and was baptized in the Clay Street Baptist Church, which the family attended regularly and which helped to nurture her faith.

She graduated from Pearl Elementary School in the country and from Benton Harbor Junior and Senior High School in Benton Harbor, Michigan. Desiring to deepen her knowledge of the Bible and to grow in her spiritual life, she attended the Moody Bible Institute in Chicago, where she felt God calling her to foreign missionary service. After graduation she continued her education at Wheaton College in Wheaton, Illinois, earning a BA in Bible. She went on to earn an MA in Religious Education from the Biblical Seminary in New York. She served as Church Missionary for one year at the Erin Avenue Baptist Church in Cleveland, which her brother pastored, to get more practical experience before engaging in foreign missionary work.

In 1951 she was appointed by the North American Baptist Missionary Society to serve in Japan with Jay and Esther Hirth as their first missionaries to Japan. She served in church planting in Ise City in Mie Prefecture, Kyoto, and Ikeda City in Osaka. She did university student evangelism in Tsu City, the capital of Mie Prefecture, and taught at the Osaka Biblical Seminary in the city of Ikeda. She taught English and Japanese Bible classes as well as English Conversation in various places, concluding her work in the Ikeda Christian Church in 1989 after 38 years of ministry in Japan. After her retirement at age sixty five, she returned to Japan ten times for short terms of service and engaged in numerous church-related ministries at her home church, Napier Parkview Baptist Church, in Benton Harbor.

Following three cancer surgeries, she is currently residing at an assisted living facility in St. Joseph, Michigan.

234

INDEX

Miller, Lillian (Wesner), 3, 4, 182, 185, 186, 192
Miller, Sherrill, 4, 100, 182
Moody Bible Institute, 1, 4, 228, 233
Moore, Fred, 103, 106-108, 113, 119, 134, 156, 158, 176, 181, 187
Moore, Pat, 103, 106-108, 113, 119, 156, 158, 176, 181
Moss, Robert, 203
Murakami, Hisashi, 93, 108, 109, 115, 117, 142, 143, 160, 166, 171, 173, 187 208, 225
Murakami, Nobuko, 143, 154, 156, 160, 166, 225
Naganuma Japanese Language School, 13, 21, 69, 106
Nakamura, Kazuo, 121, 130, 131
Naruse, Atsuko, 122, 138
Nojiri, 112, 149, 156
Nordstrom, Elaine, 88, 97, 157, 160, 165, 166, 169, 183, 205
North American Baptist General Missionary Society, 1, 6, 233
North American Baptist Seminary, Rochester, NY New York., 3
Potratz, Carol, 225
Proctor, Kenelee, 202, 203
Rhoads, John, 26, 28, 32, 33, 43-47, 51, 55, 64, 71, 78, 80, 94
Rhoads, Lydia, 26, 28, 32, 43, 71, 78,
Schauer, April, 203, 211

Schilke, Richard, 6, 23, 34, 37, 44, 61, 65, 87, 94, 117, 118, 129, 143, 146, 168, 173, 186
Shikoku, 30-34, 37-40, 43, 44, 50, 59, 80, 94, 220
Sorley, Francis, 9-11, 32
Steier, Alan, 201, 208
Steier, Judy, 201, 208
Stoller, Joan, 196-197, 201, 208, 223
Stoller, Ron, 196-197, 201, 208, 223
Sukut, Barbara, 43, 44, 47, 48, 50, 55, 61, 65, 66, 67, 69, 70, 76-79, 82, 87, 94, 106, 115, 119, 146, 151, 157, 158, 160, 172-174
Sukut, Walter, 43, 44, 47, 48, 50, 54, 55, 61, 65-67, 69, 70, 75-79, 82, 87, 94, 106, 115, 119, 146, 151, 157, 158, 160, 162, 164, 172-174
The Evangelical Alliance Mission, TEAM, 35, 201, 222, 223
Tsu, 119, 120, 128-143, 153-183, 201-208, 211, 216, 220-224
Tsu Christian Center, 121-122, 130, 133, 138, 153, 231
Uchida, Dr. 69-75, 77-79, 103, 107, 111,
Uchida, Mrs. 69-75, 77, 79, 103, 107, 109, 145, 146
Uchimura, Kanzo, 177
Wada, Mrs, 216, 221
Walth, Clarence, 99
Walth, Dorene, 99
Weick, Jeannine, 174, 176, 197

CPSIA information can be obtained at www.ICGtesting.com
Printed in the USA
BVOW08s0320220813

329082BV00008B/339/P